The Book of the
H15 and S15 4-6-0s
By
Peter Swift

Maunsell S15 30827 at Crewkerne on an up stopping passenger train in the late 1950s. The train consists of an odd formation with one brake third of the 3-set reversed and a non-corridor carriage in fourth position. transporttreasury.co.uk

Irwell Press Ltd.

Copyright IRWELL PRESS LIMITED

ISBN 978-1-906919-55-9

Bibliography

F. Burtt, *LSWR Locomotives*, Ian Allan 1949
S.C.Townroe, *King Arthurs and Lord Nelsons of the SR* Ian Allan 1949
H. Holcroft, *Locomotive Adventure* Ian Allan 1962
D.L.Bradley, *Locomotives of the LSWR Part 2* RCTS 1967
L Tavender, *Livery Register No.3 LSWR and Southern* HMRS 1970
H.C.Casserley, *London & South Western Locomotives* Ian Allan 1971
O.S.Nock, *The Southern King Arthur Family* David & Charles 1976
J.W.P Rowledge, *Heavy Goods Engines of the War Dept, Vol 1* Springmead 1977
D.L.Bradley, *LSWR Locomotives - The Urie Classes* Wild Swan 1987
P. Atkins, *Private Locomotive Builders, the Indian Connection* Atlantic Publishing 1993
J.E. Chacksfield, *Richard Maunsell, an Engineering Biography* Oakwood Press 1998

First published in the United Kingdom in 2012
by Irwell Press Limited, 59A, High Street, Clophill,
Bedfordshire MK45 4BE
Printed by Konway Press

Contents

Acknowledgements

I don't suppose that I am the only railway enthusiast whose interest occurred in two phases. My interest had been kindled from a very early age, being taken to see the daily passage of the Irish Mail during wartime years in Colwyn Bay. The interest grew with successive family moves to Evesham, replacing an LMS main line by a GWR main line and an LMS branch; then to Winchester, on a Southern main line with a GWR branch. I suppose that the next move should to have been to a place on an LNER main line with a Southern branch. As this proved difficult to find, it was beside the Waterloo-Bournemouth main line, as the Southern Railway became the Southern Region of British Railways, that I learned to recognise the different types of locomotive.

Bulleid Pacifics were beginning to appear but the majority of the passing trains were hauled by a variety of 4-6-0s, mostly with an interesting collection of names. The unnamed H15s and S15s seemed less glamorous and I never really forgave the H15s for displacing the Drummond T14 class 4-6-0s from the up van train, which struggled slowly past St Cross signalbox each day, shortly after the passage of the down Bournemouth Belle. The sight and sound of these fearsome machines, with the exhaust going straight up into the air and steam leaking from all possible points of the 4-cylinder machinery, had made quite an impression.

My railway interests waned during the 1950s but, in 1959, school was exchanged for university, with a proper railway society. I also obtained my first 35mm camera, a Pentona, which cost £9 and fell apart after two years, and set about recording what was left from my previous interests. A lot had gone; there were no Urie Arthurs left, and the Southern ones were declining fast. The M7 0-4-4Ts on the local trains had been displaced by Hampshire Diesel units the year before, although one did not need

to go far to find M7s in profusion still. The only Drummond 4-4-0s were a few T9s, which worked over the ex-GWR line to Newbury until the passenger service was taken off in March 1960. At about 5pm each day, an up goods called at Winchester to exchange wagons. During the summer of 1959, this was hauled on alternate days by one of the last two original Urie H15 4-6-0s of 1914. These were 30489, which retained its parallel boiler, and the taper boilered 30491. A number of the Southern built H15s were still around and the small wheeled S15s, of both LSWR and Southern varieties, were still plugging up and down on the freights as they had done for 40 years, and would continue to do after I left Winchester for Swindon towards the end of 1962.

Numerous books and articles have been published describing various aspects of the H15s and S15s. Those which have been of most use in preparing the text for this book are listed in the bibliography, in the order of publication. Grateful thanks are offered to the staff of the National Railway Museum and the National Archive, at Kew, who produced LSWR and Southern locomotive and boiler records, to fill in most of the story. The NRM also provided copies of General Arrangement drawings of locomotives and tenders. Apart from official records, a prime source of information is found in the notebooks of the late George Woodward of Eastleigh. He recorded every locomotive which entered and left Eastleigh Works between September 1926 and December 1966, although world events took him elsewhere between 1941 and 1947, so his records for this period were compiled retrospectively, mainly from *The Railway Observer*. George's records include details such as modifications and livery variations, which are not covered by the official records. Thanks to Ian Wilkins, the present guardian of George's notebooks, for allowing me to borrow

and photograph them, when writing my M7 book. For the provision of photographs, I am indebted to all those photographers whose material has found its way into my own collection over many years, in many cases with no record of the source of the photograph. Richard Casserley has supplied prints from the H.C. Casserley collection and Mike King has supplied prints from the Ted West collection, which he holds on behalf of a trust, and others from his own collection. Rod Blencowe has supplied prints from his collection, and has printed a number of my own negatives. The Transport Treasury has also proved a valuable well, treasury. All these cover most of the changes which occurred in the late 1950s and 1960s; Peter Groom also supplied examples of his photographs from this period. Scans of photographs from the John Eyers collection and from a set of albums of LSWR period photographs prepared by the late Don Bradley were supplied by the South Western Circle. Copies of six LSWR General Arrangement drawings are included in this book. These were provided by the National Railway Museum. Many thanks also to Paul Garratt and Mick Doleman, at the HMRS Study Centre, for identifying the relevant BR/OPC drawings from the HMRS collection.

Finally, most grateful thanks are offered to Eric Youldon and John Harvey who have long been researching the details of Southern locomotives. John's meticulous records of livery changes include inputs from many earlier observers and Eric's unerring eye for detail in photographs has brought to light many alterations which might have gone unrecorded. Both gentlemen have looked through my draft texts and tables, which are all the better for their many amendments, additions and corrections.

Peter H Swift, Spondon, Derby, June 2012

Dugald Drummond's 4-6-0 No.330, as built to Works Order F13 in 1905, at Nine Elms when new. The inverted Walschaerts valve gear driving slide valves below the outside cylinders and the casing over the firebox cross water tubes are clearly seen. The large boiler is the first of a line which, with a better firebox, superheater and a tapered front ring on all but the first sixteen boilers, would provide steam for all the Urie/Maunsell 4-6-0s. The main weakness of the design was the shallow grate, perched above the driving and rear coupled axles, with a very restricted ashpan. The F13s spent most of their life on freight trains between Exeter, Salisbury and Southampton, and their boilers and tenders were re-used on H15s E330-E334 in 1924.

335, built to order E14 in 1907, was meant to be an improvement on the F13s but turned out to be even worse, with an inordinate appetite for coal. The Walschaerts valve gear now drives piston valves above the outside cylinders, but the inside cylinders still have Stephenson's gear and slide valves. It is seen at Eastleigh on 28 September 1911, coupled to the 4,500 gallon tender which had been built for Drummond's 4-2-2-0 No.720 in 1897. 335 was out of use when Drummond died in harness in 1912 and its boiler, tender and some other parts were used by Robert Urie on an eleventh H15 in 1914. South Western Circle, Norman Collection.

1. Introduction

In 2008, Irwell Press published *The Book Of The King Arthur 4-6-0s*, to complete a sequence of three volumes on the named express locomotives of the pre-second world war Southern Railway. In this volume, we will look at the mixed traffic and freight versions of the King Arthur, which the Southern classified H15 and S15. Whilst the H15s were all basically LSWR locomotives, although the last fifteen were built or rebuilt by the Southern, the S15s, like the King Arthurs, were the products of two very different groups of locomotive designers. All three classes were initially produced from the Eastleigh based design team of Robert Urie, the last Chief Mechanical Engineer of the London & South Western Railway. All were solidly built, easily maintained and, once initial problems with heated axleboxes had been overcome, reliable. However, they did not incorporate the latest developments in boiler and valve gear design

Robert Wallace Urie was a Scot, born in 1854. After a general engineering training with Dübs & Co and other firms in Glasgow, he worked as a draughtsman at a number of the Glasgow locomotive builders. He moved to the Caledonian Railway at St Rollox Works, Glasgow, under the Caledonian's Locomotive Superintendent, Dugald Drummond. Urie became Chief Draughtsman at St Rollox in 1890 and Works Manager in 1896. Drummond had left the Caledonian in 1890 and, after a few years away from railway company employment, took the post of Locomotive Superintendent to the London and South Western Railway in 1895. The irascible Drummond and the genial Urie had clearly worked well together in Glasgow as, in 1897, Urie moved south to join his old chief, as Works Manager of the LSWR's Nine Elms Works in Battersea, moving to Eastleigh when the new Works opened in 1910. Between 1876 and 1890, Drummond had developed a series of excellent 0-6-0 goods and 4-4-0 passenger locomotives for the North British and Caledonian Railways, which were developed further by his successors on those railways, into the 1920s. On the passenger oriented LSWR, he built only one batch of thirty 0-6-0s but continued to develop the 4-4-0s and added an 0-4-4T for local passenger work.

With the introduction of corridor carriages, trains got heavier and Drummond designed a series of 4-cylinder 4-6-0s, which were mostly as bad as his 4-4-0s were good. In the days when new locomotive designs were generally produced by cautious enlargement of what went before, Drummond was not alone in failing to make a successful move from 4-4-0s to 4-6-0s. Two attributes of the Drummond 4-4-0 were an excellent firebox design and direct exhaust arrangements, giving free steaming and free running. The early 4-6-0s had neither of these attributes. The firebox was perched awkwardly, with the front of the grate above the centre driving axle and its rear above the trailing coupled axle, with an extremely cramped ashpan and no place for a rear damper. This design appears to have been governed by the need to get the locomotive, with a bogie tender, on a nominally 55 ft turntable.

The exhaust from the inside cylinders, driving the leading axle, was classic Drummond, but that from the set back outside cylinders was collected into a receptacle below the cylinders, between the frames. From there, a long exhaust pipe led forward to the smokebox, whilst another pipe led to a feedwater heater in the tender. It was probably intended that the exhaust from the inside cylinders would provide the draught for the boiler whilst that from the outside

The last of Drummond's 4-6-0s were built to orders T14 and B15 at Eastleigh in 1911-12 and were the best of a poor lot. They had smaller boilers than the F13s and E14 and had 6ft 7in driving wheels, compared with the 6ft of the earlier 4-6-0s, with all four cylinders in line. The rocking lever taking the drive from the outside Walschaerts gear to the inside piston valve is clearly seen above the front footstep. They had probably the best exhaust passages of any British 4-cylinder locomotive, but were constrained by the poor firebox, grate and ashpan arrangement. The 4,500 gallon tenders coupled, briefly, to 460 and 461 had five coal rails, in place of four. The top of one of them was transferred to H15 334 in 1930. South Western Circle, Norman Collection.

T14 461, now British Railways 30461, approaching Shawford on an up van train on 5 March 1950, probably the train on which I remember seeing them in their last days. The fireman is, no doubt, hoping that he will make the 14 miles, at 1 in 250 gradient, to Litchfield Tunnel before the ashpan gets clogged up. After that, it is downhill most of the way. Urie fitted 461 with a superheater in 1918 and Maunsell raised the platform in 1931. As usual, the exhaust is going sky high but the front end is uncharacteristically steam tight. 30461 had received a General Repair in March 1948 and still has a year to run. South Western Circle, John Eyers Collection.

cylinders would heat the water in the tender. The first batch of 4-6-0s, 330 to 334, built in 1905 to order F13, had 6ft driving wheels, for use on the undulating Salisbury-Exeter main line. They lasted one season on express passenger work, being incapable of keeping time on trains which were worked with total competence by Drummond's T9 and L12 4-4-0s. They were, however, found to be quite useful on the overnight 'market goods' service from the West Country to London and on the Salisbury to Southampton freights, which brought in coal traffic off the Great Western. The F13s were followed by a single locomotive No.335, to order E14. This was meant to be an improvement, with larger cylinders, but proved to be even worse. Its inordinate coal consumption caused it to be known as The Turkey. It was stopped for repairs in September 1912 and never ran again in its original form. These six 4-6-0s have been described in some detail, as they will re-enter the H15 story later.

Following the total failure of No.335, Drummond built two more batches of 4-cylinder 4-6-0s with 6ft driving wheels, to orders G14 and P14, in 1908 and 1910, the P14s being built at the newly opened Eastleigh Works. These had smaller cylinders and boilers and proved to be

better, if only because their proportions were not quite so far beyond the ability of the firebox to generate enough combustion gases to boil the water. However, their life was short and they were replaced by new King Arthurs in 1925, re-using just the tenders. The final batch of 4-6-0s, built at Eastleigh to orders T14 and B15 in 1911-12, had 6ft 7in driving wheels and all four cylinders in line with exhaust passages of classic Drummond design, the exhaust from the outside cylinders sweeping in a generous curve to the blast pipe. The excellent front end was still largely negated by the perpetuation of the atrocious grate and ashpan arrangement of the earlier 4-6-0s, but these were the only Drummond 4-6-0s to lead a full life. Apart from one lost to a bomb on Nine Elms shed in 1940, they lasted until 1948-51.

Drummond died in office on November 1912 and the LSWR Board appointed Robert Urie as his successor. There was one change to the remit of the Chief Mechanical Engineer. Whilst Drummond had been responsible for the provision, maintenance and running of the Company's locomotives, Urie was only responsible for their provision and maintenance. Long experience with Drummond's locomotives led Urie to

look for something simpler and more easily maintained. Many Drummond features, which added to costs, were quickly removed. These included feedwater heaters and cross water tubes in the fireboxes. Drummond had introduced these to reduce fuel consumption and to improve the steam raising capacity of his boilers. As Urie was not responsible for locomotive running, it is possible that he did not give that side of the cost balance as much consideration as the reduced maintenance.

As often occurs, a new appointment leads to other moves in the hierarchy. On Urie's promotion to Chief Mechanical Engineer, the Eastleigh Works Manager's post was filled by promoting Drummond's Chief Draughtsman, J.A. Hunter, another Scot. Urie then appointed Tom Finlayson, Chief Estimator to the North British Locomotive Company (NBL) of Glasgow, as Chief Draughtsman. A few years earlier, NBL had been involved with the design of the British Engineering Standards Association (BESA) standard range of locomotives for the Indian Railways. Of the three members of the Design Committee to be nominated by the Locomotive Manufacturers Association, two were

Robert Urie's Chief Draughtsman, Tom Finlayson, came from the North British Locomotive Company in Glasgow, and would have been familiar with the superheated BESA Standard 2-cylinder 4-6-0s supplied to the Indian Railways, although No.405 of the Great Indian Peninsular Railway was supplied by the Vulcan Foundry in 1912, and illustrated in their brochure.

from NBL. In 1906, a 2-cylinder 4-6-0 design with inside mounted valve gear appeared for heavy passenger traffic. By 1908, it had been developed with piston valves driven by outside mounted Walschaerts valve gear and, in 1912, a superheater was added.

Before Drummond's death, he had obtained authority to build two further classes of 4-cylinder locomotive, a 4-6-0 to order K15 with 6ft driving wheels

and an 0-8-0 to order H15 with 4ft 10in driving wheels, each with four 16½in x 26in cylinders. No drawings survive of the 4-6-0 but it would probably have perpetuated the grate and ashpan design of the earlier 4-6-0s. A General Arrangement of the 0-8-0 has survived. With only 4ft 10in driving wheels, it has a reasonable grate and ashpan arrangement, allied with the four cylinders in line of the T14. It might have

been quite good for heavy coal haulage but whatever would the South Western have needed it for? Urie cancelled the orders and replaced them by two more, each for five 2-cylinder 4-6-0s with 6ft driving wheels. What Urie and Finlayson produced was a BESA Standard Indian 4-6-0 chassis, with a Drummond boiler and superstructure.

Urie H15 482, new at Eastleigh in 1914. Comparison with Great Indian Peninsular Railway (GIP) No.405 shows that the Urie H15 is basically a BESA Standard 4-6-0 with a Drummond boiler and cab. The arrangement of the valve gear is identical and both designs have the frames joggled inwards in front of the driving wheels, to allow more space for the outside cylinders. Like GIP No.405, LSWR 482 is fitted with a Schmidt superheater. South Western Circle, D.L. Bradley Collection.

Urie H15 483, new in Eastleigh works yard, in April 1914, in the full Drummond grass green passenger livery with purple brown edging. 482-485 were built with Schmidt superheaters, which incorporated a damper control and a pyrometer on the right side of the smokebox. These first ten H15s initially had piston tailrods, which were later removed.

Urie H15 487 at Salisbury on 18 April 1914, in Drummond passenger livery. 486-489 were built with Robinson superheaters and had no external fittings on the smokebox, apart from the characteristic Drummond blower valve control on the near side handrail. LCGB Ken Nunn.

2. The LSWR Locomotives
The LSWR H15 Class 4-6-0s

The first ten of Urie's 4-6-0s were built at Eastleigh to works orders H15 and K15, going to traffic between January and July 1914. The H15 classification was not used in LSWR days. In his series of articles entitled 'Under 10 CMEs', published in the SLS Journal, Drummond's last 'Unindentured Premium Apprentice', E.A. Langridge, refers to them as the 486 class. It was normal on the LSWR at the time to refer to a class of locomotive by the number of the first one. The number series was 482 to 491 but, for reasons unknown, the running numbers were not applied in the order of building, and 486 was the first to be built. In Southern Railway days, most LSWR classes were given classifications based on the works order number of the first batch of each class. The works order numbers had been introduced by Drummond's predecessor, William Adams, when he re-started new construction at Nine Elms in 1887, after a period during which all new locomotives had been bought in. Apart from an initial glitch with the A12 class 0-4-2s, orders ran from A1 to Z1, then A2 to Z2 etc. Adams had previously been the Locomotive Superintendent to the Great Eastern Railway at Stratford, where a similar series of order numbers had been introduced by Robert Sinclair in 1856. Tenders were usually built to

the next order number following that for the locomotives, and orders must have been placed for other items, as locomotives and tenders used only some of the available order numbers.

In the final days of steam operation on Britain's railways, the majority of ordinary passenger and fast freight trains were hauled by superheated 2-cylinder 4-6-0s, with piston valves above the cylinders, driven by outside mounted Walschaerts valve gear. When No.486 left Eastleigh Works in January 1914, it was the first locomotive with this configuration to run on a British railway. Eastleigh had built 4-6-0s with two sets of outside mounted Walschaerts gear before; Drummond's T14 4-6-0s had two sets of valve gear, with the inside valves driven through rocking arms from the outside valve gear. His earlier 4-6-0s also had Walschaerts gear to the outside cylinders, but combined with Stephenson's gear to the inside cylinders.

Walschaerts valve gear had been patented by Egide Walschaerts of the Belgian State Railways in 1848 and locomotive designers in mainland Europe had favoured the use of outside cylinders and valve gear for many years. Their British colleagues had generally preferred the steadier running offered by inside cylinders, despite the fallibility

of 19th century crank axles and the need to get underneath for any inspection or maintenance. Even when outside cylinders were used, British designers preferred to put the valve gear between the frames. Apart from a few oddities, the first use of outside Walschaerts gear on a British 2-cylinder main line locomotive had been Gresley's Great Northern Railway H2 class 2-6-0 of 1912, later LNER class K1, followed by his O1 class 2-8-0 in 1913.

The chassis of the H15 was clearly derived from the BESA Indian Standard design. Not only was the layout of cylinders and valve gear the same, but the frames had the same inward joggle in front of the leading coupled axle, to allow more space within the loading gauge for the large outside cylinders. Above the frame, the boiler was, dimensionally, the same as that used on Drummond's F13 and E14 4-6-0s, but with a shorter firebox with a sloping grate and a decent ashpan. The lipped chimney, dome and direct loading safety valves over the firebox were also the same as those carried by the F13s. Drummond's favoured dome mounted safety valves had been moved onto the firebox on his 4-6-0s, due to loading gauge constraints. There were major differences inside the boiler. Drummond had never fitted superheaters to his

Urie H15 490 at Eastleigh, probably in 1919. It was built with a saturated boiler but received an Eastleigh superheater in 1919, being repainted into the dark goods green livery at the same time. The end of the large feedwater heat exchanger can be seen between the tender bogies.

ROD 2-8-0 2072 at Strawberry Hill in 1920. This was one of 17 locomotives hired by the LSWR during 1919/20, but they were not suited to LSWR conditions, as goods engines were also expected to work passenger trains. 2072 had been built by the North British Locomotive Co. in 1919, and never saw service in Europe. After return to store, it was sold to the GWR in 1926 as 3051, but was scrapped in 1929. On the right is one of the Beyer Peacock 0-6-0s which had been withdrawn, but were re-instated in 1917.

locomotives, apart from ineffective smokebox mounted units fitted to some of the T14s and to the D15 4-4-0s of 1912-13. Urie was a committed user of superheaters. H15s 482-485 had Schmidt superheaters, to the patents of Wilhelm Schmidt whose first superheater had been fitted to a Class S3 4-4-0 of the Prussian State Railways in 1898. 486-489 had superheaters to the design of John Robinson of the Great Central Railway whilst 490 and 491 initially used saturated steam, to enable a comparison to be made. As was frequently found on other railways, 490 and 491 were better when starting from cold, whilst the superheater was heating up on the other locomotives, but used more coal and water and their overall performance was not so good.

Whereas Drummond had always provided his locomotives with a straight platform from the front buffer beam to the rear dragbox, the platform on the H15s was raised over the coupled wheels, with a further rise over the cylinders. The cab was similar to that on the Drummond 4-6-0s, but with a more rounded side cut out and with elongated oval cab front spectacles, which remained a feature of all the Urie/Maunsell 2-cylinder 4-6-0s. The tenders supplied with the H15s appeared, superficially, to be very different from Drummond's bogie tenders, with inside framed bogies. However, apart from the use of outside framed bogies and

steel coal plates in place of Drummond's open rails, the new Urie 5,200 gallon tender was very similar to the 5,800 gallon examples which Drummond had coupled to the T14 4-6-0s during 1912.

Having built the first ten H15s, Urie turned his attention to Drummond's No.335, which was rebuilt to order M15 as an eleventh H15, leaving Eastleigh Works in December 1914. The boiler, bogie wheels and tender of the Drummond locomotive were retained, including the firebox, with its flat grate, but now provided with a proper ashpan. The tube arrangement was altered and 335 was provided with the first of Urie's 'Eastleigh' superheaters. This had been designed, it was stated, to overcome weaknesses in the Schmidt and Robinson superheaters, but the avoidance of patent royalties of £45 per loco for Schmidt or £50 for Robinson may also have influenced the change. As the firebox was longer than that on Urie's H15s, the distance between the driving and rear coupled axle was 7in longer than on the other H15s and the rear overhang, and cab, 7in shorter.

The LSWR S15s
By the time the H15s were in service, the First World War had started and new locomotive construction was out of the question, as railway workshops were turned over to armaments production. In 1916, Urie approached the LSWR Board for permission to build ten express

and five goods 4-6-0s. Nothing could be done without Government approval but, by 1918, construction could begin. First out of works in 1918-19 were ten express passenger 4-6-0s, built to orders N15 and P14. These will not be considered further, as they have been described in *The Book of the King Arthur 4-6-0s*. Following the first express 4-6-0s came four orders for freight 4-6-0s, to order numbers S15, A16, C16 and E16.

The LSWR was primarily a passenger carrying railway and its last new locomotives to be built specifically for freight work had been the thirty Drummond 700 class 0-6-0s, bought from Dübs of Glasgow in 1897. There were also William Adams's seventy 395 class 0-6-0s from the 1880s, but the LSWR had sold fifty of these to the Government in 1916, for use in the Middle East. To cover the loss of these locomotives, the LSWR re-instated a number of Beyer Peacock 0-6-0s, which had been withdrawn in 1913 but not scrapped, and hired some elderly 0-6-0s from the Great Northern and Midland Railways. Electrification of London suburban lines in 1915-16 resulted in a surplus of passenger tank engines, enabling mixed traffic locomotives to take on more freight work. In 1920, the LSWR hired seventeen ROD 2-8-0s, of Great Central design, from the Government. The LSWR considered buying its RODs, but

Urie H15 335 in Eastleigh works, with the first example of Robert Urie's Eastleigh superheater, which fills most of the smokebox. 335 is not new, for it has lost its piston tailrods.

the Government was asking £12,000 each, £2,000 more than Eastleigh's price for an S15. Six years later, unsold RODs could be had for £340! Good as the RODs were for freight traffic, they were not really what the LSWR wanted, as they were not suitable at all for passenger work.

It was not only in locomotives that the LSWR's freight facilities were inadequate. The main London goods depot was at Nine Elms but there was also a lot of traffic between the LSWR system and the railways north of the Thames. The LSWR had no suitable yard for marshalling this traffic and was having to pay for preliminary marshalling at yards such as Brent (Midland) and Willesden (LNWR). In 1911, the LSWR gained Parliamentary authority for a modern yard at Feltham, well placed for traffic to and from the LSWR via Kew Junction and the North & South Western Junction Railway. The war had prevented the yard from being built but, by 1920, a major investment in the LSWR's freight facilities was being implemented. Together with the hump marshalling yard at Feltham came the twenty S15s to move the freight on the LSWR, four 4-8-0T hump shunters to order G16 and five 4-6-2Ts to order H16, for freight transfer work. Finally, in March 1923, came a new running shed at Feltham, permitting the previous Strawberry Hill shed to be turned over to the suburban electric trains.

The twenty S15s were numbered 496 to 515, but 497 was the first to be built and 496 the last. There is a possible explanation for this. The number series 496 to 515 had been occupied by the last twenty of William Adams's 395 class 0-6-0s. Sixteen of these had been sold to the Government in 1917, leaving only 496, 506, 509 and 515. There was therefore a batch of clear numbers, starting from 497. Those responsible for the numbering must then have realised that tidiness required the use of the whole of the number series and the four 395s became duplicates as their successor S15s were put into service.

The Urie S15 was basically an H15 with smaller wheels, a tapered front ring to the boiler, and a smokebox of smaller diameter than on the H15. The taper boiler had been introduced on the N15 express 4-6-0s in 1918. The chassis, cylinders and motion of the S15 were the same as on the H15, as was the stepped platform, but it was set lower, with the boiler centreline 8ft 7½in above the rails whilst both the H15 and N15 classes, and Maunsell's later King Arthur and S15 classes, all had the boiler centreline 9ft above the rails. The low set appearance was accentuated by a tall stovepipe chimney, with a capuchon, built to the full 13ft 2½in allowed by the LSWR loading gauge. Although the tapered boiler of the S15 was the same as that used on the N15, the smokebox was shorter as the large wheeled N15 had a wheelbase 10½in longer than either the H15 or the S15. The tender was a development of that supplied with the H15s, having a wider and lower tank with 5,000 gallons water capacity. This tender had also been used first with the N15 class.

Top right. Urie S15 508, looking very new at Strawberry Hill. The low set boiler and generous LSWR loading gauge allowed for a tall stovepipe chimney, which looks strange at first sight, to those who only knew them in later days. The ribbed buffers on the locomotive to the left indicate that it is one of 17 ex-ROD 2-8-0s of Great Central Railway design, which the LSWR had on loan during 1920. Published accounts suggest that these had all left the LSWR by mid-1920, but there is clearly at least one still at Strawberry hill at the end of the year as 508 was not delivered until November 1920.

Below right. Urie S15 509 stands next to the lifting shed at Feltham, which replaced Strawberry Hill shed in early 1923. It is still in LSWR livery, which it retained until 1926. Ash heaps are beginning to accumulate at the recently opened shed.

The LSWR Feltham marshalling yard, looking east, during 1921. The line from Clapham Junction to Windsor and Reading is on the left and the control tower for the hump sidings is in the distance. 4-8-0T 495 is carrying the headcode for a train from Willesden. With the construction of Feltham yard, the LSWR no longer had to pay the LNWR to carry out preliminary marshalling of wagons for destinations on the LSWR. South Western Circle, D.L. Bradley Collection.

Urie H15 4-6-0

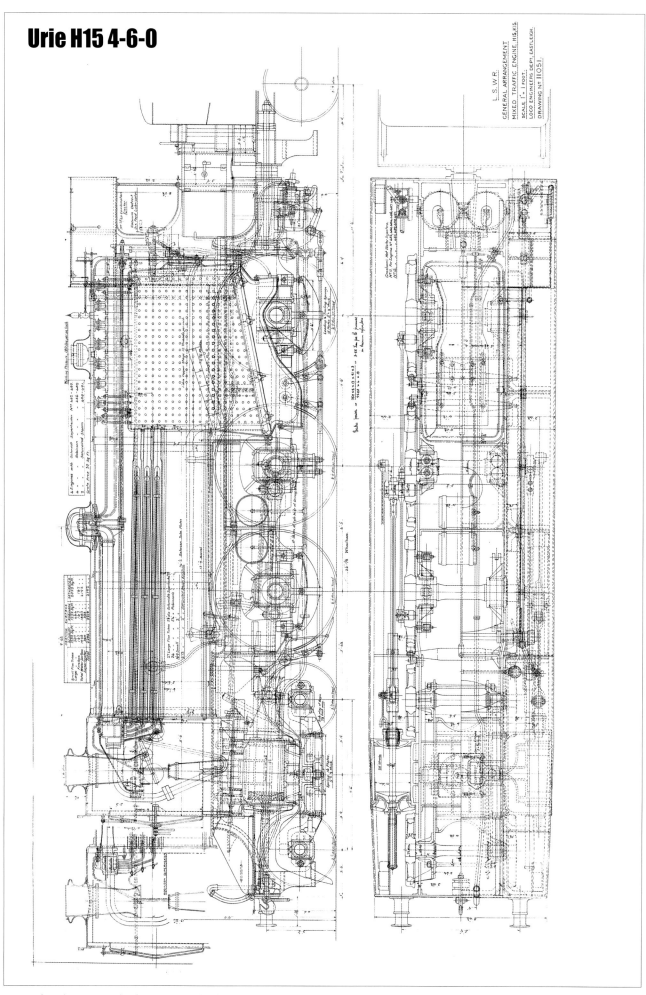

L.S.W.R.
GENERAL ARRANGEMENT
MIXED TRAFFIC ENGINE, H15,K15.
SCALE 1" = 1 FOOT,
LOCO ENGINEERS DEPT, EASTLEIGH.
DRAWING Nº 11051.

LSWR drawing 11051 for locomotives built to orders H15 and K15. The drawing shows locomotives 30482 to 30491 as built. The smokebox drawings show both the Schmidt and Robinson superheaters.

3. Drawings

Urie H15 4-6-0 No. 335

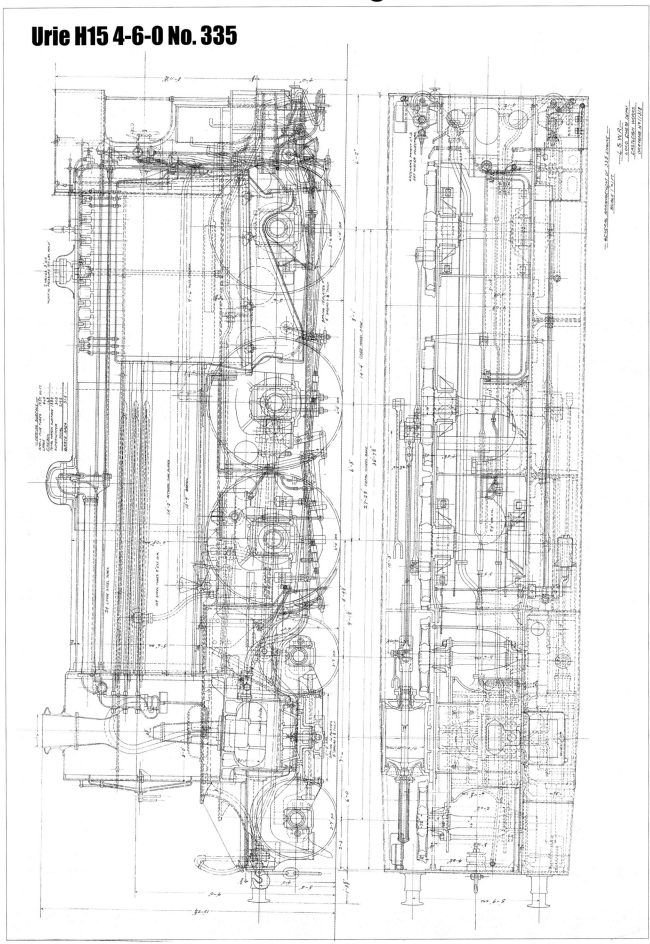

LSWR drawing 11318 for H15 30335. as rebuilt from Drummond E14 4-6-0 No.335. The Southern rebuilds 30330 to 30334 were similar, but with a 9ft wide straight platform from the cylinders to the cab, stovepipe chimneys and smaller cabside cutouts.

LSWR S15 4-6-0

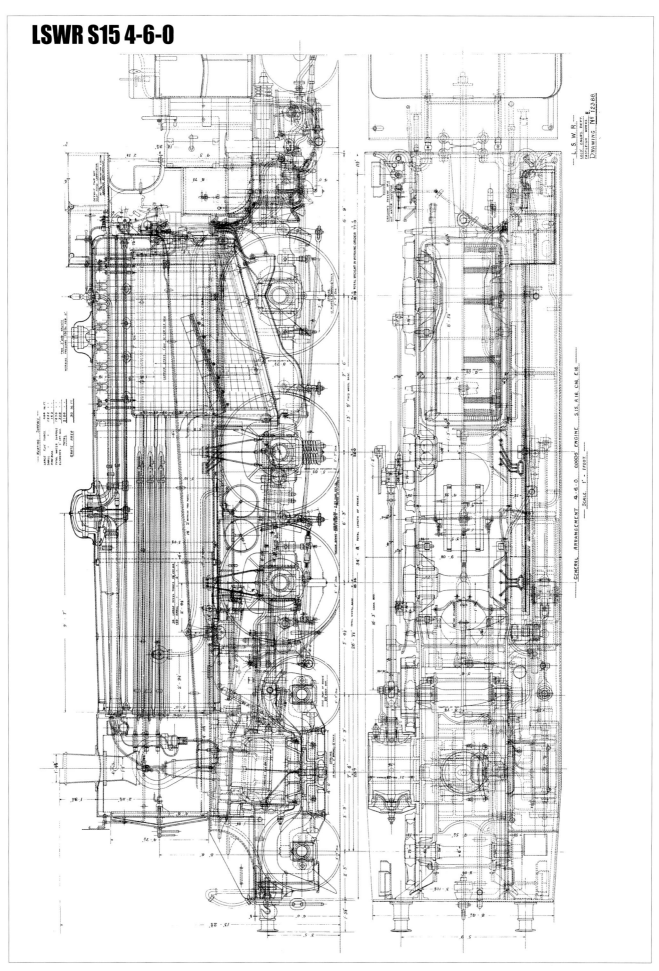

LSWR drawing 12388 for locomotives built to orders S15, A16, C16 and E16. The drawing shows locomotives 30496 to 30515, as built. Note that the space between the boiler cladding and the boiler shell widens towards the front of the boiler at the top. From about 1930, the cladding followed the shape of the boiler shell. This alteration applied to both Urie and Maunsell taper boilers.

Urie 5,200 Gallon Tender

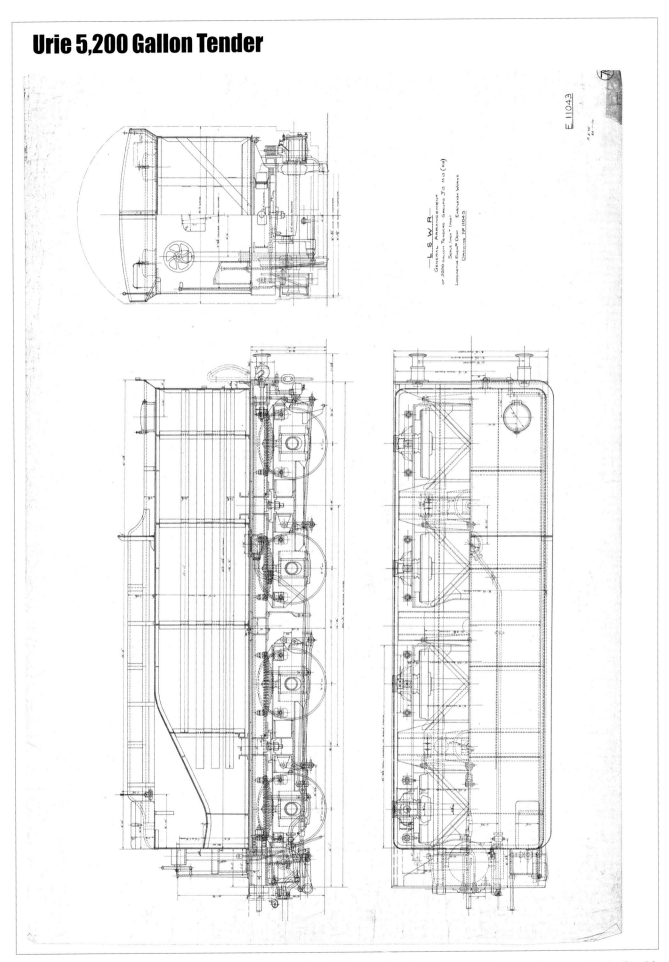

LSWR drawing E11043, dated 23 January 1914, for tenders built to orders J15 and M15. These are the examples built with locomotives 30482 to 30491. These tenders were taller and narrower than the later 5,000 gallon type. Some were coupled to Urie S15s during the 1950s and 60s.

Urie 5,000 Gallon Tender

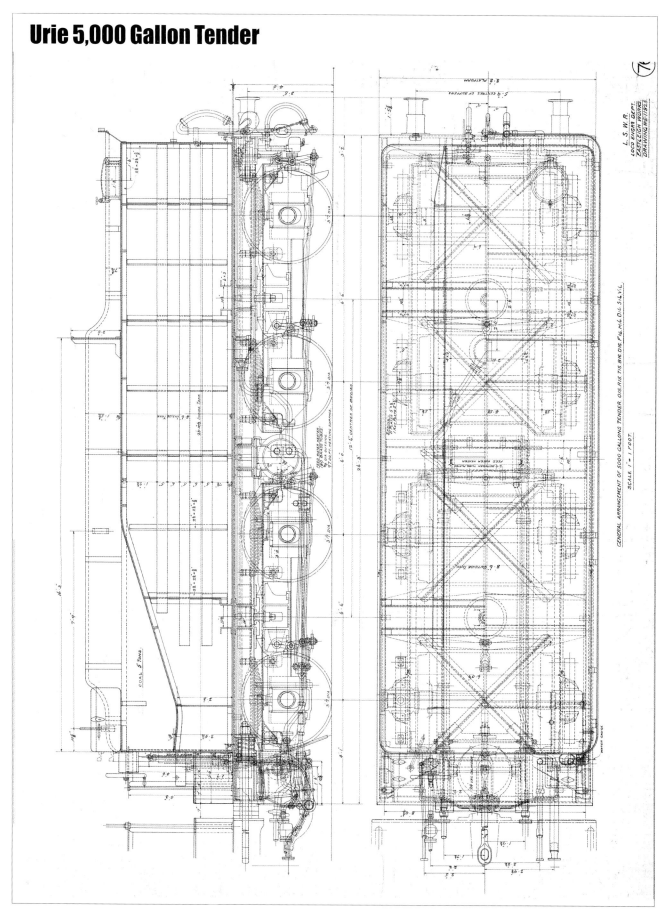

LSWR drawing E11925 for tenders built to orders O15, R15, T15, B16, D16, F16, M16, O16, S16 and V16. These are the tenders built with the LSWR N15 and S15 classes 30736 to 30755 and 30496 to 30515 and the Southern-built H15s 30473 to 30478 and 30521 to 30524. The drawing shows a feedwater heater drum, which was only carried briefly by some of these locomotives. The tenders built by the North British Locomotive Company for King Arthurs 30763 to 30792 were identical, but without the feedwater heater. Some of these NBL tenders were later coupled to S15s 30828 to 30837. The tenders coupled to S15s 30823 to 30827 were similar, but had bogie frames with arched cutouts between the wheels, whilst those coupled initially to Southern S15s E828 to E832 also had auxiliary vacuum reservoirs behind the coal space. All tenders coupled to Maunsell S15s were fitted with a conventional handbrake pedestal, replacing the brake handwheel shown in the drawing.

Drummond 4,000 Gallon Tender

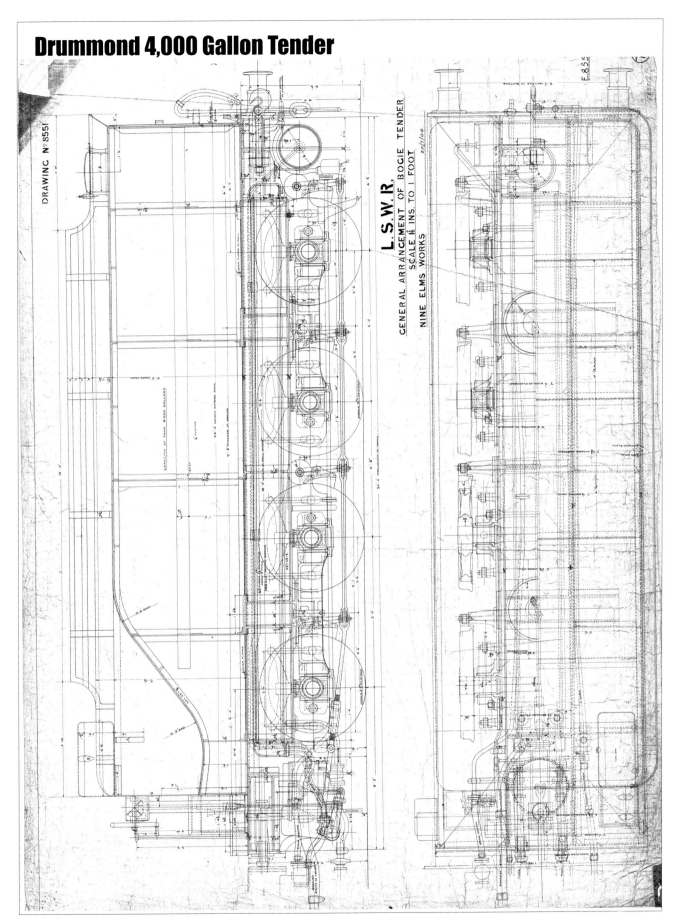

DRAWING Nº 8551

CAPACITY OF TANK 4,000 GALLONS

L.S.W.R.

GENERAL ARRANGEMENT OF BOGIE TENDER

SCALE ½ INS. TO 1 FOOT

NINE ELMS WORKS

LSWR drawing E8551, dated 20 July 1904, of a 4,000 gallon tender with a feedwater heater in a well between the frames and with double side sheeting, visible on the drawing at the rear of the sectional elevation. When no feedwater heater was fitted, the tender coping was outside the side plating. Tenders of this type were coupled to the Drummond F13 class 4-6-0s 330 to 334 and were refurbished to run with H15s 30330 to 30334. The feedwater heater well was replaced by a new flat bottom, the outer plating of the tank was removed and the handwheel operated brake was replaced by a conventional brake pedestal. In about 1930/31, these tenders were fitted with raised tops. Similar tenders, some with double sides and some without, were coupled to S15s 30504 to 30510 from 1935/6 to 1955/8. These tenders retained their handwheel operated brakes.

Southern-built H15 E473, new at Eastleigh in February 1924. It is in Southern olive green, with yellow lining, and has no cabside numberplate yet. The left-hand lower slidebar carries a crosshead driven vacuum pump. This GWR-inspired feature was carried by all the Southern-built 4-6-0s, but they were removed during the Second World War.

4. The Southern Locomotives

With the formation of the Southern Railway in 1923, Robert Urie retired and the post of Chief Mechanical Engineer to the new company went to Richard Maunsell of the South Eastern and Chatham Railway. Maunsell was born in County Dublin in 1868. He studied law at Trinity College, Dublin, and concurrently became a pupil to H.A. Ivatt, Locomotive Superintendent of the Great Southern & Western Railway (GS&WR) at Inchicore (Dublin). Having gained further experience on the Lancashire & Yorkshire and East Indian Railways, he returned to the GS&WR in 1896 as Assistant Locomotive Engineer and Works Manager and became Locomotive Superintendent in 1911. The only new locomotives built at Inchicore during his superintendence were eight 0-6-0s and a single large 4-4-0, both of them developments of designs prepared under Maunsell's predecessor, Robert Coey, by his Chief Draughtsman, Ernest Joynt. In 1913, Maunsell was appointed Chief Mechanical Engineer to the South Eastern and Chatham Railway Managing Committee.

Maunsell's appointment to the SE&CR followed a difficult period for the railway. The closure of Longhedge Works, and transfer of its workload to Ashford was not well managed and the SE&CR found itself with a severe shortage of usable locomotives at a time of increasing traffic. The Locomotive

Carriage and Wagon Superintendent, H.S. Wainwright, took the blame and retired in November 1913 at the early age of 49. For a successor, the SE&CR board were looking primarily for an able manager, and decided that Maunsell was the man to sort things out. He was, primarily, an engineering manager rather than a locomotive designer. He knew what he wanted, locomotives which would move the traffic and be easy to maintain, and he set about building up a team that could produce such locomotives. Wainwright's Chief Draughtsman, Robert Surtees, was due to retire and was replaced by James Clayton, the assistant Chief Locomotive Draughtsman of the Midland Railway at Derby. He had been involved with the design of a 2-8-0 for the Somerset & Dorset Joint Railway (S&DJR) and a 2-6-4T for the lines of the London Tilbury & Southend Railway (LT&SR) which the Midland had taken over in 1912. Both designs had superheated boilers and outside cylinders with Walschaerts valve gear, which were just becoming standard practice on British railways, although they had been normal in Continental Europe, and on British locomotives for export, for some time.

During the first decade of the 20th Century, George Jackson Churchward had been developing a new range of standard locomotives for the Great Western Railway at Swindon. These featured major advances in boiler design,

the boiler and firebox being tapered to provide the maximum steam raising capacity with the minimum weight. Superheated steam and long travel piston valves were giving performance and fuel economy which were unknown on other British railways at the time, although Churchward continued to use inside mounted valve gear at a time where the advantages of outside mounted gear were beginning to be accepted elsewhere. By 1912, the development period was over and the requirement of the GWR locomotive department was to produce more of the same, rather than continued innovation. Harold Holcroft, who had worked for Churchward on special projects, including the 43XX class 2-6-0 of 1911, moved to the SE&CR as Maunsell's personal assistant and George Pearson, the Assistant Carriage Works Manager at Swindon, became Maunsell's Assistant Chief Mechanical Engineer and Works Manager.

Maunsell's team produced drawings for a 2-6-0 (Class N) for freight work and a 2-6-4T (Class K) for express passenger work. The 2-6-4T was similar to the one designed, but not built, for the LT&S lines and the 2-6-0 could almost be described as a cross between Holcroft's 43XX 2-6-0 for the GWR and Clayton's 2-8-0 for the S&DJR. Both classes had the taper boiler and long travel piston valves of Swindon practice, but with outside mounted Walschaerts

Southern-built H15 E524 at Eastleigh on 16 July 1925. It is as built new with a Maunsell superheater, in the olive green livery, with the addition of cabside numberplates. It got a King Arthur chimney at the same time as being repainted dark green, in 1928. H.C. Casserley, courtesy R.M. Casserley.

valve gear. Superficial details, such as the cab and tender, were typical of current Midland practice. Maunsell's team also rebuilt a number of Wainwright 4-4-0s with superheaters and long lap valves, with spectacular results. Maunsell quickly realised that Urie's 4-6-0s fulfilled his dictum 'Make everything get-at-able' and took the existing Urie designs as the basis for his new designs for heavy power requirements, whilst building more of his SE&CR 2-6-0s for the lighter duties.

The Southern H15s
In May 1923 Maunsell authorised the construction of 25 more H15s, ten new ones and fifteen to be rebuilt from the Drummond 6ft 4-6-0s of classes F13, G14 and P14, but in the event only the five F13s 330-334 were rebuilt. The Western section of the Southern did not require 25 more mixed traffic engines and the G14s and P14s would have required wholly new boilers, as they carried smaller boilers than the F13s. Orders R16 and T16 were issued for the ten new locomotives and A17 for the rebuilt F13s. The new locomotives were numbered E473 to E478 and E521 to E524.

The new batch of H15s used the tapered boiler with Eastleigh superheater, which had been used on the N15 and S15 classes, with the short smokebox of the S15. They also had the straight platform of the N15, without the drop behind the cylinders of the 1914 batch of H15s or the Urie S15s. The rebuilt F13s also had the straight platform but re-used the F13 boiler, necessitating the same extended coupled wheelbase and reduced rear overhang as on 335. Two other features, which had been introduced on the N15s and S15s, were the small diameter stovepipe chimney and lack of piston tailrods. A new feature, carried by all Southern-built examples of the Urie/Maunsell 4-6-0s, was a vacuum pump mounted below the left-hand lower slidebar. This was a GWR feature, probably introduced by one of the GWR men on Maunsell's team, although it had not been used on his SE&CR 2-6-0s and 2-6-4Ts. The last of the new H15s and the rebuilt F13s had Maunsell's design of superheater, in place of the Eastleigh design. Apart from these minor alterations, the F13 with the same number. It is apparent that the boilers were taken into the boiler shop in the order in which the F13s were taken out of service, and rebuilt with Maunsell superheaters and new ashpans. They were then installed, in the same order, in the new H15s, which were numbered in order of build. The only variation was that old 333's boiler 'overtook' those from 330 and 332. As old 333 had been fitted with an Eastleigh superheater, its boiler would have required less work than the others.

F13 No	Withdrawn	Boiler to H15	H15 Completed	Tender ex-F13 No
334	20/12/1921	E330	1/11/1924	331
331	15/2/1924	E331	26/11/1924	334
333	19/8/1924	E332	11/12/1924	333
330	17/7/1924	E333	31/12/1924	332
332	12/8/1924	E334	29/1/1925	330

Southern-built H15s were to the basic Urie design, and incorporated none of the improvements which made the Southern N15s and S15s so much better than the Urie versions. They were built 9ft wide over the platform, in compliance with the Southern composite loading gauge, but had Urie cab roofs, putting them out of gauge for the Eastern section. The tender of the ten new H15s was the same as that used on the N15s and S15s but the rebuilt F13s used refurbished tenders from the old locomotives.

Although the LSWR/SR repair register suggests that locomotives E330 to E334 were rebuilt from the F13s with the same numbers, there was no re-use of components from the 'old' locomotive on the 'new' one with that number. Only E331 received the old E331's boiler, and none received the tender from the

The Southern S15s
During 1925 and 1926, Eastleigh Works was occupied with building 24 more of the N15 class express 4-6-0s. These, incorporated a higher boiler pressure and long lap piston valves, resulting in greatly improved performance. The final 14, and 30 supplied by the North British Locomotive Co, were built to the Southern composite loading gauge. This resulted in them being half an inch narrower over the platform, with shorter chimneys and with the angular eaves of the Urie cab replaced by a cab roof of SE&CR style. This merged smoothly into the cab sides and was extended back over the shovelling plate.

In May 1925 order E90 was placed on Eastleigh Works for ten more S15s, incorporating the Maunsell improvements, followed by order E158 in March 1926, for a further five. The

Southern-built H15 E330, incorporating the boiler and tender from Drummond F13 4-6-0s 334 and 331. When rebuilt for use with the H15, the double sides and feedwater heater well were removed from the tender and a conventional brake pedestal, with a handle on the top of the vertical shaft, fitted. The only obvious modification to the locomotive since rebuilding is the addition of conventional lamp irons, inserted into the LSWR sockets.

Maunsell S15 E825 in photographic grey, at Eastleigh on April 1927. The grey livery shows up detail, which is frequently lost on a fully painted locomotive, in particular the lining details. In this case, the black edging and grey main colour both represent black, whilst the white lining represents bright green. All the Southern S15s were built to the company's composite loading gauge, with rounded eaves to the cab. It has a Maunsell boiler, working at 200psi pressure with Ross Pop safety valves. The tender bogies are Maunsell's development of the Urie pattern, with arched cutouts to the frames between the axleboxes.

	H15 30330-4	H15 30335	H15 30482-90	H15 30491	H15 30473-8, 30521-4	S15 30496- 30515	S15 30823-37	S15 30838-47
Driving Wheel Dia	6' 0"	6' 0"	6' 0"	6' 0"	6' 0"	5' 7"	5' 7"	5' 7"
Loco Wheelbase	27' 2½"	27' 2½"	26' 7½"	26' 7½"	26' 7½"	26' 7½"	26' 7½"	26' 7½"
Cylinder Dia x Str	21" x 28"	21" x 28"	21" x 28"	21" x 28"	21" x 28"	21" x 28"	20½" x 28"	20½" x 28"
Boiler Pressure	175 psi	175 psi	180 psi	180 psi	180 psi	180 psi	200 psi	200 psi
Boiler Centreline	9' 0"	9' 0"	9' 0"	9' 0"	9' 0"	8' 7¼"	9' 0"	9' 0"
Platform Width	9' 0"	9' 0½"	9' 0½"	9' 0½"	9' 0"	9' 0½"	9' 0"	9' 0"
Loco Weight	80T 11cwt	81T 11cwt	80T 10cwt	79T 19cwt	79T 19cwt	79T 16cwt	80T 14cwt	79T 5cwt
Tractive Effort	25,510 lbf	25,510 lbf	26,240 lbf	26,240 lbf	26,240 lbf	28,200 lbf	29,855 lbf	29,855 lbf
Power Class								
LSWR & SR	A	A	A	A	A	A	A	A
BR 1951	4MT	4MT	4MT	4MT	4MT	6F	6F	6F
BR 1953	4P/5F	4P/5F	4P/5F	4P/5F	4P/5F	6F	6F	6F

LSWR order numbers had finished with orders B17 and C17, for the ten N15s built in 1925. The new S15s E823 to E837 were built to the SR composite loading gauge and were completed between March 1927 and January 1928. With the boiler pitch the same as that of the H15s and N15s, their appearance was very similar to that of the later N15s, although they had shorter smokeboxes, as they retained the shorter H15/S15 wheelbase. This also resulted in a number of working parts not being interchangeable between N15s and S15s. A final order, E630, for ten more S15s, was placed in March 1931 but the locomotives, 838 to 847, were not built until 1936 due to the trade depression. Robert Urie's locomotives were robustly built and, generally, somewhat heavier than locomotives of similar power built elsewhere. Maunsell's modifications

might have improved the locomotives' performance but nothing had been done to reduce the weight. The Southern N15s and S15s were a ton or more heavier than the Urie versions. With this last batch of S15s, some effort at weight reduction was made, and 1½ tons was removed.

Vital Statistics
The table above does not attempt to cover all the relevant dimensions, but is intended to summarise the differences between the various batches of H15 and S15. The weights shown are taken from the Southern weight diagrams. The LSWR figures were generally slightly lower. Tractive effort is calculated by the conventional formula, using 85% of boiler pressure. This is not strictly correct but does give some indication of the relative drawbar pull applied by each

locomotive when starting. Although all the S15s were given the same power classification, the Southern and BR Freight Train Load Tables allowed the Maunsell S15s to take five more wagons than the Urie S15s.

Maunsell S15 E832 at Salisbury on 28 April 1928. It is coupled to its original tender, with arched cutouts to the bogie frames and auxiliary vacuum reservoirs on the rear of the tender. E832 was the last locomotive to be built at Eastleigh with LSWR style lamp sockets, which may well have carried inserted lamp irons from new. Livery is black with green lining. It received smoke deflectors, a Urie tender and green livery in February 1930. H.C. Casserley, courtesy R.M. Casserley.

Maunsell S15 E834 at Feltham in 1928, with matching flat sided bogie tender and multi washout plug boiler. As usual, the green lining hardly shows up against the black. The conventional lamp irons are clear to see on the front of the locomotive. The cabside cutouts on E833 to E837 were the same as on E823-E832 and did not line up with the curve at the front of the tender side of the flat sided tenders. E834 retained its flat sided tender for less than a year, receiving a Urie tender in August 1928.

Maunsell S15 838, brand new at Eastleigh in May 1936. The final batch of S15s were built with smoke deflectors and never carried the lined black livery or E prefixes to their numbers. The driving and coupled wheels had built up balance weights, which varied from one locomotive to another. They all ran with flat sided bogie tenders which, with one late exception, they retained throughout. The cabside cutouts were shallower than on the earlier S15s, to line up with the curve at the front of the tender side.

Urie H15 E491 at Eastleigh in the late 1920s. In 1927 it was modified to carry a Urie/Maunsell taper boiler, providing a spare parallel boiler for the nine locomotives E482-E490. The initial taper boiler to be fitted was a new Maunsell example, numbered 491. E491 also received a King Arthur chimney and had its cabside cutouts reduced in depth, with the tender front panels raised to match. It retained its Urie smokebox door.

Southern-built H15 E473 approaching Clapham Junction on a special train for Portsmouth, via Woking, in about 1930. It clearly carries a Maunsell boiler, with pop valves, but no snifting valves, suggesting that it has a Urie superheater. It has received a King Arthur type chimney and smoke deflectors, with the smokebox side lamp irons moved up. George Woodward's record dated 15 August 1929 indicates that E473 left works with pop valves, and no snifting valves, but he does not mention the smoke deflectors. The boiler records confirm that Maunsell boiler 455 was fitted to E473 at that date. E473 has the smokebox door handrail separate from the boiler side handrail, the more common arrangement for the combination of smoke deflectors with a Urie smokebox door.

5. Details and Modifications

Boilers

It had been LSWR practice to have a boiler for each locomotive which, generally, remained with that locomotive. Repair durations were governed by the time taken to remove, refurbish and replace the boiler. In order to speed up repairs, Maunsell obtained additional spare boilers, so that locomotives requiring major boiler work could be fitted with boilers, which had already been refurbished. Numbers were allocated at about the time the boiler exchange scheme started in 1927, and a boiler took the number of the locomotive to which it was attached at the time. Boilers spare at the time of numbering, and later new boilers, were given numbers in the 900s and 1000s.

Four types of boiler were carried by the H15 and S15 class locomotives.

The original Urie H15s 482 to 491 carried parallel boilers, which could be fitted only to these locomotives. In 1927, E491 was rebuilt to take a taper boiler, providing one spare boiler for the remaining nine locomotives. In Southern days, these boilers were numbered 482 to 490 and 968, the original boiler from 491.

H15s E330-E335 carried the Drummond boilers from the previous F13 and E14 class 4-6-0s, which had been refurbished for use on the H15s and provided with superheaters, although the boiler on F13 333 was already so fitted. These were similar to the Urie parallel boilers on 482 to 490 but had longer fireboxes, so could be used only on 330-335. As there was never any spare boiler for these six locomotives, each one carried the same boiler throughout, and repair durations tended to be longer than for the other locomotives. These boilers worked at a pressure of 175psi.

The Urie N15s, Urie S15s and the Southern-built H15s all had identical Urie taper boilers, working at 180psi pressure and with a pair of direct loading safety valves in a rounded casing on the firebox. These were fitted initially with Eastleigh superheaters, except for H15 E524, which always had a Maunsell superheater. Maunsell superheaters were fitted to the other boilers during the 1920s. Boiler numbers were 473-478, 496-515, 521-524, 736, 738-741, 743-755, 986 and 1000. Nos.986 and 1000 were those originally carried by N15s 737 and 742, which had been fitted with Maunsell boilers in 1925. Total 50 boilers.

The Southern N15s and S15s were built with Maunsell taper boilers, dimensionally the same as the Urie boilers, but working at 200psi pressure and with Ross Pop safety valves on a flat base on the firebox. All were fitted with Maunsell superheaters, although boilers 737 and 742 initially carried Urie superheaters, as did a few others in the late 1920s. These boilers were interchangeable with the Urie taper boilers. A number of spare boilers were built or bought. Boiler numbers were: 448-457, 491 (NBL 1927), 737 and 742 (NBL 1925), 763-794 (NBL), 795-806, 823-837, 838-841 (1929), 928-931 (NBL 1927), 1001 (NBL 1927), 1047-1057 (1936), 1401-1412 (NBL 1947-49). Total 104 boilers.

All the Maunsell boilers were built at Eastleigh, except for those marked NBL, which were built by the North British Locomotive Co. Construction dates are shown only for those boilers not built as part of a specific locomotive. Boilers numbered up to 837 carried the numbers of the locomotives to which they were first fitted and boilers numbered from 838 were built as spares. When S15s 838-847 were built, they were fitted initially with new boilers 1047-1054, 1056 and 1057.

Most of the boilers had two washout plugs on each side of the firebox, above the handrail. Those on the right side were further forward than those on the left. Ten boilers 833-841 and 1057 were built with multiple washout plugs. Most of these had four plugs on the right side and five on the left, but boilers 834 and 837 had five plugs on each side. Boilers 835 and 1057 were later rebuilt with the usual arrangement of two washout plugs each side.

To summarise, any boiler carrying the number of a Urie locomotive, or a Southern H15, was a Urie boiler, with the exception of boilers 491, 737 and 742,

Urie S15 E497 at Feltham between February 1928, when it received new Maunsell boiler 931, and September 1929, when it went into works and came out with smoke deflectors. The brand new North British boiler had been put on at a Class B repair, as its previous boiler was defective. It is in lined black livery. In BR days, Maunsell boilers on Urie S15s became commonplace, as the older boilers were taken out of use. E497 retains its LSWR lamp sockets, but these now carry conventional lamp irons.

Urie S15 E499 at Eastleigh on 9 September 1933. It now has a Maunsell superheater and sloping smoke deflectors, which all the taper boilered locomotives had. When smoke deflectors were fitted to locomotives with Urie smokebox doors, the smokebox handrail was usually separate from the boiler side handrail. Some locomotives, including E499, retained the continuous boiler handrail. The smokebox lamp irons are now on the smokebox door, the chimney has lost its capuchon and passenger green has replaced its previous black livery.

which were NBL-built Maunsell boilers. Any boiler carrying the number of a Maunsell locomotive, or a number in the 9XX or 1XXX series, was a Maunsell boiler, with the exception of boilers 968, 986 and 1000, which were the original Urie boilers of H15 491 and N15s 737 and 742.

A change to the appearance of all the taper boilers occurred during the 1930s. The General Arrangement Drawing for the Urie S15 shows the top clearance between the boiler shell and the cladding on the front (tapered) ring of the boiler increased towards the front of the boiler, making the taper of the boiler appear to be less than it actually was. From the 1930s, the cladding was applied with the same clearance throughout, giving the appearance of a greater taper to the boiler.

After E491 was rebuilt to carry a taper boiler in 1927, there were 50 Urie and 104 Maunsell taper boilers for 51 Urie and 79 Maunsell locomotives. Thus, there were always some Urie locomotives running with Maunsell boilers, increasingly in later years as the older boilers were scrapped. The only Urie S15s which carried Urie boilers when they were withdrawn from service were 30499, 30504 and 30513. No Maunsell S15 ever carried a Urie boiler, although King Arthur 799 did in 1934-37.

Detail Modifications
With the exception of the reboilered 491, the H15 and S15 class 4-6-0s received no major modifications during their period of operation, but there were numerous detail alterations, which are important to modellers. These are described, approximately in order from the front to the rear of the locomotives.

Lamp Irons
At the time of the grouping in 1923, most railways used lamp irons, consisting of a vertical steel bar. A slot at the back or side (GWR) of the lamp meant it could be dropped in place securely on the iron. In earlier years, many railways had used sockets, into which a tongue on the lamp, or disc, was inserted. Of the major railways, only the LSWR and LNWR continued to use sockets in 1923. During the 1920s, the Southern built new locomotives with both types of lamp iron. New King Arthurs, with sockets, were allocated to the Eastern section of the Southern, whilst Ashford sent N class 2-6-0s, with conventional lamp irons, to the West Country. No doubt the comments of the enginemen were equally unprintable, from Ramsgate to Padstow. By the late 1920s, lamp irons had been inserted into the LSWR sockets and they were replaced by conventional lamp irons, on a random basis, during the 1930s. Many tenders retained sockets with inserted lamp irons to the end. S15s 833 to 847 were built with conventional lamp irons.

All the constituents of the Southern used headcodes defining the route of the train, rather than the Railway Clearing House train type classification used on the rest of the British railways. The LSWR and LB&SCR used six lamp, or disc, positions and the SE&CR had prepared its locomotives for the introduction of six disc codes by the Southern. On the LSWR, the smokebox side lamp sockets were on the periphery of the smokebox, at half height. On the larger boilered locomotives, a disc at the side positions was in the driver's view of the line. When smoke deflectors were fitted, the side lamp irons were raised above the deflectors, making the sighting even worse. During the 1930s, the side lamp irons were all moved to the smokebox door.

On the LSWR H15s, the top socket was initially on the periphery of the smokebox, but was moved down onto the top handrail stanchion during LSWR days and the LSWR S15s and Southern built H15s were built with the top socket on the handrail stanchion. All top lamp irons were moved onto the smokebox doors during the 1920s.

Smokebox Doors and handrails
All the H15s and the LSWR S15s were built with Urie pattern smokebox doors secured by a centre dart, with four peripheral closing 'dogs' at the bottom, where ash deposits might cause heating and distortion of the door. The

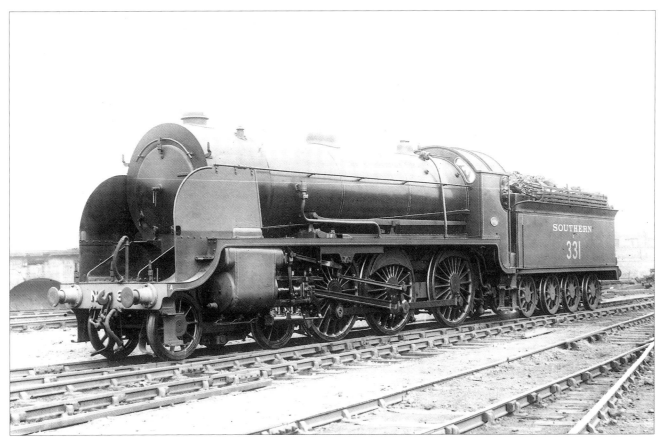

Southern parallel boilered H15 E331 at Nine Elms, between December 1929, when it received smoke deflectors, and October 1931, when it lost its E prefix. Its tender was rebuilt with a raised top and four coal rails, giving 4,300 gallons capacity, at the same time as the smoke deflectors were fitted. Most parallel boilered H15s received vertical smoke deflectors but some of the first to be fitted initially received angled deflectors, with the boiler handrail fixed to the top edge of the deflector plate. The smokebox side lamp irons have been raised, clear of the smoke deflectors but right into the driver's line of sight of the track.

Urie H15 E488 at Waterloo, on a Portsmouth train, in 1931-32. It has a Maunsell superheater and a stovepipe chimney. The smoke deflectors are vertical, which was usual on the parallel boiler locomotives. The buffer beam numerals and E prefix are in yellow serif characters. The injector steam pipe is now in line with the safety valve but E488 still has full depth cabside cutouts and Urie smokebox door, which now carries the lamp irons. The piston tailrods have gone, replaced by a small blanking plate, and the cylinder drain pipes have been extended forward, and attached to the footstep.

332 stands to the west of Salisbury station in the late 1930s with the empty stock for a train to Waterloo. It now has a Maunsell smokebox door and the tender coal rails have been plated, to avoid losing the small coal which was beginning to appear. The yellow serif buffer beam numerals now read No.332. Bournemouth Railway Club, Kelland Collection.

30485 at Eastleigh on 17 April 1949. It now has a short flared chimney and reduced depth cabside cutouts, but the side plates at the front of the tender have not been raised. It has also acquired the left-hand crosshead from a Southern-built locomotive. This still carries the rearward extension to carry the vacuum pump drive bracket. BRITISH RAILWAYS lettering and numbers, in Gill sans characters, were applied to unlined black in July 1948, at the same time as the snifting valves were removed. R.K. Blencowe Collection.

Short King Arthur type chimneys were fitted to Urie S15s 510 and 514 in 1931 but no good photograph is available. 30503 later carried a King Arthur chimney, from 1945 to 1955, and is seen at Eastleigh on 20 May 1950, a few months after receiving its BR number, with the large first emblem on the tender. It has a Maunsell boiler and the additional driving wheel balance weights, of varying shapes, added during the late 1930s, are apparent. R.K. Blencowe Collection.

smokebox handrail was a continuation of the boiler side handrail, curving over the smokebox door. When smoke deflectors were fitted, the boiler handrail was usually terminated on the top of the deflector, or behind it on parallel boiler H15s with vertical deflectors, and a separate handrail was fitted above the smokebox door. On a minority of taper boilered locomotives, the continuous handrail was retained. H15s 491 and 523 and S15s 497, 499 and 512 are noted from photographs.

The Southern S15s were all built with Maunsell pattern smokebox doors, with six closing dogs on the periphery, and no central dart. A horizontal handrail was provided, in line with the boiler side handrail, together with a small grabrail on the left side, to enable the door to be opened. When the smokebox side lamp irons were moved to the door, the small grabrail was removed and the horizontal handrail shortened.

During the 1930s, all H15s and S15s with Urie smokebox doors received Maunsell pattern doors, although the taper boilered H15 491 reverted to a Urie door for a period during 1945-46. No example has been noted of a Maunsell door on a Urie locomotive without smoke deflectors and, unlike the King Arthurs, no example of a Maunsell S15 with a Urie smokebox door has been noted.

Smoke Deflectors
As locomotive boilers got bigger, and

chimneys shorter, problems began to occur with the exhaust clinging to the boiler and obscuring the driver's view of the line. It is likely that this problem occurred with the LSWR H15s, as one reason for the small diameter stovepipe chimney fitted to the LSWR N15s and S15s is stated to have been to throw the exhaust upwards, although it restricted the exhaust and increased the back pressure. The problem returned with the Southern King Arthurs, which were designed with a free exhaust and lipped chimneys. O.S. Nock reported cases of drivers shutting off steam during a run, for no apparent reason other than to get a clear view of a signal.

Smoke deflector plates had been introduced by Richard Wagner of the German State Railways in 1925, on his Class 01 and 02 4-6-2s. Maunsell tried out an assortment of 'downdraught preventers' on King Arthurs from 1926, the most successful being a version of the large Wagner plate. Smaller plates was finally adopted and fitted to all King Arthurs in 1927-29. Similar plates were fitted to all H15s and S15s between 1929 and 1932, 838 to 847 having them from new. All taper boilered H15s and S15s had plates which sloped inwards, fixed directly to the smokebox side handrail. The first parallel boilered H15s to be fitted with smoke deflectors also had sloping plates initially but they were quickly replaced by vertical plates, fixed to the handrail by brackets, which were fitted to all the parallel boiler H15s.

Those noted with sloping plates were 331, 332, 483, 484, 485, 488 and 489. It is thought that the sloping smoke deflectors of 484 and 485 were fitted at Nine Elms, using components supplied from Eastleigh.

When smoke deflectors plates were fitted, the footsteps on the curved drop to the platform, ahead of the cylinders, were replaced by narrow steps, outside the deflector plates. The small grab rails on the outer face of the main frames were replaced by vertical stanchions above each buffer, and hand holds in the front edge of the smoke deflector plates.

Chimneys
The LSWR H15s had lipped cast iron chimneys, following the Drummond style. Probably due to problems with the exhaust obscuring the driver's view of the line, Robert Urie provided his N15 and S15 classes with narrow stovepipe chimneys, built to the full height of the LSWR loading gauge. The Southern H15s were also built with stovepipe chimneys and LSWR H15s 483, 488 and 491 carried them in late LSWR and early Southern days. The tall stovepipe chimneys of the S15s lost their capuchons during the 1930s.

There was later a return to cast iron lipped chimneys of three varieties. The parallel boilered H15s received chimneys similar to, but shorter than, those originally fitted to the 482-491 series.

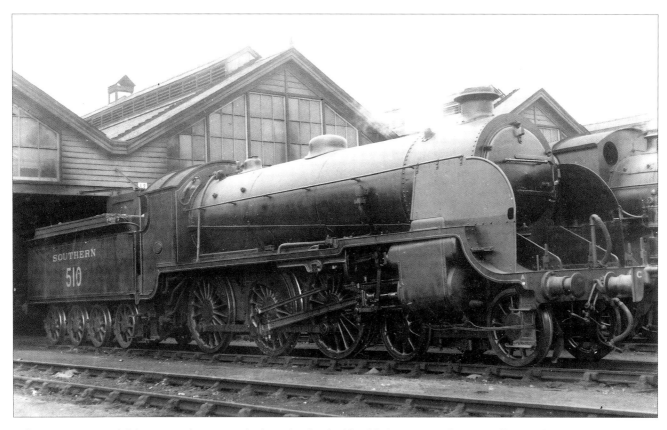

Urie S15 510 at Eastleigh on 22 July 1938. It had received a double sided Drummond 4,000 gallon tender in November 1935 and a lipped chimney of the type used on the U1 class 2-6-0s in December 1936. This became the normal chimney for Urie S15s from 1940, but it was 1948 before the last stovepipes disappeared. 510 has a Maunsell superheater and smokebox door, and has had smoke deflectors and green livery since 1931.

These were fitted to 482-490 between 1932 and 1943 and to 330-335 between 1941 and 1956.

The taper boilered H15s received King Arthur type chimneys between 1927 and 1931. After trials with King Arthur chimneys on 510 and 514 in 1931, the LSWR S15s received cast iron lipped chimneys of the type used on the U1 2-6-0s in 1936 (510) and 1940-48. 503 carried a King Arthur chimney between 1945 and 1955.

The Southern-built S15s always ran with King Arthur type cast iron lipped chimneys.

Superheaters and Fittings

The main part of any superheater, the superheater elements inside the large flues of the boiler and the superheater header inside the smokebox, are not visible from outside the locomotive, and will not be described. However, some types of superheater required visible fittings, outside the smokebox. The Schmidt superheaters, fitted initially to H15s 482-485, had superheater dampers, operated by a rod inside the right-hand boiler handrail. This required a casing and linkage outside the smokebox. There was also a pyrometer, requiring a sensing cable emerging from the top left side of the smokebox and a small plate on each side of the smokebox, below the handrail. These features were all connected with monitoring the

performance of the superheater, and were later removed.

The Robinson superheaters, fitted to 486-489, might also have been fitted with pyrometers in early days, as some photographs show blanking plates, in approximately the position of the snifting valves of the later Maunsell superheaters.

The Eastleigh superheaters, fitted to H15s 335, E473-E478, 490, 491, E521-E523 and S15s 496-515, did not betray their presence by any external evidence. Maunsell superheaters were identified by two snifting valves on the superheater header, which emerged from the top of the smoke box at either side, behind the chimney. The snifting valves were removed in late Southern and early British Railways days. On locomotives with Eastleigh or Maunsell superheaters, but not 330-335, there was also a cock for attaching a steam lance, at the front of the smokebox on the right side. It is not known how long these lasted, as they were hidden by the smoke deflectors.

Cylinders and Motion

The Urie H15s 482-491 and 335 were built with piston tailrods. These were removed during the 1920s. The exhaust pipes from the cylinder drain cocks on all H15s and the LSWR S15s initially ended level with front face of the cylinders, but were extended and

attached to the outside of the front footstep backing plates in the early 1930s. The Southern S15s were built with extended cylinder drain pipes, which were fixed to the inside faces of the footstep backing plates.

The LSWR S15s were built with fluted slidebars whilst all the H15s and the Southern S15s had plain ones. Some LSWR S15s received plain replacement slidebars, 30500 and 30512 being noted.

All Southern built-H15s and S15s were built with vacuum pumps attached below the left-hand lower slide bar, with the pump rod driven by a bracket mounted on a rearward extension to the crosshead. The pumps were removed during the Second World War but the extension to the left-hand crosshead remained for a time, until the 1950s. In early BR days, Urie H15 30485 had a left-hand crosshead from a Southern-built locomotive, with the pump drive extension.

A late British Railways period modification to a number of S15s was the replacement of the adjustable big end bearings of the connecting rods by single piece bushed bearings. These have been noted on 30507, 30508, 30510, 30511, 30826, 30827, 30830, 30842, 30843 and 30847. 841 also acquired bushed rods in preservation whilst 847 has reverted to adjustable big ends.

Urie S15 30511 at Eastleigh on 1 June 1962, shortly after a General repair, during which it received a Maunsell boiler and AWS equipment. It is also fitted with connecting rods with bushed big ends, a late modification to a number of N15 and S15 4-6-0s. The tender has left facing second emblems and electrification warning signs have been applied to the smoke deflectors and the firebox.

Urie S15 30498 at Eastleigh on 30 October 1954. It is ex-works from a Heavy Intermediate repair, during which it has received the 5,200 gallon tender from H15 30488, which would have been lined black and had suffered some accident damage (see page 232). The low sun brings out the detail below the platform, including the additional balance weights on the driving and coupled wheels. The Maunsell boiler was fitted at its previous General Repair in 1952. The tender body has been repainted, as has the smokebox, chimney and a few other bits of the locomotive. The cabside carries the 6F power classification above the number and a water treatment yellow triangle below. E.W. Fry.

Maunsell S15 30824 at Salisbury on 1 July 1950, with another variant of the additional balance weights added to the driving wheels of the S15s. In January 1950 it lost its snifting valves and received its BR number, with large first emblems on the tender. The A power classification is below the cabside numerals. R.K. Blencowe Collection.

Wheel Balance Weights

All H15s and S15s up to 837 were built with crescent shaped balance weights cast into the wheels. These were placed directly opposite the coupling rod boss and covered six spoke gaps on the leading and trailing coupled wheels and eight spoke gaps on the driving wheels. The final batch of S15s, 838 to 847, were provided with built up balance weights, with bolted plates on the front and back of the wheel. The ends of the plates were squared off slightly and lead weights were placed between the plates and the spokes. On 838, 841 and 843, the driving wheel balance weight covered eight spoke gaps but on the others they only covered seven, being cut off at the clockwise end on each side. Photographs suggest that there was no interchange of the two types of wheelsets between locomotives, unlike the Schools class 4-4-0s, where the last batch had built up balance weights, which then moved throughout the class.

From the late 1930s all the earlier S15s, of both Urie and Maunsell types, began to receive additional bolted balance weights. On the driving wheels, these consisted of either a tapered or parallel section of bolted balance weight added to the clockwise end of the cast balance weight. On the coupled wheels, some received an additional weight over one spoke gap, 90 degrees clockwise from the existing weight, whilst others received bolted weights, of various shapes, adjacent to the clockwise end

of the cast balance weight. The only H15 to receive additional balance weights was 522.

Injectors and Steam Pipes

The LSWR H15s and S15s were built with two Gresham's hot water injectors, one on each side below the cab. Maunsell fitted a Gresham's hot water injector in the right side and a Davies & Metcalfe exhaust steam injector on the left side. During British Railways days, the exhaust steam injectors were replaced by Dreadnought injectors on some locomotives.

On all H15s and S15s, steam was fed to the injectors from connections on the top of the firebox, on either side, by copper pipes which led down the sides of the firebox, to the injectors below the cab. On H15s 482-491, these pipes were close to the front of the cab, but on 330-335, they were further forward, alongside the safety valves, where they had been on the Drummond 4-6-0s. The injector steam pipes of 482-490 were later moved to the position alongside the safety valve, but some had them at an intermediate position, with the pipes just to the rear of the rearmost handrail stanchion on the boiler. This intermediate position for the injector steam pipes was standard on all the taper boilers, of Urie or Maunsell pattern. In about 1960, the injector steam pipes of some Maunsell S15s emerged from the front of the connections on the firebox and passed

ahead of the rearmost handrail stanchion. 30831, 30840 and 30842 were so noted.

Feedwater Heaters

Feedwater heaters had been used on the LSWR for many years. The cost of coal was high, due to the distance to the LSWR system from the nearest supplies of suitable locomotive coal. Barnstaple shed probably got the cheapest coal, shipped directly from South Wales to Fremington quay. Urie's predecessor, Dugald Drummond, had used Stroudley's system of feedwater heating on many of his locomotives. Part of the exhaust steam was diverted into heating pipes in the water tank(s), heating the bulk water supply.

In the mid 19th Century, the two Beatties, father and son, who had control of LSWR locomotives from 1850 to 1878, used feedwater heaters in which some of the exhaust steam heated the water, as it was being fed into the boiler. Urie adopted a system which was similar in principle, but different in practice. Whilst the final development of the Beattie system used concentric tube heat exchangers, on each side of the boiler, Urie provided a drum heat exchanger, mounted under the tender frame between the bogies. Much of the heat must have been lost from the pipes taking the exhaust steam 40ft from the smokebox to the heat exchanger, and bringing the heated water back 20ft to the injectors below the cab.

Maunsell S15 30840 at Feltham on 13 October 1964, a month after withdrawal from service. The battery box for the British Railways AWS system is alongside the firebox and the injector steam pipe has been modified, to emerge from the front of the take off point on the top of the firebox. It is fitted with BR water treatment equipment, indicated by the yellow triangle below the cabside number. This was offset on a number of S15s. The two AWS access holes can be seen, low down on the cabside. Stephen Gradidge.

Urie H15 483, probably at Nine Elms, in October 1933. The piston tailrods have gone and it was fitted with a stovepipe chimney in 1924, followed by smoke deflectors and a Maunsell superheater in 1929; it lost the E prefix in 1931. It still has a Urie smokebox door. Some timber infilling of the cabside cutout has been contrived.

It is thought that feedwater heaters may have been provided on the Urie H15s and S15s and the Southern-built H15s. The weight diagram for the Urie H15s shows a feedwater heater drum on the tender, but this is not shown on the General Arrangement drawing of the tender. Conversely, the weight diagrams for the Urie N15, S15 and Southern H15 do not show feedwater heaters, but the General Arrangement drawing for the tender does. Due to the short, 3ft 3in, length of the heat exchanger drum, it can only be seen in photographs which show the tender nearly broadside. In about 1920, H15s 486, 490 and 491 had longer heat exchangers, of rectangular section. These can be seen in photographs, as they projected outside the bogie frames. Whatever is the truth about which locomotives carried feedwater heaters when new, one thing is fairly clear; their cost outweighed any saving. Maunsell

had them removed as soon as he realised their ineffectiveness.

Oil Burning
Shortly after entering service in May 1921, S15 515 was converted to burn oil on the 'Scarab' system. An oil tank was installed in the coal space and 515 ran 7,483 miles as an oil burner between July and October 1921. It was then reconverted to coal burning, but was changed to oil again from June to December 1926, during the General Strike and the extended coal miners' strike. No H15 or S15 was involved in the oil burning programme of 1947-48.

Cabs
All the H15s and the LSWR S15s had cabs derived from Dugald Drummond practice. The edge of the arched cab roof was turned outwards, to provide pronounced eaves, above the cab side. The cab roof did not extend further back

than the cab handrail. Due to their shorter rear overhang, the cabs of 330-335 were shorter than the others. On H15s 335 and 482-491, the cabside cutout was large, resulting in the depth of the cabside being shallow, compared with the high set floor. A number of late LSWR and early Southern period photographs show timber boarding inside the lower part of the cabside cutouts. The cabside cutouts of the S15s and the Southern H15s were smaller in both width and depth, and those of 335 and 482-491 were reduced during the 1930s, the depth being reduced before the width in some cases. The altered shape varied between locomotives. A feature of the Urie cab was the pear shaped cab front spectacle glasses.

As the Southern S15s were built to fit the Southern composite loading gauge, the Urie cab roof was replaced by one derived from Ashford practice, with the

the driver's cab. If the signal was clear, an electric current sounded a bell in the cab and the brake was not applied. The other system was the Hudd system, used on the London Tilbury & Southend lines of the LMS. This used magnets on the track to pass signals to the locomotive, without requiring physical contact. A permanent magnet on the track at each distant signal applied the brake and sounded the warning horn. It was followed by an electromagnet which, if the signal was clear, cancelled the brake application. An early version of Hudd's system had been tried out on the Southern in 1931, but was not followed up.

British Railways engineers were not too keen on the physical contact required by the GWR system, which would clearly become impractical as train speeds increased. The Hudd system was also viewed with misgiving as a similar horn sound was made, whether the signal was at danger or clear, although it was shorter at a clear signal and a visual indication of the signal aspect was given to the driver. The British Railways Advanced Warning System (AWS) was developed during the 1950s, utilising the best features of each system. The use of magnets avoided the physical contact of the GWR system, the GWR bell indicated a clear signal and the Hudd yellow and black 'sunflower' indicator reminded the driver of the aspect of the last signal which he had passed. It took more time to develop a variant suitable for use on the Southern third rail electrified lines, but this was ready by about 1960. No H15s were ever fitted with AWS equipment but it was fitted between 1960 and 1962 to all S15s except for 30501, 30502, 30513, 30825 and 30828. The AWS receiver was on the front of the bogie, with a protective plate below the buffer beam to protect it from swinging couplings. The battery was in a casing on the platform, on the left side of the firebox, and other control equipment was in a casing on the front of the cab on the left side. Two access holes were cut low down in the left-hand cabside.

roof merging smoothly into the cabside, with two longitudinal rainstrips set well back from the side of the cab. Between the rainstrips, the cab roof was extended backwards, over the front of the tender. The pear shaped spectacle glasses were retained, but with a straight lower edge, whilst this was curved on the Urie cabs. No H15 or S15 ever received the visor over the spectacle glasses, which was fitted to the King Arthur class 4-6-0s.

A number of photographs of H15s around the Second World War period show blackout curtains, to make the glow from an open firebox door less visible from the air. The curtain was rolled up under the cab roof and could be unrolled, along a pair of wires fixed to stanchions on the tender. No photographs of S15s with these curtains and wires have been noted, but this might be due to the small number of photographs taken during this time. The blackout curtains appear to have been retained after the war as storm sheets, but without the wires to the tender, and some S15s also received them.

Automatic Warning System (AWS)

Systems for taking the control of the brakes of a train out of the hands of the train driver, in emergency situations, have been developed over many years, and the search for the ideal system continues today. At the formation of British Railways, two systems were in use. The first was the Great Western Railway's Automatic Train Control (ATC). This had been developed following a rear end collision at Slough in 1900 and had been installed on all GWR main lines by 1930. It relied on physical contact between a shoe on the locomotive and a ramp between the rails, at each distant signal. If the signal was at caution, the brake was applied and the inrush of air sounded a siren in

Maunsell S15 30834 at Basingstoke on empty stock of a train from Waterloo on 18 August 1962. The AWS receiver can be seen between the guard irons on the bogie, with a protective plate to prevent it being struck by a swinging coupling, which is correctly hooked up in this case. As it is summer, the steam heating hose below the buffer beam has been removed. The battery box for the AWS is alongside the firebox and the control equipment is housed in the box on the front of the cab. 30834 and 30836 were the only two S15s to retain their flat sided six wheel tenders until withdrawal.

Right. Southern H15 477 on an up train at Eastleigh on 30 July 1939. The Southern is preparing for trouble and has fitted a blackout curtain, rolled up under the cab roof, with wires to hold it down to stanchions on the tender. H.C. Casserley, courtesy R.M. Casserley.

Below. The cab of 483, at Dorchester on 14 September 1948. The new plating added to reduce the depth and width of the cabside cutout is apparent, but the tender front panel has not been raised to match. The Bulleid green shaded cabside numerals and details of the tender handbrake wheel, toolboxes and shovelling plate are well shown. A.E. West, courtesy M.S. King.

Bottom right. Southern H15 521 on a down train of empty stock at Pokesdown on 3 June 1944. 521 is in the wartime unlined black livery. The blackout curtain is not expected to be required further, and has been tied forward over the cab roof.

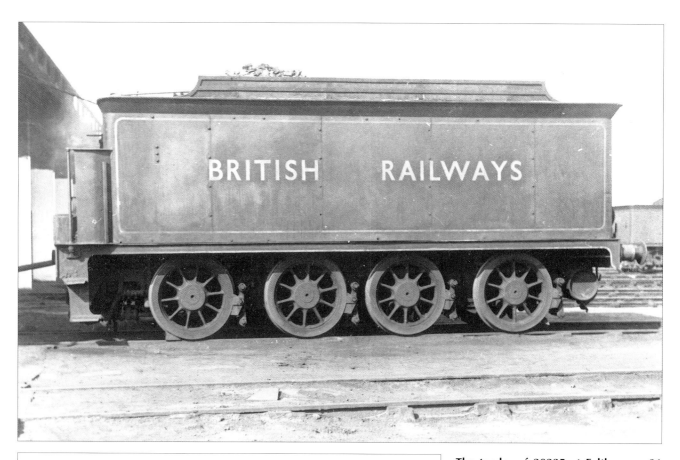

The tender of 30335 at Feltham on 21 March 1950. This was the prototype for Dugald Drummond's bogie tenders and had been built in 1897 to run with 4-2-2-0 No.720 but was moved to E14 4-6-0 No.335 in 1909; it remained with 335 when it was 'rebuilt' as an H15 in 1914. It had a water capacity of 4,500 gallons and was taller than the later Drummond 4,000 gallon bogie tenders. The front end of the platform and the side sheets were widened by the mid-1920s. The tender retained its double side sheeting, although the feedwater had not been heated since 1912. The original Drummond tender brake, applied by a handwheel, has been replaced by a conventional handbrake on a vertical shaft. A.E. West, courtesy M.S. King.

6. Tenders

In general, both the LSWR and SR built new locomotives with tenders, which stayed together throughout. However, a number of instances occurred, where changed traffic requirements resulted in groups of tenders being exchanged for others. During the 1950s, more random tender exchanges began to occur, as serviceable tenders from withdrawn locomotives were coupled to locomotives which remained in service.

Until 1927, Southern tenders were generally referred to by the number of the locomotive to which they were coupled. Separate numbers were then allocated to the tenders; those coupled to the H15s and S15s being numbered as follows:

H15s: 482 to 491, 335, 330 to 334, 473 to 478, 521 to 524, tender numbers 780 to 805.
S15s: 496 to 515, 823 to 847, tender numbers 3200 to 3244

Initially, tenders were generally still renumbered if they were transferred to a different class of locomotive. When the original tenders from S15s E828 to E837 were replaced by North British-built Urie tenders from King Arthurs in the late 1920s, the Urie tenders received tender numbers 3225 to 3234, and the original tenders from 828 to 837 received numbers in the King Arthur and Lord Nelson tender series. At later tender exchanges, the tenders retained their existing numbers.

H15s 30330-30335

The six H15s which were nominally rebuilds from Drummond 4-6-0s were coupled to the Drummond bogie tenders from these locomotives. I will deal with 30335 first, as it was the first to be rebuilt, and the most straightforward. LSWR H15 335 was coupled to the prototype Drummond 4,500 gallon bogie tender which had been built in 1897 to run with Drummond's T7 4-2-2-0 No.720. The tender was built two months after the locomotive, to order V7. Like all Drummond bogie tenders, the bogies had inside frames, but the tank was taller than the standard 4,000 gallon tenders, which followed. 720 exchanged tenders with E14 4-6-0 335 in 1908, and the tender remained with 335 when it was rebuilt as an H15. This tender, numbered 790 in 1927, kept its double sides, to retain the heat from the non-existent feedwater heater, until withdrawn. The two open coal rails were plated in the late 1930s, to prevent small coal from escaping between the rails. When running with E14 335, the tender handbrake was operated by a handwheel on a horizontal shaft. By the 1930s, a conventional brake pedestal was fitted but it is not known when this was changed.

Southern H15s E330-E334 ran with the Drummond 4,000 gallon bogie tenders, which had been built to run with the LSWR F13 class 4-6-0s 330-334. Whilst running with the F13s, they were double sided, with feedwater heater wells. When they were refurbished to run with the H15s, the feedwater heater wells and double sides were removed. The handbrake wheel, on a horizontal shaft, working the brake through bevel gears, was replaced by a conventional vertical brake pedestal. The new flat tender bottom was attached to the sides by a row of closely spaced snap head rivets. As shown in the table in Chapter 4 the number of the H15 to which each tender was coupled was not the same as the F13 from which it had come.

In 1931-32, about the same time as the locomotives got smoke deflectors, the tenders of 330-334 had raised tops and extended coal rails fitted, giving a water capacity of 4,300 gallons. At about the same time, the 4,500 gallon tenders then coupled to L11 class 4-4-0s 157, 169, 414, 436 and 437 had their capacity reduced to 4,000 gallons. Exactly what happened is unclear. George Woodward records that H15 E333 exchanged tenders with L11 E157 in January 1931 but other recorders state that the tenders were changed back in July 1933.

It would appear that the tender tops were exchanged between the tenders of

Southern H15 E332, at some date before 9 December 1926, from the postal franking on the rear of the original postcard. The 330-334 series of H15s re-used the Drummond 4,000 gallon tenders of F13s 330-334, but not in numerical order. The front of the platform was widened, the double side sheeting removed and new flat tender bottoms were fixed by a row of snap head rivets.

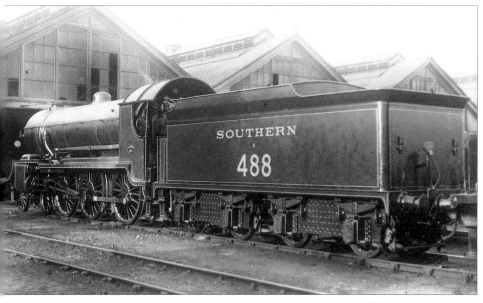

Top. Southern H15 E331, possibly at Clapham Junction, between December 1929, when it received sloping smoke deflectors, and October 1931, when it lost its E prefix and received vertical smoke deflectors. Its tender was rebuilt with a raised top and four coal rails, giving 4300 gallons capacity, at the same time as the smoke deflectors were fitted. The raised tender top can just be seen to the right of the coal rails. The tender tops appear to have been exchanged for those from five L11 class 4-4-0s, whose 4,500 gallon tenders were reduced to 4,000 gallons at the same time. G.R. Gregs.

Middle. Southern H15 334, probably waiting to go into Eastleigh works, during the 1930s. There is a Urie S15 to the left and a Drummond T14 4-6-0 on the right. Nothing else had the Urie B power classification. When the tender tops of the 330-334 series H15s were raised, 334 got five coal rails in place of four. This was a feature of the last four 4,500 gallon tenders to be built, originally coupled to T14s 460 and 461 and D15s 463 and 464 but coupled to L11 class 4-4-0s during the 1920s. The tender coal rails have been plated..

Bottom. Urie H15 E488 at Eastleigh in the late 1920s The ten tenders built with H15s 482 to 491 were narrower and taller than the later Urie and Maunsell 5,000 gallon tenders, with a water capacity of 5,200 gallons. Detail of the Southern tender livery is revealed, including the third numberplate, on the back of the tender, and the lamp irons, placed in the LSWR sockets. This arrangement lasted much longer on tenders than on the fronts of the locomotives. R.K. Blencowe Collection.

The 5,200 gallon tender of 30490 at Dorchester on 9 June 1949. Although the Urie tenders, with outside framed bogies and coal plates in place of open rails, looked superficially different from the Drummond ones, they were otherwise very similar to the Drummond 5,800 gallon tenders, built for the T14 4-6-0s in 1912. The arrangement of the handbrake, toolboxes and shovelling plate at the front was the same, as were the double water fillers at the rear. A.E.West, courtesy M.S. King.

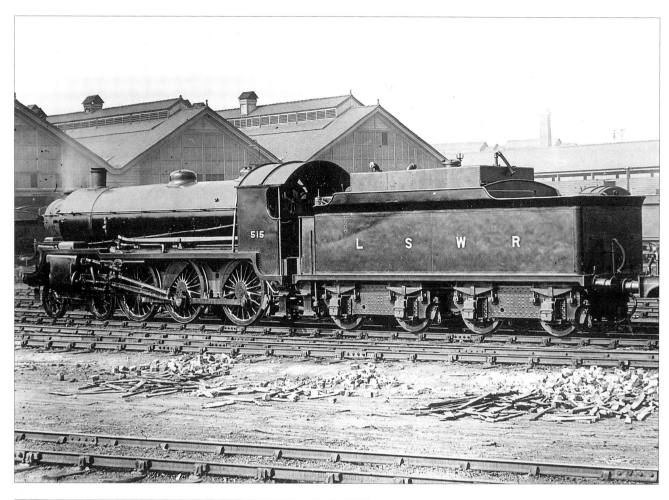

Above. Urie S15 515 at Eastleigh shed in 1921. The Urie N15s and S15s, the Southern H15s, apart from the 330 series, and the North British King Arthurs had similar Urie 5,000 gallon bogie tenders when built, wider and lower than the 5,200 gallon tenders of the Urie H15s. The tender of 515 has two variations. Between the tender bogies can be seen the cylindrical casing of the feedwater heat exchanger; fitted to the Urie S15s when new, it disappeared after a very short time. On top of the tender is an oil tank, carried by 515 from July to October 1921 and from June to December 1926. Behind can be seen the cab roof and tender of one of the ROD 2-8-0s which the LSWR hired during 1920-21.

Left. Tender of Urie S15 30506 at Ropley, on the Mid Hants Railway, 16 May 1976. Although no H15s or S15s were involved in the oil burning programme of 1947-48, the tender coupled to 30506 in 1956 had previously been coupled to Urie N15 30745, which had been an oil burner, fitted with electric lighting. The tender still carried the extended lamp irons over the electric lights, the brackets for the cable conduits and the holes in the buffer beam and platform valance for additional rear footsteps.

Urie S17 507 at Fratton on 22 May1937. In August 1935 507 gave up its Urie tender to N15X 2330 for a Drummond 4,000 gallon tender from withdrawn C8 class 4-4-0 293. The platform and side sheeting at the front have been widened. Although the C8s had never been fitted with feedwater heating, this tender has double sides, to retain the non-existent heat. The number is painted on the rear of the tender, replacing the brass numberplates when the E prefixes were removed. H.C. Casserley, courtesy R.M. Casserley.

the H15s and those of the L11s. As it is most unlikely that the rivet positions would be the same on different tenders, it is possible that the exchanged tops were welded onto the tender tanks. One pair of tenders, coupled to L11 414 and H15 334, was distinctive in having five coal rails in place of four. This was a feature of the last four of the 4,500 gallon tenders to be built.

There is no record of when the tenders were enlarged, as it took place before the introduction of the Engine Record Cards, which show tender changes. I have assumed that the enlargement took place when the pairs of locomotives were in works together, as shown by George Woodward, although there is no absolute concurrence of 332 with 437. The coal rails of these tenders were plated in the late 1930s.

30330 and 30332-30335 retained their Drummond tenders until withdrawal but, in 1956, 30331 received a hybrid Urie 5,000 gallon tender 858. This comprised the frame of tender 858, from Urie N15 30744, and the tank of tender 3214, from Remembrance 32332, which had been fitted with auxiliary vacuum reservoirs and rear footsteps. These reservoirs were retained when it was coupled to 30331, but the handrails on the rear corners of the tender were removed, as the frame had no rear footsteps.

Urie H15s 30482-30491
The original Urie H15s, LSWR 482-491,

were built with 5200 gallon bogie tenders, having outside framed bogies and flared tops, surmounted by solid coal plates, in place of the open rails of earlier tenders. Although looking superficially much more modern than the Drummond bogie tenders, these tenders were clearly developed from the 5,800 gallon tenders built the year before for the T14 class 4-6-0s. The arrangement of the tender front was the same, as were the two tank fillers at the rear. The tender front panel was short, to match the deep cabside cutouts of the Urie H15s. When 491 was rebuilt to carry a taper boiler, its cabside cutouts were reduced and the tender front panels raised to match; this was the only 5,200 gallon tender to be so modified.

It is possible that these tenders were built with feedwater heat exchanger drums mounted between the bogies. These drums are shown in the weight diagram, but not the General Arrangement drawing. Due to the short length of the drums, they are visible only in broadside photographs. In about 1920, the tenders of 486, 490 and 491 carried longer heat exchangers, of rectangular cross section. These projected outside the bogie frames, and are clearly visible in photographs. These heat exchangers had gone by early Southern days.

This type of tender was unique to the class, although, during the 1950s, some were coupled to Urie S15s, Southern H15s and one King Arthur. Tender numbers 780 to 789 were applied in 1927.

During the mid-1950s, tenders of the later standard Urie 5,000 gallon pattern were coupled to 30482, 30484 and 30488.

Southern H15s 30473-30478 and 30521-30524
The Southern-built H15s E473-E478 and E521-E524 were built with Urie standard 5,000 gallon bogie tenders, which may have been fitted briefly with feedwater heat exchanger drums between the bogies. These tenders were wider and lower than the 5,200 gallon tenders coupled to 482-491. Similar tenders were built with the LSWR Urie N15s 736-755, Urie S15s 496-515 and the Southern N15s E763-E792. During the mid-1950s, 30473 and 30474 received 5,200 gallon Urie tenders.

Urie S15s 30496-30515
The Urie S15s, LSWR 496-515, were built with Urie 5,000 gallon tenders, fitted with feedwater heat exchanger drums between the bogies. These drums were removed, probably in very early SR days.

Following the electrification of the Brighton main line in 1933, the ex-LB&SCR Remembrance class 4-6-4Ts became redundant, and were rebuilt as 4-6-0s, for the Western section, in 1934-36. They received the Urie bogie tenders from S15s 504-507, 509, 510 and 833. These S15s had Drummond 4,000 gallon bogie tenders from C8 class 4-4-0s 290-296, which were being withdrawn at the time. 833 almost immediately exchanged tenders with 508. Eric Youldon has suggested that 833, which was the first S15 to get a Drummond tender, happened to be at Eastleigh when the first rebuilt Remembrance 2329 was needing a tender, and that a decision was then made to take the tenders from the single group of S15s 504-510. These tenders retained their numbers 220-226, in the C8 series. Although the C8s had never been fitted for feedwater heating, tenders 220, 223 and 225 were double sided, and retained this feature while attached to S15s 509, 507 and 510.

By the mid-1950s, locomotive withdrawals permitted the Drummond tenders coupled to 30504-30510 to be replaced by Urie ones, and a few other S15s also had their tenders changed. 30498, 30503, 30504 and 30507 received Urie 5,200 gallon tenders while 30505, 30506, 30508, 30509 and 30510 got Urie 5,000 gallon tenders, similar to those they had lost in 1934-36.

30506 acquired the tender from Urie N15 30745 in 1956. As 745 it had been involved in the oil burning exercise in 1946-48 and had been fitted with electric lighting. This was removed when the tender was coupled to 30506 but it retained the extended lamp irons, to place route discs in front of the electric lamps. The tender also retained brackets to carry lighting conduits and had holes in the buffer beam and platform valance, where tubular rear footsteps had been fitted.

30508 and 30509 acquired the tenders from Remembrance 4-6-0s 32329 and 32328. These had originally been coupled to S15s 833 and 507 and had received auxiliary vacuum reservoirs and rear steps when coupled to 32329 and 32328. When coupled to 30508 and 30509 they retained the rear steps. The tender of 30508 lost its auxiliary vacuum reservoirs but the one coupled to 30509 retained them for a time.

Shortly before it was withdrawn, 30499 received a 4,000 gallon six wheel tender from Maunsell S15 30835. The reason for the exchange was almost certainly to provide 30835, which still had a year to run, with a bogie tender.

Maunsell S15s 30823-30847

Maunsell S15s E823 to E827 were built with tenders similar to the Urie 5,000 gallon tenders, but the bogie side frames had arched cutouts between the axleboxes and conventional handbrake pedestals were fitted. The tenders initially coupled to E828 to E832 were the same, but had three auxiliary vacuum reservoirs on the tank top, behind the coal space. The tenders coupled to E833-E837 and 838-847 were a further development of the 5,000 gallon bogie tender. The tank was of partially welded construction, with flat sides in place of the turned out coal retaining plates. Footsteps, with curved sided backing plates, were fitted at all four corners of the frame.

E828 to E837 retained their original tenders for less than two years. When Lord Nelson 4-6-0s E851-E860 were built in 1928, it had been planned to use them on the Continental boat trains, for which the 4,000 gallon six wheel tenders, built with them, would have been adequate. It was then decided to use some of the Lord Nelsons on the Western section, for which bogie tenders were required. Accordingly, the Maunsell 5,000 gallon tenders from S15s E828 to E837 were replaced by North British built Urie 5,000 gallon tenders from King Arthurs E763 to E772, which received tender numbers 3225-3234 in the S15 series. The North British tenders had been built with wheel operated handbrakes but photographs suggest that conventional brake pedestals were fitted when the tenders were coupled to the S15s. There were further subsequent tender exchanges between King Arthurs and Lord Nelsons. The final numbers of the original tenders of E828 to E832 were in the King Arthur series (885 to 889) and those from E833 to E837 in the Lord Nelson series (1001 to1005). At all subsequent tender exchanges involving S15s, the tenders retained their existing numbers.

In 1936, S15s 833 to 837 were transferred to the Central section and exchanged tenders with King Arthurs 763 to 767, which had been running with 4,000 gallon six wheel tenders, originally built with the Lord Nelson 4-6-0s. These were

Maunsell S15 30827 at Salisbury in 19th April 1959, E823 to E827 were built with tenders identical to the Urie 5000 gallon ones, apart from the bogie frames, which had arched cut-outs between the axleboxes. Note the left hand tender lamp socket has lost its inserted lamp iron. Rebuilt Bulleid Pacific 34053 carries a yellow water treatment disc on the cabside. Rebuilt light Pacifics were red engines under the Western Region route restriction coding, so the yellow disc was later replaced by a triangle. South Western Circle, John Eyers Collection.

Maunsell S15 E832 in 1928-29, probably at Salisbury. E828 to E832 were built with tenders similar to those of E823 to E827, but with auxiliary vacuum reservoirs on the rear. These were replaced by Urie 5,000 gallon tenders from NBL King Arthurs during 1929-30. E832 was the last locomotive to be built at Eastleigh with LSWR style lamp sockets, which may well have carried inserted lamp irons from new. It received smoke deflectors and green livery in February 1930.

Maunsell S15 30828 arriving at Eastleigh shed on 14 May 1961. It was coupled with the North British-built Urie 5,000 gallon tender from King Arthur E770 in 1929 and retained it until withdrawal. It had its last General repair in June 1958, at which it received forward facing second emblems. Stephen Gradidge.

a shorter version of the 5,000 gallon flat sided bogie tender.

In 1960 30847, which had been transferred to the Central section, was coupled to an SE&CR pattern 3,500 gallon six-wheel tender from an Eastern Section King Arthur. This was narrower than the 4,000 gallon tenders with the platform mounted 4ft above the rail, compared with the LSWR standard 3ft 6in above the rail. It is thought that there was enough clearance for the drawbar in the slots in the locomotive dragbox and tender front frame. The tender side frames were slotted between the axleboxes.

During the 1960s, there were a number of tender exchanges as serviceable tenders from withdrawn locomotives were attached to locomotives, which still had some way to go. 30824 received a Urie 5,000 gallon tender, replacing its Maunsell one. The only apparent difference was that it now had bogies frames with straight bottom edges. 30835 also received a Urie bogie tender, replacing its six wheeled one.

S15s 30833 and 30837 received tenders from Schools class 4-4-0s, similar to the 4,000 gallon six wheeled tenders, but

Maunsell S15 30844 at Salisbury in 1960, with flat sided tender. These were coupled to E833 to E837 and 838 to 847 when new, but E833 to E837 only ran with them for a short time. These tenders had footsteps with curved backing plates at all four corners, with handrails on the rear corners of the tender. Three auxiliary vacuum reservoirs were placed between the rear bulkhead of the coal space and the two water fillers. The cabs of 838 to 847 had reduced depth cutouts, to match the tender, but on E833 to E837, the cabside cutout was deeper than that on the tender. R.K. Blencowe Collection.

835 at Fratton on 7 May 1933, now coupled to the North British Urie tender from King Arthur 768. It is in green livery, with transfer numerals on the rear of the tender, which still has a full set of LSWR style lamp sockets, with inserted lamp irons. H.C. Casserley, courtesy R.M. Casserley.

Maunsell S15 835 at New Cross on 8 October 1938. 834 to 837 were transferred to Brighton in December 1936 and exchanged tenders for 4,000 gallon six wheel ones from King Arthurs 764 to 767. These had straight footstep backing plates, which didn't match the curved ones on the locomotives. 835 is carrying a chimney with no capuchon. The first livery changes initiated by Oliver Bulleid are apparent; the cylinders are lined with a panel.

H15 30331 at Guildford in September 1958. It was the only 330 series H15 to receive a second replacement tender, in 1956. This comprised the frame of 858, ex-30744, with the tank of 3214 ex-32332. The S15 tenders transferred to the Remembrances were provided with auxiliary vacuum reservoirs and rear footsteps. The reservoirs were retained, but the handrails on the rear corners were removed, as the frame did not have rear footsteps. South Western Circle, John Eyers Collection.

with turned in coal plates. These two tenders differed, 30833 received 708 from 30908, which had originally been coupled to a King Arthur and had straight footstep backing plates and longitudinal toolboxes. 30837 received tender 712 from 30912, with curved footstep backing plates and transverse toolboxes. While a number of H15s and S15s ran throughout with the same tender, 30833 held the record, probably the record for any Southern locomotive, with six different tenders over 38 years.

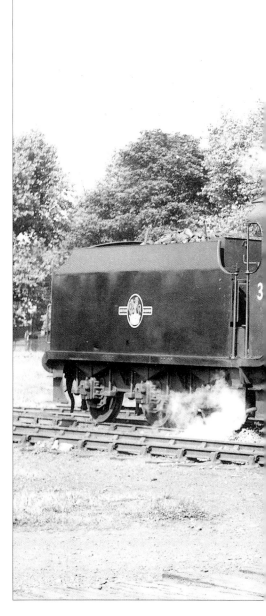

Above. Urie S15 30847 at Feltham on 18 April 1964, three months after withdrawal. At its final General repair in June 1960, it had been coupled to the Ashford style 3,500 gallon tender from withdrawn King Arthur 30805, for use on the Central section. The platform height of the tender was at the SE&CR standard 4ft and did not match the LSWR standard 3ft 6in of the locomotive. 30847 was sold for scrap to Woodham Bros of Barry. It was bought by the Maunsell Locomotive Society and restored for service on the Bluebell Railway, with a Urie bogie tender which has been rebuilt with flat sides. Stephen Gradidge.

Top right. Urie S15 30833 at Eastleigh station on 6 July 1962, shortly after receiving the 4,000 gallon 6-wheel tender, with sloping coal plates, from Schools class 4-4-0 30908. With straight edged footstep backing plates and LSWR style longitudinal toolboxes, this tender was initially coupled to a King Arthur.

Right. Urie S15 30837 at Eastleigh on 31ˢᵗ August 1962, coupled to the 4000 gallon 6-wheel tender from Schools class 4-4-0 30912. This tender has curved edged footstep backing plates and Ashford style transverse toolboxes. Peter Groom

Urie H15 488, as built in the Drummond grass green passenger livery, with purple brown edging and black and white lining. Unfortunately, the difference in shade between the green and the purple brown is hardly apparent in most photographs; the purple brown edging to the boiler bands is almost lost. South Western Circle, Norman Collection.

Urie H15 335, posed for the official photograph, when new in December 1914. It appears to be in the dark green goods livery, with black edging and a single fine light green line, which does not show up well in most photographs. The cover over the right hand piston tailrod is clearly shown.

7. Liveries

At the start and the end of their service, the H15s and S15s could be differentiated by their carrying different liveries, although they all carried the same liveries during the 1930s and 1940s. However, it was far from as simple as that!

LSWR Liveries

The first ten H15s, LSWR 482 to 491, were the last new locomotives to be painted in Dugald Drummond's passenger livery. This was a bright, grass-green using a type of paint called Royal Green. A coloured postcard of 486 was issued in the F.Moore series, although it has a few inaccuracies. The green was applied to the boiler, dome casing, splashers, cab and tender sides, cab front and tender rear, platform valance, footstep backing plates and wheels. The edges of the cab and tender structure were purple brown, with white-black-white lining between the green and the purple brown. Boiler bands were white-black-white with purple brown to either side, and white-black-white bands at front and rear of the cylinder casing. The splashers, platform valance and footstep backing plates were edged in black with a fine white line. The outside frames of the tender bogies were purple brown, with a lined panel, which was probably green, as the other lined areas.

The F.Moore card omits the lined panel entirely. The flared top of the tender was purple brown but the tender coal plates were green. Buffer beams and buffer housings were red, the rest was black. The tender was lettered LSWR in 8½in gilt sans serif letters with black shading. The running number was applied to the cabside in 6in numerals and to the buffer beams in 8½in numerals with No to the left of the coupling and the running number to the right.

H15 335 was painted in the LSWR goods livery, which had remained more or less unchanged from the 1880s to the Grouping. Where the passenger livery was grass green, the goods livery was dark holly green. No contemporary representation of this colour is known. The edging of the green panels was black, with a single bright green line between the green and the black. Boiler bands and cylinder lining were green-black-green. Tender bogies were unlined black, and remained so for all future liveries. Lettering and other details were as for the passenger livery. It is thought that the 482-491 series H15s received goods green at their first General Repair. Some sources refer to the livery being unlined, but the fine green line is frequently not apparent in photographs.

S15s 496 to 515 were painted in LSWR goods green livery, with green lining, when new. Urie had introduced a power classification system in which the largest locomotives were classified A with successively higher letters, up to K, for smaller locomotives. Unlike the Midland/LMS/BR system, no provision was made for the future construction of more powerful locomotives, but the Urie power classification was retained by the Western section of the Southern until about 1950. The A power classification appeared on the running plate valance, by the front buffer beam, on all H15s and S15s.

Southern Liveries

Until November 1923, Eastleigh works continued to repaint locomotives in full LSWR livery. Maunsell then introduced new liveries, derived from those of the LSWR. The Southern retained the old companies' numbers but added A (Ashford) to Eastern section locomotives, B (Brighton) to Central Section locomotives and E (Eastleigh) to Western Section mainland locomotives. New locomotives were lettered according to their maintenance workshop. The goods livery was black, but retained the fine green lining of the LSWR goods livery. H15 E487 received lined black in December 1923 and the LSWR S15s E496 to E515 were repainted

Urie H15 490 at Nine Elms in the early 1920s, after it was fitted with a superheater in December 1919. It is now in the dark green goods livery, probably unlined. The injector steam pipe has been moved forward, but not as far as the later position alongside the safety valve. The rectangular casing of the feedwater heat exchanger is visible between the tender bogies.

Above. Urie S15 498, the second S15 to be completed, was selected for the official photograph, in photographic grey livery. Maybe the fact that it was completed in April 1920, rather than February for 497, influenced the choice. The white lining shows up much better than the green on the finished goods livery.

Left. Urie S15 513 at Strawberry Hill when new, but with the black edging hardly differentiated from the dark green, and the light green lining almost lost.

Urie H15 E487 at Nine Elms in 1924. In December 1923, E487 was the first H15 to receive the new Southern livery and was erroneously painted black. The black livery should carry fine green lines, but these are frequently not picked up by photographs. Southern cabside numberplates are yet to appear.

Top. Southern H15 E473, new at Eastleigh in February 1924. It is in Southern olive green, with yellow lining, and as yet has no cabside numberplate.

Middle. Urie H15 E486 at Nine Elms in the mid-1920s, in Southern dark green livery with cabside numberplates. H. Gordon Tidey.

Bottom. Urie S15 E501 at Nine Elms in the mid-1920s. It is in the black goods livery with green lining, which does show up on the cab and tender in this photograph, and has a cabside numberplate. The headcode, which would indicate Waterloo-Bournemouth after 1934, is for Nine Elms loco yard to Clapham Junction.

Above. Maunsell S15 E836 in 1927-28, at Feltham in the black goods livery with green lining. It is coupled to its original flat sided tender, which it lost in October 1928. Both engine and tender have curved footstep backing plates but the deep cabside cutout does not match the shallow drop of the tender side.

Left. Urie H15 491 at Nine Elms in the early 1930s. It was fitted with smoke deflectors and lost the E prefix to its number in November 1931. The wide spacing between the SOUTHERN lettering and the number suggests that its paintwork was only touched up, with the E prefix painted over. Having a taper boiler, the smoke deflectors are of the sloping variety. 491 retains the continuous handrail rail over the smokebox front.

Southern parallel boiler H15 332 at Eastleigh, immediately after a General repair and full repaint, probably in January 1937. Panchromatic film clearly differentiates the green from the black. It now has a Maunsell smokebox door and the coal rails have been plated.

into lined black during 1924-26. The Southern S15s E823 to E837 carried the lined black livery when new.

Passenger locomotives were painted in Robert Urie's olive green passenger livery, with black edging to the green panels, but with yellow lining replacing the single white line, which had been used on the LSWR. H15s E330-E334, E473-E478 and E521-E524 were delivered new in this livery and LSWR H15s E335, E482, E483, E485 and E486 received it, at General Repairs, during 1923-24. In February 1925 the olive green of the passenger livery was altered to a darker shade and the white lining returned. All the H15s received this livery during 1925-1928. In about 1924/25, oval brass number plates were fitted to the cab sides and tender rear. These carried the wording SOUTHERN RAILWAY around the top, the running number at the bottom and the E between.

On the Drummond, Urie, and Urie-style tenders with flared tops, the lined panel on the tender side was limited to the flat area of the tender side. The flared top and coal plates were painted green and changed to black in February 1931, although they remained green when the tender paintwork was only touched up after a repair. On flat sided tenders, both the six wheeled and bogie varieties, the lined panel followed the whole tender side. The frames of six wheeled tenders were painted green and lined, although the outside frames of tender bogies remained unlined black.

The lettering on both green liveries and the black livery was the same.

SOUTHERN was placed on the tender side in 6½in primrose serif lettering, known as 'Expanded Egyptian' with the running number below in 18in sans serif characters. In between was a 3in letter E, indicating that the locomotive was maintained at Eastleigh. In October 1924 S15 505 received cabside numberplates, replacing the transfer numerals of its LSWR livery. The tender got 12in Southern style numerals, with no E-prefix, below the LSWR lettering. Although the Southern officially used yellow serif buffer beam numerals, Eastleigh continued to use LSWR gilt sans serif numerals, No and number, for some years.

In December 1929 the Southern decided to paint the S15s in the passenger green livery. Shortly afterwards, in 1931, the letter prefixes were removed. Most S15s ran briefly in green with E-prefix numbers but 507, 508, 825, 826 and 835 went straight from black with E-prefix to green without; 829, 830, 833 and 834 lost their prefixes, whilst still in black

With the loss of the prefixes, 1000 was added to Eastern Section numbers, 2000 to Central Section numbers and 3000 to LSWR duplicate numbers, which had previously been prefixed by a 0. On the H15s and S15s, the only effect of this was the disappearance of the E, which was ground off the cabside numberplates. On newly painted locomotives, the spacing between SOUTHERN and the number on the tender was reduced but, probably due to the financial situation, many locomotives only underwent partial repaints at this time, and retained wide

spacing, with the E painted out. By this time, yellow serif buffer beam numerals were being used and the number plates on the rear of the tenders were replaced by transfer numerals. Buffer beam lettering was No to the left of the coupling with the running number on the right but locomotives which received the serif numerals before the elimination of the prefixes had E to the left and the number to the right. With the serif lettering, the underlining of the o of No had a dot below it.

The final batch of S15s, 838 to 847, were delivered in dark green, without prefixes, and all the other H15s and S15s received this livery in 1931-35.

Bulleid SR Liveries

The arrival of Oliver Bulleid on the Southern in 1937 heralded a series of changes to the locomotive liveries. The first was relatively simple, the replacement of the two vertical lining bands on the cylinders by a rectangular panel. This variant to the Maunsell green livery was applied between December 1937 and April 1939 to H15s 333, 474, 476, 483, 484, 487, 489, 490, 521 and 522 and S15s 496, 497, 502, 509, 513, 515, 823-828, 831, 832, 835 and 837.

The Southern Railway Board wished to brighten up the railway's dark green image and Bulleid tried various brighter locomotive liveries, mainly on express passenger locomotives. The mixed traffic 4-6-0s did not escape the period of chaos which followed, until the Second World War enforced a dull uniformity. Some of the new liveries retained the Maunsell style of lettering

Maunsell S15 829 at Salisbury on 20 May 1935. It had been the last of the black S15s to be repainted green, a couple of weeks earlier. All of the tender coping and the coal plates are painted black. Two 20 ton steel coal wagons of coal factor Stephenson Clarke, who supplied the Southern with locomotive coal, stand on the ramp to the coal stage. These would have been brought from South Wales by the GWR, which encouraged the use of high capacity wagons by offering better rates than for the usual 12 ton mineral wagons. H.C. Casserley, courtesy R.M. Casserley.

Left. Urie S15 499 at Eastleigh in the late 1930s. It is now in lined green livery, with a Maunsell superheater and smoke deflectors. Its stovepipe chimney has lost its capuchon and it has a Maunsell smokebox door. R.K. Blencowe Collection.

Below. Maunsell S15 831 on Eastleigh works yard on 19 June 1938, following a Class A repair. At this date, additional balance weights are beginning to appear on the driving and coupled wheels. The cylinders have been lined with a panel, in place of the previous vertical lines front and rear. No explanation is offered for the missing smoke deflector, but it does show that the smokebox side handrail did not depend on the smoke deflector to hold it.

Urie H15 486 at Eastleigh on 7th January 1941. This was one of five H15s repainted in 1938/9 in the Maunsell dark green livery with black/white lining, but with Bulleid lettering. The SOUTHERN lettering was centrally placed in the green panel on the tender and the number was on the cabside. B. Anwell, R.K.Blencowe collection

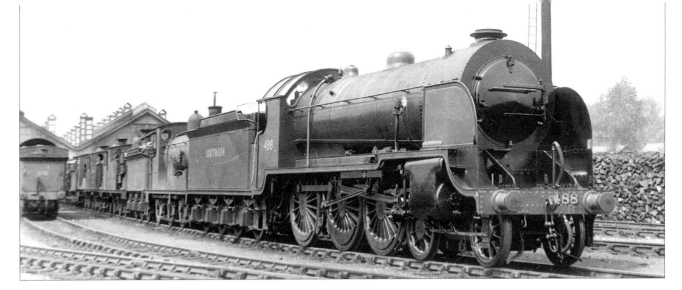

Above. Urie H15 488 heads a line of locomotives at Eastleigh shed on 30 July 1939. It has just left works in Bulleid's olive green livery with black edging and white lining, with a short flared chimney. Only the upper parts of the smoke deflectors are green and the tender is lined in a single panel, including the coal plates, with the SOUTHERN title in line with the cabside number. The stanchions and wires for a blackout curtain can be seen on the front of the tender. H.C. Casserley, courtesy R.M. Casserley.

Right. Maunsell S15 844 at Eastleigh on 11 May 1940. In August 1939 it took boiler 837 with multiple washout plugs and was repainted in Maunsell dark green livery, but with yellow lining in place of white. This photograph shows that the livery included half green smoke deflectors. The crosshead mounted vacuum pump, removed during the Second World War, is still there at this time. A.C. Wells, Eric Youldon Collection.

H15 332 near Pirbright Junction on a Salisbury train in 1939. It is in light olive green with black edging and yellow lining, with Bulleid lettering. On the Drummond tender, the green is limited to the tankside and the SOUTHERN title is placed centrally, at a lower level than the cabside numerals. The train consists of two ex-LSWR 4-car lavatory sets of 1906-10, the leading one reduced to three cars, with two Maunsell corridor thirds in the centre. M.S. King Collection.

Top. Southern-built H15 523 at Eastleigh on 11 May 1940, recently repainted in unlined dark green with Bulleid lettering. No photograph has been located of an H15 or S15 in the unlined malachite green livery, which was also used between late 1939 and early 1941. A.C. Wells, R.J. Harvey Collection.

Middle. Maunsell S15 834 at Eastleigh on 4 April 1941, recently repainted in unlined black with gilt Bulleid lettering. This was changed to the Bulleid 'sunshine' style around August-September 1941. R.K. Blencowe Collection.

Urie S15 507 with Drummond bogie tender, in June 1947, shortly after a second repaint in unlined black with green shaded sunshine lettering. R.K. Blencowe Collection.

whilst others used Bulleid's style. Some retained the dark green but olive green and a bright green known as malachite were also introduced.

Bulleid's style and layout of lettering used 9in gilt sans serif lettering and numerals. The letters had a fine black line inside the outer edge while the numerals had plain black shading. SOUTHERN was placed centrally in the lined panel on the tender side and the number was centrally placed on the cabside. Buffer beams carried just the number, in 6in numerals, to the left of the coupling.

Between December 1938 and February 1939 five H15s, 330, 473, 475, 486, 524 were repainted in the Maunsell dark green livery with black/white lining, but with Bulleid lettering. The SOUTHERN lettering was centrally placed in the green panel on the tender and the number was on the cabside.

In May 1939 H15s 332 and 491 were repainted in olive green with green/yellow lining, Bulleid lettering and half green smoke deflectors. They were followed in July-Sept 1939 by H15s 477, 482, 485, 488 in the same livery, but the black/white lining returned. It is known, from photographs, that 332 had the SOUTHERN lettering placed centrally on the lined panel on the tender. On 488, the lining on the tender followed the whole of the tender side and the SOUTHERN lettering was aligned with the cab side numerals.

Between June and August 1939 four S15s, 510, 843, 844 and 847, were repainted in Maunsell dark green with Maunsell lettering and the number on the tender. The white lining was replaced by yellow. Only the sloping part of the smoke deflectors was painted green, with black edging and yellow lining. These were followed in September by 846, in the same livery but with Bulleid lettering, with the number on the cabside, probably with green smoke deflectors.

Between September and November 1939, three S15s, 501, 504 and 832, left works in unlined dark green with Maunsell lettering. It is likely that these had received touching up to their existing livery.

From October 1939 to February 1941 H15s and S15s were repainted in unlined green, with Bulleid lettering. The SOUTHERN lettering was aligned with the cabside numerals.
Initially, unlined dark green was applied to H15s 334, 335, 478, 483, 487, 490, 523 and S15s 497, 498, 502, 505, 506, 507, 511, 512, 513, 824. 826, 829, 830, 838, 839, 840, 841, 842. From October 1940, H15s 474, 476, 489 and S15s 500, 508, 825, 827, 831, 833, 836 received Bulleid's light (malachite) green.

In March 1941 unlined black became the standard livery for H15s and S15s. The H15s remained thus until early British Railways days and no S15 ever again carried any livery but unlined black, except for some of those now in preservation. Between March 1941 and August 1941, H15s 333, 475, 486, 521 and 522, and S15s 499, 509, 823 and 834 were repainted unlined black with gilt Bulleid lettering. The lettering was changed to the Bulleid 'sunshine' style around August-September 1941. For black locomotives, these were yellow (referred to as old gold) with a black interior line and green shading. By 1946, all H15s and S15s had this livery.

British Railways Liveries
At the start of the British Railways period in January 1948, all the H15s and S15s were in unlined black with Bulleid green shaded sunshine lettering. Although the livery remained black, the next two years were as confusing as the 1939-40 period, as different lettering styles, and combinations of them, were applied.

Between January and March 1948 H15s s335, s482 and S15s s837, s838 were repainted with s prefixes to their Southern numbers and with the tenders lettered BRITISH RAILWAYS in Southern lettering.

Between March and June 1948, H15 30489 and S15s 30509, 30825 and 30837 were repainted with 30XXX numbers and BRITISH RAILWAYS tender lettering, all in Southern style

In June 1948 H15s 30334 and 30476 and S15 30505 were repainted with Southern cabside numerals, with the green shading removed from the transfers, but Gill Sans BRITISH RAILWAYS tender lettering.

Between July and December 1948 H15s 30330, 30475, 30477, 30485 and 30486 and S15s 30496, 30497, 30501, 30514, 30515, 30823, 30832, 30841 and 30847

Southern H15 473 at Eastleigh on 4 September 1948, in unlined black livery with green shaded sunshine lettering. The ex-LB&SCR E2 class 0-6-0T, on the left, has had a 3 added to its Southern number 2102, replacing an S prefix, on the side and rear of the bunker. A.E. West, courtesy M.S. King.

Above. Unlined black Urie H15 S335 being coaled by a temporary crane and bucket at Exmouth Junction in 1948. The S prefix and BRITISH RAILWAYS tender lettering was applied in March 1948. This locomotive was unique in carrying two of the British Railways transitional liveries. J.H. Aston.

Left. Urie H15 30489 at Nine Elms in June 1949. BRITISH RAILWAYS tender lettering and number, both in Southern style characters on unlined black, appeared in May 1948. The number is also on the front buffer beam. It lost its snifting valves at the same time. R.K. Blencowe Collection.

Maunsell S15 S838 at Eastleigh in June 1949. 837 and 838 were the only S15s to get S prefixes to Southern numbers, in early 1948. Lettering is in Southern style, with hand painted characters where the letters could not be derived from SOUTHERN. The snifting valves were removed at the same time. R.K. Blencowe Collection.

Top. Urie H15 30476 at Nine Elms in June 1949, with a Drummond T14 4-6-0 behind. Livery is unlined black with running number in Southern style numerals; BRITISH RAILWAYS tender lettering in Gill sans, a combination also carried by H15 30334 and S15 30505. R.K. Blencowe Collection.

Left. Southern H15 30475 at Exmouth Junction in June 1949, now with BRITISH RAILWAYS and number in Gill sans characters, on unlined black. The smokebox plating must be new, as there is no patch where the snifting valves have been removed. The A power classification is still at the front of the platform valance. R.K. Blencowe Collection.

Urie H15 30335 at Exmouth Junction in April 1949. In November 1948 it lost its snifting valves and was renumbered 30335 in lined black with Gill sans characters. Was this a full repaint or was the new lettering and lining applied to its eight month old paintwork? The cabside cutout has been reduced in depth and the snifting valves have been removed, with a cover patch on the smokebox. R.K. Blencowe Collection.

Urie S15 30500 at Eastleigh on 29 November 1949. The BR number on the SOUTHERN livery appeared in October 1948. Cabside and bufferbeam numerals are in 'sunshine' style and a smokebox numberplate has been added later. The 3 on the cabside is much clearer than the rest, suggesting that a combination of transfer 3 and hand painted 0500. A.E. West, courtesy M.S. King.

were repainted unlined black with Gill sans cabside numerals and BRITISH RAILWAYS tender lettering.

In November 1948 H15s began to appear with the BR lined black mixed traffic livery, derived from that of the L&NWR. Three H15s, 30335, 30484 and 30490, were repainted lined black with Gill sans numerals and BRITISH RAILWAYS on the tender. The BRITISH RAILWAYS, whether in Southern or Gill sans style, was always hand painted. When the Southern style was reproduced, the internal line in the characters was omitted, although it is believed that some Southern H, R, S and T transfers were incorporated.

Whilst these full repaints were taking place, H15s 30331, 30333, 30474, 30487, 30491, 30521, 30522, 30523, and 30524 and S15s 30500, 30504, 30511, 30831, 30833, 30835, 30836, 30839 and 30843

Southern parallel boiler H15 30332 at Basingstoke on a down train about 1950. It had acquired a short flared chimney in 1947. In May 1949 it lost its snifting valves and received lined black livery, with an unlettered tender. The A power classification is below the cabside number. D.L. Bradley.

Urie S15 30512 with unlettered tender at Feltham in June 1949, shortly after a Class A repair, during which it received a Maunsell boiler and BR number. The boiler is 835; built with multiple washout plugs it has clearly been rebuilt with just two each side. 30512 has lost its superheater snifting valves but the 700 class 0-6-0 on the left still has them. The lower fluted slidebar has been replaced by a plain one. R.K. Blencowe Collection.

Southern parallel boiler H15 30333 at Eastleigh on 23 December 1949, showing its new lined black livery with the large first emblem; power classification A below the cabside number. D.L. Bradley.

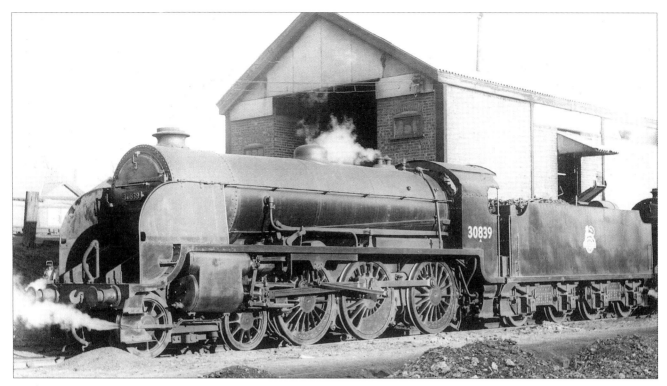

Southern S15 30839 at Eastleigh on 25 March 1950. The crosshead driven vacuum pump has gone, but the extension to the crosshead, to carry the pump drive, is still there. This was one of the first S15s to receive the first BR emblem on the tender, in large form. The A power classification is below the cabside number. R.K. Blencowe Collection.

received their new 30XXX numbers, in Southern style numerals, on their existing Southern livery. On 30522 and 30523, the transfers were of the type intended for use on green locomotives, as supplies of green shaded transfers began to run out.

During 1949 the standard livery was lined black for H15s and unlined for S15s. The hand painting of BRITISH RAILWAYS on the tender ceased and,

pending delivery of transfers for the new BR emblem, tenders were unlettered. Locomotives which received these livery styles were lined black H15s 30332, 30478, 30487, 30488, 30521 and 30523 and unlined S15s 30499, 30506, 30508, 30510, 30512, 30826, 30827, 30829, 30834, 30836, 30838, 30840, 30842* and 30843.
*30842 probably never ran with an unlettered tender; it received the large first emblem almost immediately.

In late 1949 transfers of the first British Railways emblem, depicting a lion standing on a wheel, became available, and were applied to all H15s and S15s between October 1949 and March 1953, and at subsequent repaints until early 1957. Initially, the large emblem was used but the small one was applied from March 1950. The lion faced forward on both sides of the locomotive. From March 1957, the large version of the second British Railways emblem was

Urie H15 30485 at Eastleigh on 2 July 1951. It had been painted in lined black in January 1951, with A power classification below the cabside number and small first emblem on the tender. This was in line with the number, though a central location in the tender panel was more usual. The crosshead, with a rearward extension for the vacuum pump drive, has come from one of the Southern-built locomotives. D.L. Bradley.

used, with the lion standing upright on a crown, holding a wheel in its front paws. Cynics commented that the change of emblem represented the change from British Railways carrying the public to the public carrying British Railways.

Initially the second emblem was produced in right facing and left facing versions, and was applied with the lion facing forwards on both sides of the locomotive. The College of Arms then pointed out that the upright lion on a crown (heraldically described as a demi lion rampant), was the crest of the British Transport Commission's full coat of arms, and should always face left. From late 1958, left facing lions were applied to both sides of the locomotive. The second emblem was only carried by six H15s, 30475, 30476, 30486, 30491, 30521 and 30522, the latter being the only one to carry left facing lions on both sides. All the S15s received the second emblem except for 30505.

Urie H14 30489 at Eastleigh on 15 February 1958, after a Heavy Intermediate repair. The tender was changed for one from 30487, but it is still the 5,200 gallon type used on the original batch of H15s. The power classification is now 4P5FA, above the cabside numerals. The cabside lining is cut where it reaches the platform. This was the usual arrangement from 1954 but some H15s still received continuous cabside lining. E.W. Fry.

On lined black H15s the cabsides initially had continuous lining, which followed the whole shape of the cabside. From 1954 the line was interrupted where the front vertical line on the cabside reached the platform and reappeared as a horizontal line, aligned with the bottom line of the tender panel. However, continuous lining was applied subsequently to some H15s

During the British Railways period the following subsidiary lettering or symbols were applied.

Buffer beam numerals were generally carried by locomotives, which were repainted into unlined black. Smokebox numberplates began to appear in 1949

and were fitted retrospectively to unlined black locomotives. At about the same time, the A power classification was moved to a position below the cabside numerals. In about 1951, the H15s were classified 4MT and the S15s 6F, but only the Southern A classification was displayed on the locomotives. In 1953, the H15s were reclassified 4P/5F. The power codes were generally displayed as 4P/5FA on H15s and 6F on S15s, above the numerals. Shedplates began to appear on the smokebox doors in about 1951.

Overhead line warning flashes appeared on a number of S15s, with 30500, 30504, 30507, 30508, 30511 and 30839 all noted. These were all based at Feltham and

might have found themselves under the overhead wires of the Great Eastern Section. The usual location of the warning flashes were the bottom front corner of the smoke deflectors and the top of the firebox. Some also had flashes on the tender toolboxes.

A number of S15s were fitted with British Railways water treatment equipment during the 1950s. These locomotives were identified by a yellow disc painted on the cabside below the number. The yellow disc was later replaced by a triangle, to avoid confusion with Western Region route restriction discs. The yellow triangle can appear to be similar to the A power classification, when this was placed below the cabside number.

Maunsell S15 30829, probably at Eastleigh, immediately after a General repair. The period would likely enough be June 1951 as it carries the Southern A power classification below the cabside number and small first BR emblems on the tender.

Urie H15 486 passing Raynes Park on a West of England express when new, with shelters on the front platform for the test crew, who will be taking indicator diagrams of the steam pressures in the cylinders. The shelters have lined passenger livery! The driver, who cannot be getting a very good view of the line, can be seen through the cab spectacle glass and there is another man, probably a third member of the test crew, on this side of the cab. All three test crew appear to have expected their photograph to be taken at Raynes Park. Although the first stage of the suburban electrification did not start operation until 1915, the third rail is already in position on the local lines. Bournemouth Railway Club, Kelland Collection.

Urie H15 487 on the curve leading from Eastleigh carriage works to the Portsmouth line with US Ambulance Train No.62 in April 1918. Although posed, this photograph is an illustration of the considerable use made of H15s on military trains during the First World War. See also page 119.

8. Allocation and Use

The H15s

The Urie H15s entered service during 1914, on both passenger and freight work on the main lines to Bournemouth and Exeter. Initially, 488 and 489 were based at Salisbury, the rest at Nine Elms. When new, they gained a reputation for fast running, despite having only 6ft driving wheels. They were, of course, considerably larger than any of the Drummond 4-4-0s, all with saturated boilers at that time but much easier on the firemen than the Drummond 4-6-0s, with their awkward grates and ashpans. After the outbreak of the First World War, all were based at Nine Elms and were used mainly for freight and military traffic. There were initially numerous problems with overheated bearings, although all achieved mileages between 100,000 and 200,000-plus before their first General Repairs.

After initial allocation to Eastleigh and Nine Elms, rebuild No.335 was based at Salisbury, where it was joined later by the Southern rebuilds, E330-E334. Although occasionally moving elsewhere, these six locomotives were always associated with Salisbury, enabling regular firemen to become accustomed to their high set flat grates. The 330 series were a common sight West of Salisbury on stopping trains until February 1950, when a general revision of engine working diagrams saw many of the stopping passenger and some goods workings incorporated into West Country diagrams.

When the new Southern H15s appeared, E473-477 went initially to Nine Elms, E478 and E521-524 to Bournemouth, where they were not well received. By this time, the Drummond D15 class 4-4-0s had been provided with superheated boilers and proved superior to the H15s on the Bournemouth expresses. E478 was tried briefly on the Victoria to Dover boat trains, to compare it with the North British-built King Arthurs, which were not totally satisfactory when new. It was thought that the smaller wheels of the H15 would be useful on the gradients, but it failed to perform as hoped. Its cab was out of gauge for the Eastern Section, but is not reported to have struck anything.

What had gone wrong, following the high hopes with the first H15s in 1914? It seems likely that the 1914 batch of H15s suffered from the driver's view of the line becoming obscured by the exhaust steam clinging to the boiler. On 18 October 1914 488 was heading an up overnight West Country goods, when it collided with another goods train, which was halted at Andover Junction. It was concluded that the smooth running of the new engine had caused the driver to underestimate his speed, but had falling steam caused him to miss the distant signal? Along with the Urie N15s and S15s, the Southern H15s were provided with small diameter chimneys to lift the exhaust, but this also constrained the draughting. Maunsell's design team had to sort out the steaming problems on the Urie N15s. The Urie stovepipe chimney was replaced by the wider, lipped, chimney fitted to the Southern King Arthurs, with an improved petticoat pipe and a wider blast pipe nozzle. These alterations overcame most of the steaming problems but the problem of steam obscuring the driver's view returned, until smoke deflector plates were added. As noted under Smoke Deflectors in Chapter Five, O.S. Nock (in his *Southern King Arthur Family*) recorded that drivers of King Arthurs tended to shut off steam briefly when running at speed, simply in order to get a view of an obscured signal. He also noted some excellent runs between Salisbury and Exeter with the 330 series H15s, still with narrow stovepipe chimneys, suggesting other possible contributory factors to the steaming problems.

The Schmidt and Maunsell superheaters had a single transverse header at the top of the smokebox, well out of the path of the combustion gases

Parallel boilered Southern H15 E330 heads a down express past Hewish Gates on 2 August 1928. E330's Drummond boiler, bogie wheels and tender have passed this way thousands of times over the previous 23 years, but mainly as parts of a Drummond F13 class 4-cylinder 4-6-0... As with most Eastleigh repaints during the 1920s, the buffer beam numerals are in LSWR gilt sans serif style. H.C. Casserley, courtesy R.M. Casserley.

Top. Southern H15 E522 heading a Bournemouth express, thought to be between Raynes Park and New Malden, in the 1920s. It still has a stovepipe chimney and Eastleigh superheater and the lamp sockets do not yet contain lamp irons. Not often seen in photographs is the switchgear on the third rail on the right. This complicated arrangement, which would look at home on a Hornby Dublo train set, was not perpetuated in the Southern Railway's electrification schemes.

Middle. Southern H15 474 passing the Town Quay in Southampton during the 1930s on a boat train from the New Docks. 474 received smoke deflectors, a King Arthur chimney and a Maunsell superheater in June 1931. It still has a Urie smokebox door. Buffer beam numerals are in yellow serif style. The first carriage was initially an LSWR corridor brake third; it became an ambulance carriage during the first world war and was then rebuilt as a luggage van. There are at least three Pullman carriages in the train. R.K. Blencowe Collection.

Below. Southern H15 521 heading a down goods at Millbrook in the 1940s. It is in unlined black with green shaded 'sunshine' lettering and was renumbered 30521 (Southern livery) in June 1948. The tracks on the right lead into Southampton's New Docks. South Western Circle, John Eyers Collection.

Top. Parallel boilered Southern H15 30333 arriving at Seaton Junction on an up stopping train. It appears to have its Southern number 333 on the buffer beam but 30333 on the cabside, applied in October 1948. The train consists of an ex LSWR non-corridor 4-car lavatory set of 1906-10, reduced to three cars by the Southern in the 1930s. A.E. West, courtesy M.S. King.

Middle. Urie H15 30490 heading the 7.02 Waterloo-Bournemouth parcels train in Clapham cutting in June 1949. 30490 received lined black livery, with **BRITISH RAILWAYS** lettering and number in Gill sans characters, in November 1948. Clapham cutting signalbox closed in May 1936, but remained in place for the next thirty years.

Below. Taper boilered Urie H15 30491 near Winchfield on milk empties for the West of England in 1949-50. It had been renumbered in March 1949, using Southern style numerals, on its existing unlined black livery. It is now carrying a Urie taper boiler, with a Maunsell smokebox door, and has lost its snifting valves.

71

Above. Southern H15 30475 leaving Southampton Central on the 12.10 Birmingham Snow Hill to Bournemouth Central via Reading and Basingstoke on 20 June 1959. 30475 received the second BR emblem, forward facing on both sides, at its last General Repair in August 1958. E.W. Fry.

Middle. Southern H15 30521 passing Eastleigh on a Southampton boat train, via Northam, on 24 July 1954. It is in lined black with the first BR emblem, applied in 1952. Stephen Gradidge.

Bottom. Urie H15 30489 approaching Eastleigh on an up goods on 25 July 1960. The 1/125 second fastest shutter speed of my Pentona has just about stopped 30489, but had less success with the down express. By this date, 30489 was the only one of the original 482 to 491 batch still in service with a parallel boiler. Apart from the smoke deflectors, its appearance, under the dirt, is little changed from when it was new in 1914.

Southern H15 30522 leaving Eastleigh on the Romsey line with empty ballast hoppers for Meldon Quarry on 17 August 1959. 30522 has a Maunsell boiler and the two visible hoppers are from the Southern's final batch, built at Ashford in 1947, with cast steel bogies.

from the tubes to the chimney. The Eastleigh superheater had two transverse headers in the smokebox, above and below the large boiler tubes. These were connected by vertical distributing pipes, to which the superheater elements in the large tubes were fixed. The lower header was right in front of the lower small tubes of the boiler and the vertical distribution pipes were in front of the large tubes, containing the superheater elements (see page 11). This can only have impeded the free flow of the combustion gases, although it must be noted that Maunsell's investigators concentrated on the blastpipe and chimney and did not immediately change the superheater arrangements. Another possible contributory factor might be the reduced smokebox volume of the H15s. The smokebox of the taper boilered H15s and S15s had a smaller diameter than that of the parallel boilered locos and was shorter than that of the N15s. These factors might explain why the 330s, with Maunsell superheaters, apparently did better than the new Southern-built H15s, all with Eastleigh superheaters except for E524.

Maunsell's testing was carried out on N15 and King Arthur locomotives. S.C.Townroe quotes maximum indicated horsepower of 950 for unmodified Urie N15 742, 1,250ihp for 742 with modified draughting and 1,500ihp for King Arthur 451. Results obtained under test conditions are never the same as those achieved in normal service but the figures are likely to be a reasonable indication of the relative

maximum power developed in service by the three types. It can be assumed that similar improvements resulted from the application of modified draughting to the H15s. The additional power of the King Arthur can be ascribed to longer valve travel, higher boiler pressure and enlarged ashpan air openings. The Maunsell S15s also had the benefit of these improvements.

By the late 1920s there were enough King Arthur 4-6-0s to work most of the express traffic and the H15s were used mainly on goods or stopping passenger trains, with some express work, particularly on Southampton boat trains and holiday relief trains, for which their performance was quite adequate. However, most of the available photographs of H15s in service, particularly in the earlier days, show them on passenger trains. Many of the Western section's principal goods trains ran overnight and the H15s would tend to be on passenger work on summer Saturdays, when the photographers were about. Loading gauge constraints ensured that they remained on the Western section and axle loads limited them to the main lines, including the single track Alton-Winchester line, which was an alternative route to Southampton. Salisbury's Southern H15s 475 and 476 appeared regularly at Exeter, with occasional visits by other H15s from further east.

The first H15 to be withdrawn from service was 30485. On 22 January 1955 it was approaching Bournemouth Central on the 6.30pm from Weymouth to Waterloo when the driver of King

Arthur 30783 misread signals and the two engines collided, front right to front right, on a crossover, fortunately at low speed. 30783 lost its right-hand cylinder and 30485 was knocked on to its side. It was taken to Eastleigh and withdrawn three months later. 30490 was withdrawn in June 1955, on arrival at works. Presumably, it also had some defect, which was not worth putting right. The remaining H15s were withdrawn from service between 1957 and 1961. The introduction of British Railways Standard 4-6-0s had taken away much of their work and the first part of the Kent Coast electrification in 1959 displaced more Bulleid Pacifics and Standard 4-6-0s to the Western Section.

The Urie S15s

The S15s were always primarily main line goods engines, although able to take a hand with passenger traffic at holiday times. When new, 496 was allocated to Salisbury, 497-506 to Nine Elms and 507-515 to Strawberry Hill, moving to the new shed adjacent to Feltham marshalling yard in 1923. Although occasionally moving elsewhere, Nine Elms and Feltham remained the main bases for Urie S15s throughout. Loading gauge and weight constraints restricted them to Western section main lines. Once the Maunsell S15s were in service, Urie S15s did not generally run west of Salisbury but did turn up occasionally at Exeter.

In February 1942 496-499 were loaned to the Great Western Railway and were given Red route restriction and power classification D. They were based initially

Left. Urie S15 501, approaching Boscombe on a down goods train in the early 1920s. It is not clear whether 501 is in LSWR or Southern livery, but it does not yet have a Southern cabside plate.

Middle. Urie S15 502, in LSWR livery, passing Esher on a Basingstoke-Waterloo train in the early 1920s. The train consists of an LSWR 4-car lavatory set, made up from new brake thirds and older intermediate vehicles in 1911, with a van on the rear. Although built primarily as goods engines, the Western section S15s always did some passenger work, particularly on summer Saturdays.

Below. Urie S15 507 passing Weybridge on freight from Southampton Docks to Nine Elms via the main line. The date is between January 1932, when 507 acquired smoke deflectors, and 1934, when a different headcode was in use. Maunsell smokebox door. H Gordon Tidey.

Left. 30496 passing Headbourne Worthy, north of Winchester, on a freight from Southampton to Nine Elms on 29 June 1950. It had received its BR number and BRITISH RAILWAYS tender lettering, in Gill sans characters, late in 1948. R.K. Blencowe Collection.

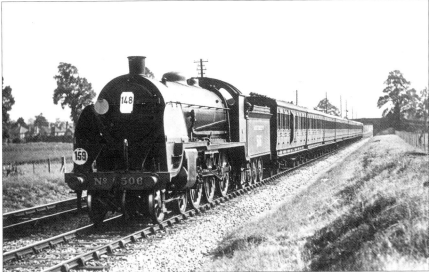

Middle. Urie S15 506 heading a special train for Portsmouth, between April and August 1935. Another photograph, clearly taken on the same occasion, shows 507 on a similar train, but with a Urie tender. 506 received a Drummond tender in April 1935 and 507 in August. The train is a scratch set of LSWR non corridor vehicles, led by a brake composite with a centre brake compartment, giving lots of passenger accommodation, but little luggage space. The trains are probably taking visitors to a Royal Navy event, connected with King George V's Silver Jubilee.

Below. Urie S15 30507 on freight for Southampton in the late 1950s. The location is between Woking and Sturt Lane Junction as the slow lines are electrified, but not the fast lines. The date is between October 1955, when 30507 received a Urie 5,200 gallon tender, and December 1957, when it got a Maunsell boiler.

Urie S15 30501 passing Millbrook on freight from Bournemouth on 22 April 1960.

at Old Oak Common and Southall but 496 and 498 later moved to Exeter and 497 to Tyseley. They all returned to Feltham between March and May 1943.

The Urie S15s remained main line goods engines throughout but, on summer Saturdays into the early 1960s, they took their turn on the semi-fasts from Waterloo to Basingstoke and Salisbury, enabling the Standard 5MTs which usually worked those trains to work the holiday reliefs. They were not superseded until the D6500 Crompton Type 3 diesel electric locomotives began to appear in the 1960s, followed by a rapid decline in rail freight traffic. The Urie S15s were withdrawn between 1962 and 1964.

The Maunsell S15s
Unlike the H15s and the Urie S15s, the Maunsell S15s were all built to the Southern Railway composite loading gauge, so could work on the Central and Eastern sections of the Southern, as well as the Western section. They were 9ft wide across the platform, compared with 9ft 0½in for the LSWR ones (was there actually any difference?). The chimney height was reduced from 13ft 2⅜in to 12ft 11½in and the projecting eaves of the LSWR cab roof were replaced by a roof which merged smoothly into the sides, following Ashford practice. Even so, the Southern S15s were always primarily Western Section engines, with only small numbers working briefly on the other two sections.

The first batch of fifteen were allocated thus: E823-E827 to Exmouth Junction, E828-E832 to Salisbury and E833-E837 to Feltham. This started a long association with the Exeter-Salisbury main line, on both freight and passenger trains. From February 1944 they were permitted to run to Okehampton, with a 40mph speed limit, primarily for the Meldon ballast traffic. They had to run tender first in one direction, until a 70ft turntable was installed at Okehampton in 1947. In 1936 833-837 were provided with six wheeled tenders and transferred to Brighton. They were used on main line goods workings on the LB&SCR main line, providing greater power than the native K class 2-6-0s. Unlike S15s on the Western section, they were restricted to 45mph and not permitted to work passenger trains. A 45mph speed limit for an S15 is equivalent to a 53mph speed limit on a King Arthur, which was certainly never imposed. The Western section Maunsell S15s were always likely to appear on passenger duties, particularly at holiday times.

The 1936 batch of S15s went to Hither Green (838-842) and to Feltham (843-847) raising the question – why was the 1936 batch not sent in its entirety to the Central and Eastern sections, leaving the Feltham allocation where it was? The Hither Green S15s worked main line freight between Bricklayers Arms, Hither Green, Ashford and Dover. Like the Central section engines, they provided increased power compared with the N class 2-6-0s, were limited to 45mph and restricted to goods work. In 1939 838-842 moved to Feltham and, in 1940, 833-837 moved to New Cross Gate, to reduce the number of engines at vulnerable coastal sheds. In 1942, 833-837 also moved to Feltham, putting all the S15s on the Western section.

In 1946-48 841-846 moved to Exmouth Junction and, in 1951, 30835-30837 moved back to the Central Section, to Redhill. They were joined in 1959 by bogie tender 30847. In 1960 this was replaced by a 3,500 gallon six wheel tender. One wonders why those responsible for these moves didn't transfer 30833 or 30834, which already had six wheel tenders. As with the Urie S15s, the Maunsell S15s did not begin to lose work until the arrival of the Cromptons and the decline in rail freight traffic. They were withdrawn from service between 1962 and 1966.

Preservation
None of the H15s survived into preservation and the only Urie/Maunsell 4-6-0 on the official BR list for preservation was King Arthur 30777. Traditionally, the scrapping of redundant locomotives had been dealt with at the railways' own workshops, enabling components and material to be recycled. The large number of locomotives being withdrawn in the 1960s was beyond their ability and neither the components nor the material were required as steam repairs declined. Many locomotives were therefore sold to commercial scrapyards. One of these yards was Woodham Bros of Barry Island, in South Wales which, by 1968, contained over 200 locomotives. A drop in scrap prices and a concentration on scrapping wagons resulted in most of these locomotives still being in the yard when the proprietor, Dai Woodham, realised that he had customers for them in the

Urie S15 30504 passing Queens Road, Battersea, on an evening parcels train to Basingstoke or Southampton on 7 June 1961. 30504 now has the 5,200 gallon tender from H15 30487 and carries overhead line warning plates. H.F. Wheeler Collection.

Urie S15 30499 standing in the loop on an up goods at Brockenhurst on 27 September 1961. The distinctive guards lookout of an Ironclad carriage indicates that the photographer is in a pull-push set, being propelled either to Lymington or Bournemouth via Wimborne. 30499 was one of only three Urie S15s to be withdrawn from service with a Urie boiler. L.R. Freeman, transporttreasury.co.uk

Loco	Left Barry	Purchaser and Current (2010) status
30499	11/1983	Urie Locomotive Society, restoration in progress at Bury and Ropley
30506	4/1976	Urie Loco Soc, ran on Mid Hants Rly 1987-2001, repair in progress
30825	11/1987	To traffic on North Yorkshire Moors Railway 2011, boiler from 30841
30828	3/1981	Eastleigh Rly Preservation Soc, in service 1993-2002, to Mid Hants 2004
30830	9/1987	Maunsell Loco Soc, now being rebuilt on North Yorkshire Moors Railway
30841	9/1972	To traffic Chappell 1975, ran later on North Yorkshire Moors Railway
30847	10/1978	Maunsell Locomotive Soc, ran on Bluebell Railway 1993-7, under repair

growing railway preservation movement. Amongst these were Urie S15s 30499 and 30506 and Maunsell S15s 30825, 30828, 30830, 30841 and 30847. The frames of 30841 were found to be out of line and its boiler has been used to return 30825 to service. The above list summarises what happened to them.

Left. Urie S15 30506 approaching Basingstoke on the 2.47 pm Salisbury-Waterloo on 18 August 1962. The train comprises a 3-set of BR Mk 1 carriages, with a strengthening Maunsell SK.

Below. Maunsell S15 E826 between Wilton and Salisbury on an up goods in the period 1927-31, in lined black. It took the green livery with smoke deflectors and lost the E, in late 1931.

Maunsell S15 E831 heading a West of England express, somewhere west of Salisbury, in the late 1920s. It received smoke deflectors and green livery, and lost its original tender, in December 1929. All the visible carriages are ex-LSWR, suggesting a summer Saturday additional train. Although used regularly on the Salisbury-Exeter stopping trains, the use of S15s on the expresses was not usual, except at times of peak traffic. R.F. Mack.

Maunsell S15 E836 passing Clapham Junction on 5 April 1928 with a lightweight Portsmouth train, via Woking. An ex-LSWR 4½ set has been strengthened by two Thirds, the leading one most of 40 years old. H.C. Casserley, courtesy R.M. Casserley.

Top. Maunsell S15 E827 approaching Exeter Central on a down stopping train comprising an LSWR 4-car lavatory set of 1906-10 and a tail load of vans. The date is between January 1930, when E827 received smoke deflectors and green livery, and December 1931, when it lost its E prefix. The odd vehicle on the right is thought to be a vacuum cleaner van, converted from an ex-LSWR covered carriage truck.

Middle. Maunsell S15 E827 approaching Honiton tunnel on a West of England express in 1930-31. The pair of dining cars at the front of the train and the fifth carriage are new Southern Railway vehicles; the rest are all LSWR timber bodied vehicles.

Below. Maunsell S15 838 heading a goods train, at the start of its journey from Dover to Bricklayers Arms via Ashford, Tonbridge and Chiselhurst, in the late 1930s. Vans and a container wagon are at the front of the train, although it is not possible to see whether they are piped up to provide a fitted head. Bulleid Pacific Preservation Society.

Maunsell S15 842 passing Tonbridge on an up goods in the late 1930s. The headcode indicates the route to be from Dover or Ramsgate to Bricklayers Arms via Sevenoaks, Otford, Swanley and Chiselhurst. Unlike the Western section of the Southern, the use of S15s on passenger trains on the Eastern or Central sections was not permitted. R.K. Blencowe Collection.

S15s were permitted to run from Exeter to Okehampton from 1944, subject to a 40mph speed restriction. 30831 is at Exeter St David's on the Exmouth Junction to Yeoford goods during the 1950s. The reason for the passenger carriage at the front of the train is not known but it might be the Meldon Quarry workmen's coach, which was coupled to the stone trains between Okehampton station and the quarry, returning to Okehampton after maintenance. Unless it is to return tender first to Exeter, 30831 will have to go on to Okehampton to turn. E.S. Youldon Collection.

30331 approaching Farnborough on a train for Basingstoke or Southampton Terminus in July 1949. The wide spacing between all four tracks suggests that it is approaching the aqueduct carrying the Basingstoke Canal, which has separate arches for each track. Until the Bournemouth electrification, the third rail on the relief lines went as far as the bridge over the Reading-Redhill line, to allow for electric train movements onto the main line from the Ascot-Ash Vale line. R.K. Blencowe Collection.

H15 The Record

The primary sources of information are the SR and BR engine and boiler record cards, held by the National Railway Museum (NRM), and the LSWR Engine repair and boiler registers, held by the National Archive at Kew. The LSWR engine repair registers were updated to about 1931 and the Southern repair category has been added retrospectively for some repairs. The SR engine record cards were introduced in about 1935, leaving a gap in between. The NRM has a full set of SR S15 record cards but not one for an H15 was located. The BR 9215 cards for most of the H15s are available, but only cover the period after 1952. Eric Youldon kindly provided copies of some SR H15 engine record cards. It has been possible to interpolate some missing repairs from the boiler record cards or from the records of George Woodward, indicated by (GW) in place of the repair category. From September 1926 to September 1940, when he was called up into the army, George Woodward, as mentioned in the Acknowledgements, lived between Eastleigh shed and the loco works, and recorded the date at which each locomotive entered and left Eastleigh works. Between 1941 and 1947, his records were written retrospectively from information published in *The Railway Observer*, and other local sources. I have checked these entries in the RO and put (RO) in place of the repair category.

Between 1948 and 1966, George was no longer living in sight of the works but visited the shed every Sunday, to update his records. Although still reliable, his post-war entries are less detailed than those for the 1926-1940 period. He recorded details such as modifications and liveries, which were not recorded on the ERCs. I have generally shown the repair dates shown on official records, where they are available. However, the official dates were frequently 'optimistic', being the means by which the works got paid for repairs carried out. Some works visits went unrecorded in the ERCs, but were noted by George. These include 'Shed to Shop' repairs, arranged locally between Eastleigh shed and the shop foreman, and some returns for rectification following a Works Repair.

Don Bradley makes reference to some instances of repairs to S15s at Ashford, Brighton and Swindon Works. Where these are not confirmed by the ERC, I have put (DB) in place of the repair category. Some of these entries fill otherwise unexplained gaps in the repair chronology.

The LSWR boiler register shows boiler movements to and from each locomotive, and was updated until the early 1920s. However, its only relevance

to this book was to show the movement of boilers between the 330-334 series, when they were rebuilt. From about 1926, permanent numbers were allocated to each boiler, and boiler record cards were introduced, most of which are at the NRM. Until boilers started to be exchanged at Class A repairs, the boiler carried the same number as the locomotive. I have shown the boiler number at the entry for the first repair shown on the Boiler Record Card, and at each repair when the boiler was changed. 30330-30335 always kept the same boilers.

The Southern Railway classified its repairs or overhauls by the letters A, B, C and D. At a class A repair, the locomotive would be lifted off its wheels, worn or damaged components brought back to standard, modifications carried out and the boiler, generally, exchanged for one which had already been refurbished. The locomotive would generally be repainted into the current livery. The scheduled mileage between class A repairs was 85,000, after about two years of service. The interval was increased during the Second World War. Class B Repairs were carried out at about the half way stage between class As, but examination of the record cards shows that, in practice, they seldom occurred. Class C repairs were carried out to rectify defects, which had occurred in service, and Class D repairs covered specific work such as out of course repainting, accident damage repair or weighing.

In British Railways days, the class A became a General Repair , Class B became a Heavy or Light Intermediate Repair (H/Int or L/Int) and Class C and D became Casual or Non-Classified Repairs (H/Cas, L/Cas or N/C). With the increased mileage between General repairs, Intermediate and Casual repairs became much more common.

When examining the 'Record' pages, the following points should be noted:
All repairs took place at Eastleigh Locomotive Works, unless another

works or running shed is indicated. Mileages shown are the mileage since the previous Class A, or General, repair. Dates shown are the dates between which the locomotive was recorded out of service.

Notes on renumbering and livery changes are taken from tables prepared by John Harvey from various primary sources, including wartime observations by the late John Fairman and Tony Sedgewick and the post-nationalisation records of Barry Fletcher. Liveries are noted in the tables only when there was a change and it can be assumed that the livery concerned was retained, through successive repaints and touchings up, until the next livery change is shown. In early British Railways days, both Southern and Gill sans characters were used, identified in the tables by (S) or (G). From the late 1950s, the second British Railways emblem was applied, facing forward on both sides from March 1957 to late 1958, then facing left on both sides. This is indicated by (F) or (L) in the tables, although not all cases have been checked against photographs.

Shed allocations for the LSWR and Southern period are taken from Don Bradley's *LSWR Locomotives - The Urie Classes*, Wild Swan Publications, 1987. Don quotes allocations for H15s when new, at 1915, 1925, 1939 and 1940, together with a number of intermediate movements. For the S15s, he gives allocations when new and at 1928 and 1940 with other movements. For the years 1948 and 1950, I have referred to *British Railways Steam Locomotive Allocations 1948-1968* by Jim Grindlay, Modelmaster Publications, 2006. For later movements, I have referred to Tony Walmsley's *Shed by Shed Part Five* which lists all monthly movements between August 1950 and 1968, as recorded in *Trains Illustrated* and *Modern Railways*. Ultimately, any errors caused by my accepting incorrect information, or by mis-interpreting correct information, are mine.

332 at Salisbury in the late 1930s, now with the coal rails plated to avoid the loss of small coal. Behind it is a wagon belonging to coal factor Stephenson Clarke, who had the contract to supply the Southern Railway with locomotive coal.

30330

Built Nine Elms 9/1905   Order No. F13-1   Works Serial Number 768
Rebuilt Eastleigh 11/1924 Order No. A17-1   Works Serial Number 108
Rebuilt as ᴇ330 11/1924, renumbered 330 1/1932, 30330 9/1948

Individual repairs as Class F13 are not shown.

9/1905		New 4-cylinder Locomotive 330
17/7/24-1/11/24	A	Rebuilt as H15, boiler ex 334, tender ex 331, olive green, ᴇ330
9/6/25-3/7/25	C	Tyres & Axleboxes
2/11/25-18/11/25	C	Tyres & Axleboxes, boiler 330
26/5/27-3/9/27	A	Full repaint, dark green, tender 791.
11/1/29-11/1/29	D	Weighing
16/7/29-31/8/29	A	General repairs
15/12/31-30/1/32	A	General Repair, smoke deflectors, full repaint, renumbered 330
16/2/32-5/3/32	(GW)	Tender enlarged to 4300 gallons
11/10/33-15/11/33	(GW)	Part repaint
17/9/34-6/11/34	(GW)	Boiler removed for repair.
15/7/35-27/7/35	C	27,546
31/12/36-6/2/37	A	76,977, full repaint
23/12/38-15/2/39	A	81,620, full repaint, lined dark green, Bulleid lettering
27/9/41-12/11/41	A	88,661, unlined black, sunshine lettering
10/2/44-18/3/44	A	70,995
4/5/46-31/8/46	B	66,501
5/8/48-4/9/48	A	135,728, snifting valves off, BRITISH RAILWAYS 30330 (G)
30/9/48-2/10/48	C	Return
20/12/50-5/1/51	H Cas	35,252, not repainted
5/3/52-19/4/52	Gen	83,738, short flared chimney, lined black, first emblem
11/5/54-15/5/54	L Cas	47,879, not repainted
24/2/55-19/3/55	L Int	70,889, not repainted
11/5/57		Withdrawn
6/7/1957		Scrapped at Eastleigh, 1,043,516 miles

Allocation
1925	Salisbury
6/1935	Nine Elms
10/1935	Salisbury
8/1950	Feltham
9/1950	Salisbury

330 at Exmouth Junction on 27 July 1948. It now carries smoke deflectors, a Maunsell smokebox door and conventional lamp irons. With the addition of smoke deflectors, the small handrails on the main frames have been replaced by short stanchions above each buffer. The crosshead driven vacuum pump disappeared in the early 1940s. The tender now has a raised top and four coal rails, which have been plated. Livery is unlined black with green shaded sunshine lettering. R.K. Blencowe Collection.

30330 at Nine Elms in June 1949. At an overhaul in September 1948, it lost its snifting valves and was renumbered BRITISH RAILWAYS 30330, in Gill Sans characters, still in unlined black. 30330 retained its stovepipe chimney until April 1952, when it received lined black livery. The rearward extension to the crosshead, to carry the vacuum pump drive, is still in place. R.K. Blencowe Collection.

30331

Built Nine Elms 9/1905   Order No. F13-2   Works Serial Number 769
Rebuilt Eastleigh 11/1924 Order No. A17-2   Works Serial Number 109
Rebuilt as E331 11/1924, Renumbered 331 11/1931, 30331 3/1949

Individual repairs as Class F13 are not shown.

9/1905		New 4-cylinder Locomotive
15/2/24-26/11/24	A	Rebuilt as H15, boiler ex 331, tender ex 334, olive green, E330
9/6/25-12/6/25	D	Trailing axleboxes
4/10/25-10/10/25	D	Driving axleboxes, boiler 331
7/4/26-23/4/26	C	Light Repairs
24/5/27-8/10/27	A	Full repaint, dark green, tender 792.
10/5/28-29/5/28	D	Right driving bearing
21/10/29-14/12/29	A	Sloping smoke deflectors, tender enlarged to 4300 gallons
2/10/31-19/11/31	A	Renumbered 331, tender not repainted, straight smoke deflectors
27/11/31-3/3/32	(GW)	In store.
11/6/34-26/7/34	(GW)	Boiler removed for repair, tender and wheels not repainted
17/3/36-25/4/36	A	63,080
1/7/37-24/7/37	B	49,847
26/2/38-26/2/38	D	
16/9/38-9/11/38	A	96,849, full repaint
13/6/41-15/10/41	A	88,095, Short flared chimney, unlined black, sunshine lettering
17/3/42-21/3/42	D	10,995
29/1/44-9/2/44	C	79,654
8/1/45-24/2/45	A	108,908
28/10/46-14/12/46	A	73,521
14/3/48-1/4/48	B	44,543, at Salisbury
17/2/49-18/3/49	L Int	71,453, SOUTHERN 30331
10/4/51-30/5/51	Gen	135,433, snifting valves off, lined black, first emblem
27/3/53-1/5/53	H Int	Not repainted
22/10/54-6/11/54	L Cas	114,021, not repainted
12/8/55-2/8/55	L Cas	129,407, not repainted
9/2/56-31/3/56	Gen	5000 gallon tender 858 ex 30744 *, full repaint
?-31/8/57	(GW)	
1/4/58-26/4/58	H Int	not repainted
3/61		Withdrawn, 1,149,690 miles
3/6/61		Scrapped at Eastleigh

*This tender had the frames of tender 858 and the tank from tender 3214, ex 32332, and retained the additional vacuum reservoirs.

Allocation
1924	Salisbury
6/1935	Nine Elms
10/1935	Salisbury
8/1950	Feltham
9/1950	Salisbury

331 at Nine Elms in the mid-1930s. The tender was enlarged to 3,400 gallons in 1929 and the four coal rails are now plated to prevent loss of the fine coal, which was beginning to appear, although that precaution should not be necessary with the large lumps on 331's tender. Buffer beam numerals are in Southern black shaded yellow serif characters, with a dot below the underlining of N<u>o</u>.

30331 at Eastleigh, probably immediately after its General Repair in May 1951. It had acquired a flared chimney in 1941, getting a Maunsell smokebox door and losing its vacuum pump at about the same time. The extension to the crosshead, to carry the pump drive, has been removed. It has now lost its snifting valves and has received lined black livery with a small first BR emblem. D.L. Bradley.

30332

Built Nine Elms 10/1905   Order No. F13-3   Works Serial Number 770
Rebuilt Eastleigh 12/1924 Order No. A17-3   Works Serial Number 110
Rebuilt as ᴇ332 12/1924, Renumbered 332 9/1932, 30332 5/1949

Individual repairs as Class F13 are not shown.

10/1905		New 4-cylinder Locomotive
13/8/24-11/12/24	A	Rebuilt as H15, boiler and tender ex 333, olive green, ᴇ332
7/5/25-16/5/25	D	Big ends
15/2/26-4/3/26	C	Light repair, boiler 332
7/4/27-17/8/27	A	Full repaint, dark green, tender 793,
23/5/28-12/6/28	D	Piston valve liner
6/11/29-3/1/30	A	Sloping smoke deflectors, tender enlarged to 4300 gallons.
12/11/30-13/12/30	C	Tubes repaired in situ
21/7/32-9/9/32	A	General repair, vertical smoke deflectors, repaint, renumbered 332
17/9/34-12/11/34	(GW)	Boiler removed for repair
2/12/36-9/1/37	A	87,659, full repaint
13/4/37-22/4/37	D	384, light repairs
16/12/37-8/1/38	C	31,461, touch up only
1/6/38-1/6/38	D	41,954, repair in paintshop
4/4/39-10/5/39	A	74,049, olive green, Bulleid lettering, half green smoke deflectors
20/12/39-11/1/40	C	20,339, touch up only
8/11/41-11/5/42	A	77,357, unlined black, sunshine lettering
21/10/44-18/11/44	A	87,503
14/3/47-3/5/47	A	89,690, short flared chimney
12/4/49-20/5/49	A	68,878, snifting valves off, lined black, unlettered, 30332
13/12/51-26/1/52	Gen	70,891, repainted, first emblem
7/2/52 -14/2/52	Return	
17/1/55-5/2/55	H Int	67,758, not repainted
26/4/55-30/4/55	L Cas	73,253
3/11/56		Withdrawn, 968,484 miles
10/3/57		Scrap at Eastleigh

Allocation
1924	Salisbury
8/1950	Nine Elms
10/1950	Salisbury

E332 backing the leading coaches of a Waterloo express onto the rear portion at Exeter Queen Street in the 1920s. Steam from the short cylinder drain pipes hides the front coupling, but it looks like a three link one. E332 is as built, with LSWR style lamp sockets and refurbished 4000 gallon Drummond tender. The visible carriages are all ex-LSWR, including a close coupled bogie block set in the Exmouth bay.

30332 at Guildford on19th April 1952. It now carries a small first BR emblem on the tender, still with the Southern A power classification. The extension to the crosshead, to carry the vacuum pump drive, is still in place. D.L. Bradley.

30333

Built Nine Elms 10/1905   Order No. F13-4   Works Serial Number 771
Rebuilt Eastleigh 12/1924 Order No. A17-4 Works Serial Number 111
Rebuilt as E333 12/1924, Renumbered 333 4/1934, 30333 10/1948

Individual repairs as Class F13 are not shown.

10/1905		New 4-cylinder Locomotive
8/11/18-5/6/20		Superheater fitted to boiler
19/8/24-31/12/24	A	Rebuilt as H15, boiler ex 330, tender ex 332, olive green, E333
1/9/25-5/9/25	D	Left leading bearing, boiler 333
25/4/27-12/8/27	A	Full repaint, dark green, tender numbered 794
9/3/29-7/5/29	B	Boiler re-tubing in situ
3/12/30-17/1/31	A	Smoke deflectors, repaint, 4500 gallon tender 260 ex L11 157
15/10/32-2/11/32	C	
24/6/33-17/7/33	(GW)	Repainted, tender 794 ex 157, enlarged to 4300 gallons
28/8/33-7/9/33	(GW)	Very dirty
2/1/34-2/1/34	(GW)	Weighing only
24/2/34-21/4/34	(GW)	Boiler removed for repair, part repaint, renumbered 333
27/2/36-11/4/36	A	76,980, full repaint
23/7/37-19/8/37	B	55,271, repair in paint shop
2/7/38-24/8/38	A	86,565, full repaint, cylinders lined in panel
3/4/39-4/5/39	C	27,600, part repaint
23/9/40-16/7/41	A	76,432, unlined black, gilt lettering
18/3/43-16/4/43	C	56,685, sunshine lettering
18/8/43-23/8/43	C	67,520
24/11/43-22/12/43	C	78,104
25/5/44-27/6/44		92,054, repair at Salisbury
13/11/44-19/1/45	A	105,016
29/5/47-20/9/47	A	92,409, snifting valves off
12/10/48-30/10/48	C	35,825, not repainted, SOUTHERN 30333
3/11/49-9/12/49	A	71,668, lined black, first emblem
26/8/52-7/11/52	Gen	84,363, not repainted, short flared chimney
4/11/55-3/12/55	H Int	75,269
25/10/1958		Withdrawn,1.064,166 miles
8/11/58		Scrap at Eastleigh

Allocation
1924	Salisbury
6/1935	Nine Elms
10/1935	Salisbury
10/1940	Feltham
1/1943	Eastleigh
3/1944	Salisbury
8/1950	Nine Elms
10/1950	Salisbury

333 on a down train at Yeovil Junction in 1935. The cabside numberplate originally had the E prefix above the number, but this was chiselled off when the prefixes were abandoned. Note that the side plate at the front of the tender is curved out, to match the width of the cab. Folding doors between cab and tender closed.

30333 at Eastleigh on 29 March 1958. It received a short flared chimney in late 1952. It still carries the A power classification, but with the BR classification 4P/5F added above the number. It retains its large tender emblem but has received discontinuous cabside lining. E.W. Fry.

30334

Built Nine Elms 12/1905   Order No. F13-5   Works Serial Number 772
Rebuilt Eastleigh 1/1925   Order No. A17-5   Works Serial Number 112
Rebuilt as ᴇ334 1/1925, Renumbered 334 11/1932, 30334 6/1948

Individual repairs as Class F13 are not shown.

12/1905		New 4-cylinder Locomotive 334
20/12/21-29/1/25	A	Rebuilt as H15, boiler ex 332, tender ex 330, olive green, ᴇ334
30/6/25-14/7/25	C	Left driving bearing
14/8/25-22/8/25	D	Right driving bearing
22/8/27-29/10/27	A	General repairs, dark green, boiler 334, tender 795
16/7/28-1/8/28	D	Right trailing bearing
12/9/28-25/9/28	D	Right leading bearing
6/5/29-13/6/29	C	Right driving bearing
30/1/30-15/3/30	A	Smoke deflectors, tender enlarged to 4300 gallons
1/10/32-5/11/32	A	Full repaint, renumbered 334
27/2/33-27/2/33	(GW)	
31/10/33-30/11/33	(GW)	
17/2/34-23/2/34	(GW)	Cab roof straightened
10/4/35-7/6/35	(GW)	Boiler removed for repair, part repaint
16/9/36-14/10/36	B	54,340
16/3/37-25/3/37	C	65,807
19/8/37-22/9/37	A	80,912, full repaint
17/3/39-19/4/39	C	72,614
22/1/40-28/2/40	A	92,652, full repaint, unlined dark green, Bulleid lettering
5/11/42-13/1/43	A	91,241, unlined black
16/11/44-2/3/45	A	64,526. Boiler removed for repair after other work due to leaks.
22/2/46-29/6/46	B	30,549
20/5/48-19/6/48	A	95,235, snifting valves off, BRITISH RAILWAYS (G) 30334 (S)
3/2/50-10/2/50	L Cas	49,635
4/10/50-27/10/50	L Int	69,079
16/1/53-13/2/53	Gen	144,397, lined black, first emblem
9/1/56-28/1/56	L Int	55,509, short flared chimney
21/6/58		Withdrawn
2/8/58		Scrapped at Eastleigh. Mileage 1,028,883

Allocation
1924	Salisbury
8/1950	Nine Elms
10/1950	Salisbury

E334 leaving Honiton Tunnel on an up express on Saturday 4 August 1928. The locomotive is as rebuilt, with no smoke deflectors and 4,000 gallon tender. The train is clearly a holiday extra, with a 30 year old 2-car non-corridor set at the front, which should have been confined to one of the West Country branches. H.C. Casserley, courtesy R.M. Casserley.

30334 at Feltham on 18 March 1950. The tender has been enlarged, with five coal rails. In June 1948 30334 lost its snifting valves and was re-lettered/numbered BRITISH RAILWAYS 30334, using Southern transfer numerals and hand painted lettering, to the Southern style but without shading. An L11 class 4-4-0 stands on the right. H.C. Casserley, courtesy R.M. Casserley.

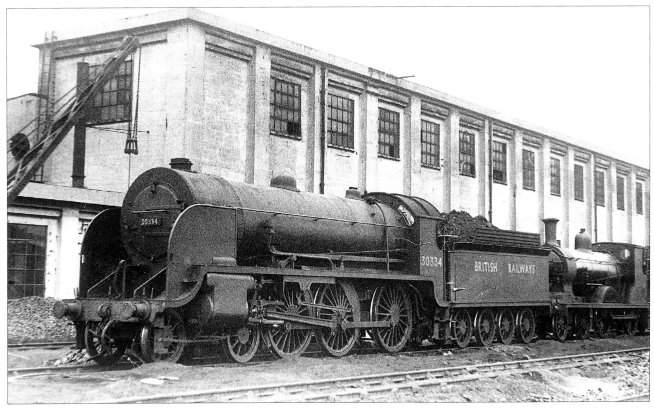

30335

Built Nine Elms 11/1907   Order No. E14   Works Serial Number 807
Rebuilt Eastleigh 12/1914 Order No. M15   Works Serial Number 48
Renumbered E335 12/1923, 335 9/1932, s335 3/1948, 30335 11/1948

Individual repairs as Class E14 are not shown.

Date	Code	Description
11/1907		New 4-cylinder Locomotive 335
1/1908		4,500 gallon tender ex 720
16/9/12-5/12/14		Rebuilt as 2-cylinder 4-6-0 335, Urie goods green
21/12/15-24/12/15		Left leading box heated
2/5/16-6/5/16		Slipper blocks etc.
9/10/17-16/2/18		97,694 miles, General repairs
12/6/18-22/6/18		Left driving axlebox
6/9/18-12/10/18		Various light repairs
27/4/20-15/5/20		Boxes and leaking tender
22/6/20-3/7/20		Left driving axlebox heated
21/3/21-30/7/21		General repair
24/10/22-28/10/22		Left trailing axlebox
20/7/23-15/12/23		General repairs, olive green E335
22/9/24-26/9/24	D	Trailing bearing
7/7/25-16/7/25	D	Alterations to brake gear
27/11/25-27/3/26	A	General repair, boiler 335
2/6/27-13/12/27	A	Maunsell superheater, tender numbered 790, dark green
18/2/30-4/4/30	A	General repair, tender not repainted, smoke deflectors
12/11/30-10/12/30	B	
26/7/32-3/9/32	A	Full repaint, renumbered 335,
16/8/33-25/8/33	(GW)	
26/3/35-8/5/35	(GW)	Boiler removed for repair, part repaint
27/8/35-27/8/35	D	
12/10/36-6/11/36	B	49,407, mileage extended by 5,000, part repaint
10/3/37-25/3/37	C	63,011
8/4/37-15/4/37	(GW)	Boiler work carried out in situ.
24/1/38-30/3/38	A	97,727, part repaint
12/7/40-21/8/40	A	85,362, full repaint, unlined dark green, Bulleid lettering
25/3/43-19/5/43	A	87,859, unlined black
28/6/43 – 6/7/43	D	
1/8/44-11/8/44	C	35,222
1/8/45-15/2/46	A	66,664, experimental axle boxes with rolled finish (Test 1984)
16/1/47-6/3/48	B	67,232, tender repainted, BRITISH RAILWAYS s335 (S)
19/10/48-27/11/48	A	87,498, snifting valves off, new cylinders, lined black, 30335
17/1/50-27/1/50	L Cas	27,247
31/7/50-11/8/50	L Cas	37,826
11/12/51-18/1/52	Gen	83,884, short flared chimney, first emblem
14/3/52-22/3/52	NC	4,266
28/5/53-13/6/53	L Cas	41,083
4/8/53-18/9/53	H Cas	43,484
13/12/54-8/1/55	L Int	60,416, not repainted
6/6/59		Withdrawn
29/8/59		Scrapped at Eastleigh, mileage 1,327,650

Allocation

1914	Eastleigh
6/1914	Nine Elms
1915	Salisbury
1/1943	Eastleigh
3/1944	Salisbury
8/1950	Nine Elms
10/1950	Salisbury

E335 approaching Raynes Park on an up train from Southampton Terminus via the main line consisting of an LSWR 4½ set and a 4-car set of non corridor stock. The snifting valves on the smokebox show that it now has a Maunsell superheater; this was fitted in December 1927. Buffer beam numerals still in LSWR gilt sans serif style and lamp irons in the LSWR sockets.

30335 in 1949-50. In March 1948, it was repainted in unlined black as s335, with **BRITISH RAILWAYS** tender lettering in Southern style. In November 1948 it lost its snifting valves and was renumbered 30335, in Gill sans characters, in lined black. Was this a full repaint or was the new lettering and lining applied to its eight month old paintwork? Two features shown in this photograph are the plated tender coalrails and the cabside cutout, which has been reduced in depth. D.L. Bradley.

30473

Built Eastleigh 2/1924   Order No. R16-1   Works Serial Number 98
Built as ᴇ473, renumbered 473 11/1931, 30473 1/1950

11/2/1924		New Locomotive E473, olive green, boiler no. 473, tender 796
1/7/24-5/7/24	D	Right trailing axlebox
23/7/24-31/7/24	D	New footplate
2/3/25-10/3/25	D	Left trailing bearing
28/2/27-4/6/1927	A	Dark green, King Arthur chimney
4/7/27-6/7/27	D	Left driving bearing
27/6/28-31/7/28	C	Tubes etc.
5/9/28-14/9/28	D	Left driving bearing
20/6/29-15/8/29	A	General repair, Maunsell boiler 455, Full repaint.
20/10/31-28/11/31	A	General Repair, Boiler 514, smoke deflectors, full repaint 473
2/12/31-4/3/32	(GW)	Stored in Paintshop
21/4/34-26/5/34	(GW)	part repaint
3/7/36-15/8/36	A	94,303, boiler 745, part repaint
10/11/38-7/12/38	A	95,603, boiler 521, full repaint, dark green, Bulleid lettering
8/12/1941-21/1/42	A	80,580, boiler 744, unlined black
18/5/44-5/8/44	A	85,066, Maunsell boiler 826
3/4/46-11/5/46	C	62,893
2/4/47-10/5/47	A	83,576, boiler 753
5/12/49-13/1/50	A	72,124, boiler 746, snifting valves off, lined black, first emblem, renumbered 30473
31/7/52-8/8/52	L Cas	67,549, not repainted
16/9/52-4/10/52	H Int	68,094
3/5/54-8/5/54	L Cas	116,068
8/11/54-27/11/54	Gen	133,592, boiler 506
12/4/56-27/4/56	L Cas	47,344
1/8/57-24/8/57	H Int	5200 gallon tender 786 ex 30483, not repainted
1/8/1959		Withdrawn 1,182,612 miles
5/9/59		Scrapped at Eastleigh

Allocation
1924   Nine Elms
1/1945   Feltham
1948   Eastleigh

473 at Nine Elms on 20 May 1932. It carries a Urie boiler, with a Maunsell superheater and King Arthur chimney. It still has a Urie smokebox door, but this now carries the side lamp irons. After leaving works in November 1931, with smoke deflectors and no E prefix, it was stored in Eastleigh paintshop and did not return to service until March 1932.

30473 at Eastleigh on 7th September 1957, shortly after a heavy intermediate repair, during which it was coupled to 5,200 gallon tender 786, from 30483. This has the small version of the first BR emblem, in a raised position to align with the cabside numerals. Power classification is now 4P5FA. The cab lining is continuous. Bolted plates were added to the cylinder casings of many Urie/Maunsell 4-6-0s during the 1950s. E.W. Fry.

30474

Built Eastleigh 2/1924   Order No. R16-2   Works Serial Number 99
Built as ᴇ474, Renumbered 474 6/1931, 30474 2/1949

23/2/1924		New Locomotive, Southern olive green
22/7/25-29/7/25	D	Left trailing bearing
18/1/26-11/6/26	A	General Repair, dark green, boiler numbered 474, tender 797
17/11/27-5/12/27	D	Left trailing bearing
2/10/28-3/1/29	A	General Repair, boiler 501
7/6/29-21/6/29	D	Left trailing bearing
14/5/31-27/6/31	A	Boiler 755, smoke deflectors, Maunsell s'heater, KA chimney, repaint, renumbered 474
18/7/33-29/8/33	(GW)	Boiler 506, part repaint
16/2/35-6/3/35	(GW)	part repaint
12/2/36-13/3/36	A	Maunsell boiler 798, part repaint
9/5/36-5/6/36	C	2,631
27/7/36-1/8/36	D	5,377, repair in yard
6/1/37-26/1/37	C	24,707, repair in paint shop
12/10/38-8/11/38	A	90,707, boiler 743, full repaint, panelled cylinders
5/10/40-30/10/40	A	77,866, boiler 473, unlined light green, Bulleid lettering
1/11/43-8/12/43	A	105,346, boiler 497, unlined black
20/11/46-21/12/46	A	89,900, boiler 499
17/1/47-15/2/47	B	97, new right hand cylinder
9/9/47-25/9/47	C	16,749
6/4/48-17/4/48	D	31,621
19/1/49-25/2/49	H Cas	52,553, boiler 744, Snifting valves off, SOUTHERN 30474
4/9/51-29/9/51	Gen	127,757,boiler 741, repainted lined black, first emblem
21/4/52-26/4/52	L Cas	16,266
26/5/53-13/6/53	L Int	50,515
20/1/55-12/2/55	Gen	102,903 M boiler 1055, 5200 gal tender 782 ex 30484, repainted
7/1956-16/9/56	(GW)	
11/2/57-15/2/57	L Cas	50,884
21/4/58-16/5/58	H Int	73,503, not repainted
30/4/60		Withdrawn mileage 1,115,567
14/5/60		Cut up at Eastleigh

Allocation
1924	Nine Elms
1/1945	Feltham
1948	Eastleigh

E474 at Nine Elms during the 1920s. It still has no cabside numberplate. By the state of the covered coaling stage roof, it is probably around 1927.

30474 on the turntable at Bournemouth shed, 24 July 1951. It received its British Railways number, on Southern unlined black livery, at a Heavy Casual Repair in February 1949 and is now due for a General Repair. R.K. Blencowe Collection.

30475

Built Eastleigh 2/1924   Order No. R16-3   Works Serial Number 100
Built as E475, renumbered 475 7/1932, 30475 10/1948

No SR Engine Record Card available

15/3/24		New Locomotive E475, olive green.
7/7/24-14/7/24	D	Trailing axlebox
25/11/24-29/11/24	D	Left driving axlebox
18/1/26-24/4/26	A	General repair
17/2/27-2/3/27	C	Light repair, boiler numbered 475, tender 798
14/9/27-6/10/27	C	Right trailing bearing
23/2/28-28/7/28	A	General repair, Boiler 740, full repaint, dark green
15/4/30-14/6/30	A	Maunsell s'heater, KA chimney, smoke deflectors, repaint
8/6/32-23/7/32	A	Boiler 524, loco renumbered 475
25/10/34-1/12/34	(GW)	Boiler 746, part repaint
13/10/36-19/11/36	(GW)	Boiler 521, part repaint
24/10/38-23/12/38	(GW)	Boiler 476, full repaint, dark green, Bulleid lettering
? – 21/3/41		Boiler 740, unlined black, gilt lettering
2/1943-?	(RO)	Unlined black, sunshine lettering
?-3/11/45		Maunsell Boiler 772
9/1947-?	(RO)	
10/1948-23/10/48	(GW)	Boiler 523, snifting valves off, BRITISH RAILWAYS 30475 (G)
2/1952-?	(GW)	
19/9/52-18/10/52	Gen	Boiler 750, repainted, lined black, first emblem
5/1954-23/5/54	(GW)	
1/4/55-30/4/55	Gen	Boiler 747, repainted
6/3/57-23/3/57	H Int	not repainted
31/7/1958-23/8/58	Gen	repainted, second emblem (F)
1/10/59-2/10/59	L Cas	not repainted
12/1961		withdrawn, mileage 1,309,376
10/3/62		Cut up at Eastleigh

Allocation
1924	Nine Elms
6/1939	Salisbury
8/1950	Eastleigh

E475 at Nine Elms, with no cabside numberplate but the newness is wearing off the paint. The late LSWR and early Southern olive green had a reputation for not weathering well.

30475 at Eastleigh on 17 February 1955. It is in lined black with a small first emblem on the tender, with 4P/5F power classification above the cabside numerals and the Southern A classification below. The cabside lining is continuous.   Peter Groom.

30476

Built Eastleigh 4/1924   Order No. R16-4   Works Serial Number 101
Built as E476, Renumbered 476 12/1932, 30476 6/1948

12/4/1924		New Locomotive E476, olive green E476
31/8/25-5/9/25	D	Left driving bearing
12/9/25-3/10/25	C	
13/10/26-5/2/27	A	General repair, dark green, boiler numbered 476, tender 799
5/12/27-13/12/27	D	Left driving axlebox
17/10/28-26/1/29	A	General repair, Maunsell s'heat, KA chimney, repainted
9/10/29-9/10/29	D	Weighing
26/11/30-10/1/31	A	General repair
14/1/31-24/1/31	(GW)	Smoke deflectors
4/11/32-10/12/32	(GW)	Boiler 496, loco renumbered 476
4/1/33-5/1/33	(GW)	
16/10/33-21/11/33	(GW)	
29/4/35-31/5/35	(GW)	Boiler 513, smokebox burnt
28/7/36-25/8/36	C	52,725, part repaint
26/11/37-5/1/38	A	98,628, boiler 497, full repaint, cylinders panelled
24/10/40-27/11/40	A	83,167, boiler 513, unlined light green, Bulleid lettering
13/3/43-14/4/43	A	89,973, boiler 474, unlined black
17/7/44-4/8/44	C	50,226
6/2/46-30/3/46	A	110,271, Urie boiler 986
19/5/48-10/6/48	A	86,579, boiler 510, sn valves off, BRITISH RAILWAYS (G) 30476 (S)
3/3/50-24/3/50	L Int	64,878
30/7/51-25/8/51	Gen	110,856, boiler 736, lined black, first emblem
23/1/53-5/2/53	L Cas	50,241
?-13/2/54	(GW)	
1/4/54-24/4/54	Gen	80,832, boiler 507, repainted
17/2/55-19/2/55	L Cas	28,232
15/6/56-7/7/56	L Int	65,844
9/8/57-10/8/57	L Cas	92,544
3/12/57-18/1/58	Gen	104,708, Maunsell boiler 774, repainted, second emblem (F)
13/10/58-16/10/58	NC	not repainted
1/12/59-19/12/59	L Int	not repainted
?-23/1/60	(GW)	
12/1961		withdrawn, mileage1,263,643
3/3/62		Scrapped at Eastleigh

Allocation
1925	Nine Elms
1/1936	Eastleigh
3/1944	Salisbury
8/1950	Nine Elms
10/1950	Eastleigh

E476 at Nine Elms in the mid-1920s. It is as built, but has gained a cabside numberplate.

30476 at Nine Elms on 31 May 1960. It had received Maunsell boiler 774, continuous cabside lining and the second BR emblem, facing forward on both sides, during its last General Repair in January 1958. Peter Groom.

30477

Built Eastleigh 4/1924   Order No. R16-5   Works Serial Number 102
Built as ᴇ477, Renumbered 477 9/1931, 30477 9/1948

10/5/1924		New Locomotive ᴇ477, SOUTHERN olive green.
21/4/25-25/4/25	D	Left leading axlebox hot
14/9/26-15/1/27	A	General repair dark green, boiler numbered 477
4/4/27-9/4/27	D	Trailing axleboxes
24/4/28-3/8/28	B	Light repairs
21/10/29-14/12/29	A	General repair, Maunsell boiler 929, tender 800, full repaint
25/7/31-5/9/31	A	Boiler 521, KA chimney, smoke deflectors, renumbered 477
28/1/33-2/3/33	(GW)	Boiler 508
17/7/33-26/7/33	(GW)	
6/10/34-9/11/34	(GW)	
29/10/35-21/11/35	C	Repair at Nine Elms
27/11/36-2/1/37	A	77,708. boiler 747
29/3/38-18/5/38	B	38,526
16/8/39-13/9/39	A	69,623, boiler 746, olive green, black/yellow lining, half green smoke deflectors, Bulleid lettering
23/3/43-5/5/43	A	96,094, boiler 986, unlined black
29/1/44-22/2/44	C	21,914
9/10/45-8/12/45	A	79,279, boiler 523
6/8/47-30/8/57	C	62,091
14/8/48-11/9/48	A	89,565, boiler 503, snift valves off, BRITISH RAILWAYS 30477 (G)
11/4/51-19/5/51	Gen	74,121, boiler 498, repainted unlined black, first emblem
31/10/52-22/11/52	H Int	50,457, repainted lined black
30/12/53-13/1/54	L Cas	84,620
10/1954-17/10/54	(GW)	
18/11/54-2/12/54	L Cas	110,056
17/2/55-26/2/55	L Cas	116,253
12/10/55-11/11/55	Gen	134,784, boiler 750
24/2/56-8/3/56	NC	5,873, derailment damage
10/4/57-18/4/57	L Cas	47,375
2/1958-15/2/58	(GW)	
13/6/58-11/7/58	H Int	56,408
4/7/59		Withdrawn, Mileage 1,020,549
8/8/59		Cut up at Eastleigh

Allocation
5/1924	Nine Elms
1/1936	Eastleigh
3/1944	Nine Elms
8/1950	Eastleigh

30477 at Eastleigh on 1 October 1950. It is in unlined black, with Gill sans lettering.

30477 at Eastleigh in BR lined black, with the A power classification below the cabside number, and the small first emblem on the tender. This livery was applied at a Heavy Intermediate Repair in November 1952. D.L. Bradley.

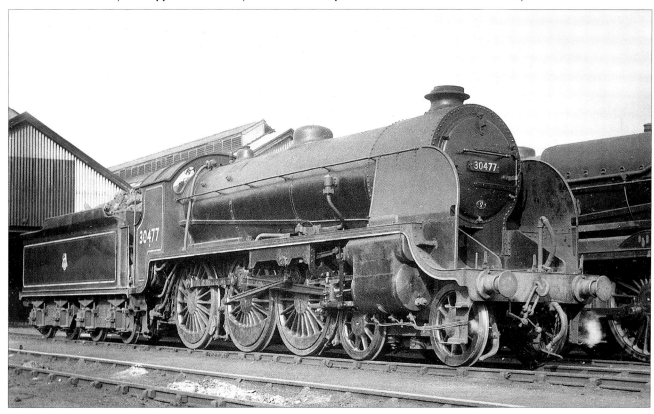

30478

Built Eastleigh 6/1924   Order No. T16-1   Works Serial Number 103
Built as E478, renumbered 478 4/1932, 30478 12/1948

No SR Engine Record Card available

5/6/1924		New Locomotive E478, SOUTHERN olive green
25/8/24-30/8/24	D	Right trailing bearing
19/10/25-7/11/25	B	Axleboxes and springs
15/9/26-8/1/27	A	Full repaint dark green, boiler numbered 478, tender 801
7/3/28-7/3/28	D	Springs changed
30/4/28-15/8/28	A	General repair, KA chimney, part repaint
18/3/29-28/3/29	D	Left driving bearing
21/3/30-24/5/30	A	Boiler 750, Maunsell superheater, smoke deflectors, full repaint
11/11/31-12/11/31	(GW)	
1/3/32-7/4/32	A	Boiler 736, part repaint, renumbered 478
13/9/34-22/10/34	(GW)	Full repaint
17/12/35-31/1/36	(GW)	partial repaint
18/1/37-18/2/37	(GW)	Boiler 498, partial repaint
12/6/39-15/7/39	(GW)	partial repaint
13/6/40-22/7/40	(GW)	Boiler 986, full repaint, unlined dark green, Bulleid lettering
?-31/3/43		Boiler 751, unlined black
?-5/10/45		Boiler 498
3/1946-?	(RO)	
10/1947-?	(RO)	
4/1948-1/5/48	(GW)	Boiler 744, snifting valves off, not painted
11/1948-11/12/48	(GW)	Maunsell boiler 829, Repainted lined black unlettered, 30478
?-21/1/50	(GW)	not painted
24/12/52-23/1/53	Gen	Maunsell boiler 771, repainted, first emblem
16/3/55-9/4/55	H Int	tender 801 to 30448, tender 797 ex 30474 fitted
8/1955-6/8/55	(GW)	
26/6/56-7/8/56	L Cas	At Nine Elms
12/2/57-2/3/57	L Int	not painted
3/1959		Withdrawn, mileage 1,107,597
18/4/59		Cut up at Eastleigh

Allocation

6/1924	Bournemouth
9/1925	Eastleigh
2/1927	Battersea
1927	Eastleigh
12/1941	Old Oak Common (GWR)
1948	Basingstoke
3/1944	Feltham
1948	Eastleigh
6/1955	Nine Elms

E478 passing Vauxhall on a Bournemouth express in about 1925, before receiving cabside numberplates. It must be a peak loading period, as three elderly non-corridor thirds have been added to the front of the corridor train. The driver's head can be seen through the cab spectacle glass. Compare its position with that of the side route disc. It must have created quite a blind spot for his view of the line.

30478 at Eastleigh on 9 July 1949; it has a Maunsell boiler and lined black livery with an unlettered tender acquired in December 1948. ELGH has been painted on the buffer beam in LNER fashion. This was done when Stephen Townroe was the Eastleigh Shedmaster, to remind Nine Elms which locos were his! D.L. Bradley.

107

30482

Built Eastleigh 3/1914   Order No. H15-3   Works Serial Number 40
Built as 482, Renumbered E482 4/1924, 482 3/1932, s482 2/1948, 30482
12/1950

No SR Engine Record Cards available

14/3/1914		New Locomotive, 482, Drummond passenger green.
21/4/14-25/4/14		Left leading bearing heated
2/5/14-23/5/14		Left driving bearing heated
3/5/15-15/5/15		Boiler leaking
15/1/17-17/2/17		Light repair
8/3/17-16/3/17		Right leading bearing hot
11/9/19-27/9/19		Scored piston
13/9/20-22/1/21		196,426 miles, general repair, goods green
5/4/21-9/4/21		Right driving box hot
5/4/22-8/4/22		Right leading box hot
15/11/23-5/4/24	A	General repair, Southern olive green, E482
12/4/24-16/4/24	C	Right driving axlebox hot
26/7/24-31/7/24	D	Left trailing bearing
1/7/25-18/7/25	D	Axleboxes
14/4/26-27/4/26	C	Right driving axlebox, boiler numbered 482
29/12/26-18/6/27	A	Dark green, new chimney, tender numbered 780
9/8/28-6/9/28	D	Right driving bearing
3/2/30-15/3/30	A	General repair, Boiler 483, repainted, smoke deflectors
5/2/32-12/3/32	A	Short flared chimney, renumbered 482
3/9/34-9/10/34	(GW)	Boiler 482, Maunsell superheater
9/4/35-15/4/35	(GW)	
21/9/36-22/10/36	(GW)	part repaint
16/12/36-28/1/37	(GW)	Boiler removed for repair, part repaint
9/3/37-18/3/37	(GW)	light repair
31/1/38-18/3/38	(GW)	Boiler repairs in situ, part repaint
?-5/7/39	(GW)	Boiler 483, olive green, black/yellow lining, half green smoke deflectors, Bulleid lettering
4/1942-1/6/42	(RO)	Boiler 484, unlined black
8/1945-8/9/45	(RO)	Boiler 486
1/1948-21/2/48	(GW)	Boiler 483, Snifting valves off, BRITISH RAILWAYS s482
11/1950-2/12/50	(GW)	Boiler 486, repainted, lined black, first emblem, 30482
1/1951-17/2/51	(GW)	not painted
5/12/52-27/12/52	Int	not painted
1/11/54-20/11/54	Gen	Boiler 484, 5200 gal tender 780 replaced by 5000 gal 3202
15/8/56-8/9/56	H Int	
9/1/58-8/2/58	L Cas	At Nine Elms
8/1958-20/9/58	(GW)	
5/1959		withdrawn, Mileage 1,471,917
22/8/59		Cut up at Eastleigh

Allocation
Nine Elms throughout

482 passing Earlsfield on a special to Bournemouth. The black centred disc over the near buffer indicates a special train. The photograph is not dated, but is probably after the First World War, with 482 in the dark LSWR goods green livery.

30482, after November 1954, when it received a 5,000 gallon tender and a second repaint in lined black.

30483

Built Eastleigh 4/1914   Order No. H15-4 Works Serial Number 41
Built as 483, Renumbered ᴇ483 4/1924, 483 10/1931, 30483 8/1950

2/4/1914		New Locomotive 483, Drummond passenger green.
25/5/14-30/5/14		Left leading bearing heated
17/5/15-22/5/15		Pistons etc.
31/8/15-4/9/15		Hot box
4/10/15-9/10/15		Motion & coupling rods
2/8/16-12/8/16		Right trailing bearing hot
14/5/17-2/6/17		General repairs
17/8/18-12/10/18		Hot boxes
8/7/20-15/1/21		187,645 miles, general repair, goods green
12/6/22-24/6/22		Left driving tyre loose
12/10/22-14/10/22		Left driving box heated
24/11/22-25/11/22		Right leading bearing heated
21/6/23-23/6/23		Right trailing box hot
28/12/23-26/4/24	A	General repair, stovepipe chimney, olive green, ᴇ483,
20/10/26-2/4/27	A	General repair, boiler 483, tender 781, dark green
23/7/29-18/9/29	A	Boiler 490, Maunsell s'heater, sloping smoke deflectors, repaint
28/8/31-31/10/31	A	Boiler removed for repair, vertical smoke deflectors, repaint, 483
31/11/32-11/5/32	B	
26/2/34-3/4/34	(GW)	Boiler 968, part repaint
25/3/36-2/5/36	A	92,627
9/3/38-6/4/38	A	85,182, boiler 485, repainted, cylinders panelled
13/4/40-15/5/40	A	86,575, boiler 490, unlined dark green, Bulleid lettering
19/5/42-/7/42	C	Mileage extended by 5,000 at Nine Elms
24/9/43-24/11/43	A	115,184, short flared chimney, unlined black
2/2/46-9/3/46	A	81,202, boiler 483, new right hand cylinder
31/1/47-29/11/47	A	65,686, boiler 489, snifting valves off
13/6/50-11/8/50	A	96,560, boiler 485, lined black, first emblem, 30483
10/1951-?	(GW)	
7/1952-5/7/52	(GW)	Not repainted
20/11/52-17/12/52	Gen	72,294, Boiler 489, repainted
17/8/55-10/9/55	H Cas	95,873, boiler 482, tender 786 ex 30485, repainted
11/1955-26/11/55	(GW)	not repainted
19/4/56-21/4/56	L Cas	112,306, not repainted
13/6/57		To Works, but no work done
28/6/57		withdrawn, mileage 1,467,889
2/7/57		Cut up at Eastleigh

Allocation
1914	Nine Elms
8/1950	Eastleigh
11/1950	Nine Elms

483, new in Eastleigh works yard, in April 1914, in the full Drummond grass green passenger livery with purple brown edging. 482-485 were built with Schmidt superheaters, which incorporated a damper control and a pyrometer on the right side of the smokebox.

30483 at Eastleigh, newly painted in BR lined black, with small first emblem on the tender and A power classification below the cabside number, in August 1950. No shed plate has yet been attached, but it remained at Eastleigh for three months, before going back to Nine Elms. W. Gilburt.

30484

Built Eastleigh 5/1914   Order No. K15-1   Works Serial Number 43
Built as 484, renumbered ᴇ484 11/1926, 484 12/1931, 30484 11/1948

23/5/1914		Built as 484, Schmidt superheater, Drummond passenger green
14/4/16-22/4/16		Slipper blocks etc.
2/10/16-14/10/16		Various slight repairs
8/7/18-13/7/16		Angle irons
5/12/19-3/4/20		180,913 miles, general repair, goods green?
7/9/21-17/9/21		Right trailing bearing hot
30/9/21-29/10/21		Tubes
8/6/22-10/6/22		Left trailing bearing hot
27/1/23-12/5/23		General repairs, LSWR goods green
20/9/23-29/9/23		Left trailing bearing
2/9/24-25/9/24	B	All tyres loose
16/10/24-24/10/24	D	Driving axlebox
24/2/26-25/11/26	A	General repair, boiler 484, tender 782, dark green ᴇ484
22/1/29-25/3/29	A	General repair, repainted.
9/12/30-31/1/31	B	Tubeplate, Maunsell superheater, straight smoke deflectors *
14/11/31-19/12/31	A	Boiler 482, repainted, renumbered 484
6/6/32-1/7/32	B	
24/4/34-6/6/34	(GW)	Boiler 490, part repaint, short flared chimney
30/3/36-16/5/36	A	86,950, boiler 489, full repaint
17/8/36-24/8/36	D	7,451, light repair
9/7/38-24/8/38	A	92,222, boiler 487, full repaint, dark green, cylinders paneled.
24/7/40-24/7/40		Mileage extended by 15,000 at Nine Elms
16/8/41-1/10/41	A	102,036, boiler 489, unlined black
10/12/42-18/12/42	C	47,472, at Nine Elms
1/2/43-3/3/43	C	51,082, at Nine Elms
19/8/43-23/8/43	C	69,658, at Nine Elms
6/7/44-28/7/44	C	103,864, mileage extended by 30,000 at Nine Elms
10/2/45-24/3/45	A	124,273, boiler 487
29/11/46-16/1/47	B	63,496
10/7/48-30/10/48	A	103,369, boiler 490, Snifting valves off, lined black, BRITISH RAILWAYS 30484 (G)
21/2/51-30/3/51	Gen	82,953, boiler 968, repainted, first emblem
29/5/52-21/6/52	H Cas	45,145, not painted
2/9/52-1/10/52	Cas	50,411 at Guildford
30/11/54-15/1/55	Gen	127,432, boiler 486, 5000 gal tender 3206 ex 30502
21/8/57-14/9/57	H Int	89,304, not painted
9/5/1959		withdrawn, mileage 1,517,013
11/7/1959		Cut up at Eastleigh

*Evidence suggests that sloping smoke deflectors were fitted between 25/3/29 and 8/12/30, so they may have been fitted at Nine Elms.

Allocation
1914	Nine Elms
10/1940	Feltham
1/1945	Nine Elms

484 heading a West of England train, running on the down slow line somewhere between Farnborough and Basingstoke, in the late 1940s. It has smoke deflectors, a short flared chimney and a Maunsell smokebox door and is in Southern unlined black livery.

30484 at Eastleigh on 12 August 1955. It had a General Repair in January 1955, during which a 5,000 gallon tender was attached. Both depth and width of the cabside cutout have been reduced. R.K. Blencowe Collection.

30485

Built Eastleigh 6/1914   Order No. K15-3   Works Serial Number 45
Built as 485, renumbered ᴇ485 2/1924, 485 10/32, 30485 7/1948

20/6/1914		Built as 485, Schmidt superheater, Drummond passenger green
10/8/14-15/8/14		Hot Box
15/3/16-25/3/16		Springs, slipper blocks, port faces etc.
27/2/17-17/3/17		Repairs
3/3/20-18/9/20		190,247 miles, general repairs, goods green
14/7/21-30/7/21		Right driving wheel shifted etc.
23/1/22-18/2/22		Superheater tubes
3/12/23-22/2/24	A	General repair, SOUTHERN olive green, ᴇ485
18/3/24-21/3/24	B	Left driving bearing
8/7/24-4/7/24	C	Trailing axlebox
12/4/26-2/10/26	A	General repair, boiler numbered 485, full repaint, dark green
24/4/28-26/9/28	A	Maunsell superheater, boiler 968, tender 783,
12/8/30-19/8/30	D	Right trailing bearing, straight smoke deflectors *
21/2/31-4/4/31	A	General repair
8/9/32-5/10/32	B	short flared chimney, renumbered 485
11/7/33-22/8/33	(GW)	Boiler 485, repaint, Schmidt superheater
19/7/35-30/8/35	A	87,888, boiler 488, Maunsell superheater, part repaint
18/10/37-13/11/37	A	85,631, boiler 486, repaint
14/7/39-23/8/39	A	73,585, repaint, olive green, black/yellow lining, half green smoke deflectors, Bulleid lettering
18/3/42-18/3/42		Mileage increased by 10,000 at Nine Elms
17/11/42-12/12/42	A	101,805, boiler 483, unlined black
17/9/45-13/10/45	A	98,000, boiler 484
26/8/46-19/10/46	B	39,499, new right hand cylinder
30/11/46		Tender 786 ex 488 at Nine Elms
6/10/47-13/19/47	D	69,590, repair at Nine Elms
5/5/48-17/7/48	A	76,538, boiler 968, snift valves off, BRITISH RAILWAYS 30485 (G)
3/1/1951-27/1/51	A	87,977, boiler 483, lined black, first emblem
18/2/53-14/3/53	Gen	71,961, boiler 485
22/1/1955		Damaged in collision at Bournemouth Central
2/1955	(GW)	To Works
13/4/1955		Withdrawn, mileage 1,303,990
6/8/1955		Cut up at Eastleigh

*Evidence suggests that sloping smoke deflectors were fitted between 26/9/28 and 12/8/30, so they may have been fitted at Nine Elms.

Allocation   1914 Nine Elms throughout

E485 at Nine Elms between February 1924, when it received Southern olive green livery, and July 1925, when T9 718 lost its LSWR livery. E485 has no cabside numberplate and the only modification has been the replacement of its Schmidt superheater by an Eastleigh one.

30485 at Eastleigh on 21 March 1953, immediately after a General Repair. It had received lined black with the first BR emblem at its previous General Repair in September 1951 and George Woodward noted it as 'not repainted' in 1953. However, it has been well cleaned and the paintwork has probably been touched up and re-varnished. Leslie Freeman, transporttreasury.co.uk

30486

Built Eastleigh 1/1914   Order No. H15-1 Works Serial Number 38
New as 486, renumbered E486 9/1924, 486 3/1932, 30486 9/1948

17/1/1914		New, Robinson superheater, Drummond passenger green
23/3/14-4/4/14		Valves & whitemetal packing
1/5/14-9/6/14		Piston Valves
23/6/14-4/7/14		Fitted with indicating gear
27/7/14-25/7/14		Indicating gear removed
18/11/16-2/12/16		Left trailing bearing hot etc.
24/7/17-25/8/17		Tubes etc.
17/8/18-12/10/18		Left trailing axlebox heated
17/8/20-28/8/20		Right leading bearing
8/3/21-20/8/21		228,971 miles, general repairs, goods green
8/5/22-20/5/22		Left driving tyre loose
23/5/23-9/6/23		Right leading bearing
22/10/23-3/11/23		Right trailing axlebox hot
22/11/23-24/11/23		Coupling rod bushes examined
18/3/24-22/3/24	B	Left trailing bearing
30/6/24-9/9/24	A	General repair, repaint SOUTHERN olive green, E486
24/1/27-30/8/27	A	General repairs, dark green, boiler 486, tender 784
3/2/30-22/3/30	A	Maunsell superheater Smoke deflectors, repaint.
18/1/32-2/3/32	A	short flared chimney, loco renumbered 486
?-11/2/33	(GW)	Entry on boiler card, but no work done
26/9/34-14/12/34	(GW)	Boiler 483, repainted
19/10/36-21/11/36	A	88,192, partial repaint
21/10/38-23/11/38	A	82,482, boiler 489, repaint dark green, Bulleid lettering
15/3/41-30/4/41	A	86,045, boiler 488, unlined black, gilt lettering
20/7/43-8/9/43	A	85,433, boiler 482, sunshine lettering
18/8/45-3/9/45	C	84,189, repair at Nine Elms
9/1/46-31/1/46	C	100,834, mileage extended by 5,000 at Nine Elms
22/2/46-2/3/46	C	102,196, mileage extended by 10,000
1/4/46-27/4/46	A	195,338, boiler 490
12/5/48-4/9/48	A	64,653, boiler 484, snift valves off, BRITISH RAILWAYS 30486 (G)
8/6/49-1/7/49	L Cas	31,729
5/9/50-16/9/50	L Cas	69,571
2/10/50-6/10/50	NC	72,887
30/7/51-7/9/51	Gen	102,258, boiler 482, lined black, first emblem
10/6/53-4/7/53	Gen	66,031, boiler 483, not repainted
11/1953-15/11/53	(GW)	not repainted
8/12/55-31/12/55	L Int	87,491, not repainted
13/5/57-8/6/57	Gen	Boiler 487, repainted, second emblem (F)
8/1958-23/8/58	(GW)	not repainted
7/1959		withdrawn, Mileage 1,512,324
5/9/1959		Cut up at Eastleigh

Allocation
1914   Nine Elms 10/1940   Feltham   1/1945 Nine Elms

486 at Exmouth Junction in 1923. It is in LSWR goods green livery and the injector steam pipe has been moved forward, in line with the safety valve. A patch on the smokebox shows where a pyrometer had been fixed, for measuring temperatures in the Robinson superheater. It is fitted with feedwater heating, the end of the heat exchanger can be seen between the tender bogies.

30486 on an up train at Eastleigh during the mid-1950s. It is in BR lined black with small first emblem and 4P5FA power classification. It has undergone the usual modifications; smoke deflectors, short flared chimney, Maunsell smokebox door, although that can't be seen, and reduced depth cabside cutouts.

30487

Built Eastleigh 2/1914   Order No. H15-2   Works Serial Number 39
New as 487, renumbered ᴇ487 12/1923, 487 8/1931, 30487 7/1948

21/2/1914		New, Robinson superheater, Drummond passenger green
2/9/14-19/9/14		Left cylinder broken etc.
26/11/14-5/12/14		Hot Box
28/10/15-6/11/15		Leading boxes
5/2/16-12/2/16		Buffer plate repairs etc.
10/1/17-27/1/17		
19/12/17-9/3/18		137,837 miles, general repairs, goods green
9/4/18-13/4/18		Tubes etc.
27/7/18-3/8/18		Various slight repairs
15/8/19-13/9/19		Tubes & axleboxes
12/10/20-12/2/21		General repairs
24/3/22-22/4/22		Right driving tyre loose
4/9/23-8/12/23		General repair, Southern lined black, numbered ᴇ487
27/11/24-3/12/24	D	Right leading bearing
20/7/25-30/7/25	C	Trailing bearings
17/9/25-1/10/25	D	Left driving bearing, boiler 487
26/7/26-12/2/27	A	General repairs, dark green, boiler numbered 487, tender 785
21/3/29-1/6/29	A	General repairs, Maunsell superheater, partial repaint, sloping smoke deflectors.
13/7/31-29/8/31	A	General repair, Boiler 488, straight smoke deflectors, repaint, renumbered 487
27/9/33-9/11/33	(GW)	Boiler 488, part repaint
10/4/35-21/5/35	(GW)	Boiler 484, part repaint
24/8/36-3/10/36	B	51,753, boiler 490, mileage extended by 10,000, part repaint
18/11/37-18/12/37	A	102,793, full repaint, dark green, cylinders panelled.
28/12/39-7/2/40	A	77,034, boiler 968, unlined dark green, Bulleid lettering
11/6/41-28/6/41	C	35,410
5/6/42-6/7/42	C	63,948
18/12/42-3/2/43	A	81,517 unlined black
28/2/44-17/3/44	C	40,306
13/2/45-14/4/45	A	73,047, boiler 489
25/4/47-7/6/47	B	66,205. boiler 485, snifting valves off
22/6/48-26/6/48	D	99,763, not repainted, SOUTHERN 30487
30/5/49-15/7/49	A	126,815 boiler 488, lined black, unlettered
5/10/51-3/11/51	Gen	77,934, boiler 484, first emblem
5/1952-?	(GW)	
22/4/54-29/5/54	Gen	90,283, boiler 490
20/12/55-14/1/56	H Int	58,962
2/1956-?	(GW)	
23/11/57		Withdrawn, mileage 1,419,965
7/12/57		Cut up at Eastleigh
Allocation		Nine Elms throughout

487, new in Eastleigh Works yard in 1914. It has a Robinson superheater and is painted in the Drummond grass green livery with purple brown edging. As usual, a monochrome photograph does not differentiate between the two colours. The headcode indicates that it is going to Eastleigh shed, just across Campbell road, but it must go to the station and back to get there. South Western Circle D.L. Bradley Collection.

487, now in goods green livery, posed on the curve leading from Eastleigh carriage works to the Portsmouth line with US Ambulance Train No.62 in April 1918. This 16 vehicle train had been rebuilt from LSWR corridor carriages. When these were returned to the LSWR in 1919, they became passenger brake vans (see also page 68).

30488

Built Eastleigh 4/1914   Order No. H15-5   Works Serial Number 42
Built as 488, renumbered ᴇ488 7/1925, 488 3/1933, 30488 3/1949

No SR Engine Record Card available

25/4/1914		New Engine, Robinson superheater, Drummond passenger green
18/6/14-27/6/14		Tender bearings heated
17/10/14-31/10/14		Collision at Andover
11/11/14-14/11/14		Left leading bearing melted
29/9/15-9/10/15		Conn, Coupling & Piston Rods
12/12/16-30/12/16		Axeboxes refitting
11/8/17-1/9/17		Left trailing bearing hot
12/9/17-29/9/17		Driving boxeshot
31/7/18-24/8/18		Left driving box hot etc.
11/11/19-24/4/20		178,669 miles, general repairs, goods green
17/5/20-22/5/20		Right piston rod scored
28/5/20-5/6/20		Left leading bearing heated
7/7/20-10/7/20		Boxes & Connecting rods
17/11/21-17/12/21		Superheater tubes
30/8/22-28/10/22		General repairs
9/2/25-22/7/25	A	General repairs, stovepipe chimney, SOUTHERN dark green
14/9/27-24/9/27	D	Right trailing bearing
10/10/27-9/3/28	A	General repair, Maunsell s'heater, boiler 488, tender 786
28/6/29-28/6/29	D	Weighing
17/10/29-16/12/29	B	Framing, sloping smoke deflectors, repaint
16/2/31-18/4/31	A	General repairs, boiler 484, straight smoke deflectors?
23/1/33-8/3/33	(GW)	Repainted, renumbered 488
4/4/35-4/5/35	(GW)	Boiler 486
4/7/37-21/5/37	(GW)	Boiler 484, Repainted
14/6/39-25/7/39	(GW)	Short flared chimney, repainted, olive green, black/yellow lining, Bulleid lettering, half green smoke deflectors
4/1942-9/5/42	(RO)	Boiler 487, Unlined black
?/1944-16/9/44	(RO)	Boiler 488
1/1946-?	(RO)	
11/1946		Tender 783 ex 485 at Nine Elms
1/1947-?	(RO)	
12/1948-12/3/49	(GW)	Boiler 487, repainted lined black, unlettered, 30488
10/1949-?	(GW)	
3/1952-23/3/52	(GW)	Boiler 488, lined black, first emblem
31/3/53-4/4/53	L Cas	Accident damage, not repainted
23/12/53-16/1/54	L Int	repainted
4/1954		5000 gallon Tender 869 ex 30754
5/5/55-3/6/55 Gen		Boiler 986, repainted
?-17/3/56	(GW)	not repainted
1/10/57-19/10/57	L Int	Not repainted
4/1959		Withdrawn, Mileage 1,500,637
23/5/59	(GW)	Cut up at Eastleigh

Allocation
1914	Salisbury
3/1915	Nine Elms

488 in the late 1930s, now with vertical smoke deflectors and a Maunsell smokebox door. The injector steam pipe is in line with the safety valve, the depth and width of the cabside cutouts has been reduced and the cylinder drain pipes have been extended to the front footsteps.

30488 passing Shawford Junction on a train for Southampton Terminus. The date is after April 1954, when 30488 received a 5,000 gallon tender. The track to the right leads to Winchester Chesil and the GWR line to Didcot whilst the near track to the left by-passes Shawford station, leading into the down slow where the Southern main line becomes four track.

30489

Built Eastleigh 5/1914   Order No. K15-2   Works Serial Number 44
Built as 489, renumbered E489 5/1926, 489 3/1932, 30489 5/1948

No SR Engine Record Card available

Date	Code	Description
30/5/1914		New engine, Robinson superheater, Drummond passenger green
1/10/14-3/10/14		Coupling rod cap broken
27/2/15-6/3/15		Piston valves
12/4/16-22/4/16		Slipper blocks etc.
11/4/17-28/4/17		Repairs
23/8/17-8/9/17		Axleboxes
10/1/18-19/1/18		187,892 miles, general repairs
16/7/18-27/7/18		Left trailing bearing hot
25/4/19-17/5/19		Superheater
12/10/20-21/1/21		General repairs, goods green
27/9/22-30/9/22		Left trailing box hot
2/11/22-17/2/23		Left driving wheel loose on axle, General repair
9/5/23-19/5/23		Left driving box heated
29.7.24-20/8/24	D	Trailing axlebox
9/7/25-18/7/25	D	Leading axleboxes
9/10/25-1/5/26	A	General repairs, boiler 489, Southern dark green renumbered E489
25/10/27-12/11/27	C	Right driving bearing, tender 787
14/11/28-14/2/29	A	General repairs, boiler 485, Schmidt superheater
4/11/29-21/12/29	B	Right driving wheel, sloping smoke deflectors
27/4/31-14/5/31	D	Left driving bearing
28/1/32-5/3/32	A	Boiler 487, Maunsell superheater, short flared chimney, vertical smoke deflectors, renumbered 489.
5/2/3-10/3/34	(GW)	part repaint
27/11/35-6/1/36	(GW)	complete repaint
26/2/36-10/3/36	(GW)	
22/4/38-23/5/38	(GW)	Boiler 968, complete repaint, dark green, panelled cylinders
9/6/39-27/7/39	(GW)	Boiler 482, touch up only
12/1940	(RO)	Unlined light green, Bulleid lettering
?-29/6/43		Boiler 486, Unlined black
?/1945-14/7/45	(RO)	Boiler 968
3/1946-?	(RO)	
2/1948-15/5/48	(GW)	Boiler 486, snifting valves off, BRITISH RAILWAYS 30489 (S)
7/1950-9/9/50	(GW)	Boiler 489, repainted, lined black, first emblem
19/5/52-21/6/52	Gen	Boiler 487, repainted
4/5/54-29/5/54	L Int	
15/2/55-3/3/55	L Cas	At Nine Elms
4/4/56-28/4/56	Gen	Boiler 488, repainted,
20/1/58-8/2/58	H Int	tender 787 replaced by 785 ex 30487
1/1961		Withdrawn, Mileage 1,521,178
2/1961	(GW)	To Eastleigh
11/3/61		Cut up at Eastleigh

Allocation

1914	Salisbury
3/1915	Nine Elms
8/1950	Eastleigh
11/1950	Nine Elms

489, new at Eastleigh works in May 1914. It was the last of the 486-489 batch, fitted initially with Robinson superheaters.

30489 at Eastleigh on 17 February 1958, after a Heavy Intermediate repair, during which it had received the tender from 30487. Power classification is now 4P/5FA and the cabside lining is discontinuous. Peter Groom.

30490

Built Eastleigh 7/1914   Order No. K15-4   Works Serial Number 46
Built as 490, renumbered ᴇ490 12/1926, 490 8/1931 , 30490 11/1948

No SR Engine Record Card available

Date	Code	Description
11/7/1914		New Locomotive, Saturated boiler, Drummond passenger green
20/7/14-25/7/14		Hot box
26/4/15-28/4/15		Steam tube cleaner fitted?
13/9/15-18/9/15		Coupling rod brasses and bushes
16/12/15-18/12/15		Hot box (left leading)
22/5/16-27/5/16		Bogie spring & ? gear
24/8/16-2/9/16		Heated bearings
9/10/16-4/11/16		In collision at Andover, goods green
31/5/19-13/12/19		169,257 miles, general repairs, Eastleigh superheater fitted
17/7/22-16/9/22		General repairs
5/5/24-11/7/24	B	Right driving tyre loose
3/10/24-9/10/24	D	Trailing boxes
1/7/25-10/7/25	D	Left driving bearing
23/6/26-18/12/26	A	General repairs, dark green E490, boiler 490, tender 788
4/3/29-16/5/29	A	General repairs, boiler 489, Maunsell superheater
8/7/31-15/8/31	A	Smoke deflectors, boiler removed for repair, repainted, renumbered 490
28/8/33-14/10/33	(GW)	Boiler removed for repair, partial repaint
21/3/34-3/4/34	(GW)	Boiler repaired in situ
16/12/35-13/2/36	(GW)	Boiler 485, short flared chimney, full repaint
10/1/38-14/2/38	(GW)	Boiler 488, part repaint, panelled cylinders
22/4/40-29/5/40	(GW)	Boiler 485, repainted, unlined dark green, Bulleid lettering
?-1/6/41		Boiler 490
9/1943-6/10/43	(RO)	Boiler 485, repainted unlined black
12/1943-?	(RO)	
6/1945-?	(RO)	
31/5/46-31/8/46	A?	Boiler 482, tender 788
15/10/48-20/11/48	Gen	Snifting valves off, lined black, BRITISH RAILWAYS 30490 (G)
24/4/51-26/5/51	Gen	Boiler 490, first emblem
31/10/52-22/11/52	Int	not repainted
1/2/54-13/2/54	H Cas	Boiler 482, not repainted
25/6/55		Withdrawn, Mileage 1,397,637
2/7/55		Cut up at Eastleigh

Allocation
Nine Elms throughout

E490 at Waterloo on a Portsmouth train between May 1929, when it received a Maunsell superheater, and July 1931, when it went into works, and came out with smoke deflectors. It has lost its piston tailrods and has lamp irons in its LSWR sockets.

30490 at Eastleigh, probably shortly after it was repainted with the first BR emblem in May 1951. It still carries the A power classification below the cabside number. D.L. Bradley.

30491

Built Eastleigh 7/1914   Order No. K15-5   Works Serial Number 47
Built as 491, renumbered ᴇ491 5/1925, 491 11/1931, 30491 3/1949

No SR Engine Record Card available

31/7/1914		New Locomotive, Saturated boiler, Drummond passenger green
9/11/14-14/11/14		Alterations to valves
8/12/14-23/12/14		Firebox crown
14/9/15-18/9/15		Axleboxes & coupling rods
25/10/15-6/11/15		Derailed at Honiton
14/6/17-6/10/17		116,614 miles, Eastleigh superheater, short stovepipe chimney, goods green
23/1/18-23/2/18		Broken footplate
5/10/18-19/10/18		Left driving bearing hot
31/10/18-9/11/18		Right leading bearing hot
21/2/19-1/3/19		Left leading bearing hot
25/6/20-26/6/20		Left trailing bearing
24/2/22-27/5/22		Left driving horn checks
23/7/23-28/7/23		Hot trailing boxes
21/12/23-29/12/23	C	Left leading bearing melted
18/10/24-25/10/24	D	Hot trailing boxes
13/12/24-16/5/25	A	General repairs, SOUTHERN dark green, numbered ᴇ491
18/7/25-24/7/25	D	Left leading bearing
10/8/25-19/8/25	D	Light repairs
1/2/27-13/6/27	A	Maunsell boiler 491, King Arthur chimney, tender numbered 789
9/5/29-4/7/29	A	General repairs
14/10/3-27/11/31	A	Maunsell boiler 454, smoke deflectors, repainted, renumbered 491
6/6/32-7/7/32	(GW)	
25/4/34-13/6/34	(GW)	Urie taper boiler 503, part repaint
9/6/36-23/7/36	(GW)	full repaint
25/1/39-15/2/39	(GW)	Derailment damage
4/4/39-11/5/39	(GW)	Boiler 745, olive green, green/yellow lining, half green smoke deflectors, Bulleid lettering
?-30/6/42		Boiler 477, unlined black
?-26/1/44		Boiler 512
9/1945-?	(RO)	
12/1947-1/1948		Boiler 476, snifting valves off
3/1949-19/3/49	(GW)	Unlined black SOUTHERN 30491
8/1950-30/9/50	(GW)	Boiler 505, repainted lined black, first emblem
15/9/53-10/10/53	Gen	Boiler 515, repainted
23/11/55-10/12/55	H Int	
3/4/57-4/5/57	Gen	Maunsell boiler 788, repainted, Second emblem (F)
7/4/59-25/5/59	L Int	not repainted
2/1961		Withdrawn, Mileage 1,539,740
4/4/61	(GW)	Cut up at Eastleigh

Allocation
1914	Nine Elms	8/1950	Eastleigh	11/1950	Nine Elms

491 at Eastleigh in the early 1920s. It was built with a saturated boiler but received an Eastleigh superheater and stovepipe chimney in 1917, being repainted into the dark goods green livery at the same time. Even at this oblique angle, the end of the feedwater heat exchanger can be seen between the tender bogies.

491 at Eastleigh for General Repair on 11 April 1939. In 1927, it had been modified to carry a standard Urie or Maunsell taper boiler, providing a spare boiler for Nos.482 to 490. It now carries a Urie taper boiler with a Maunsell smokebox door and smoke deflectors. R.K. Blencowe Collection.

30521

Built Eastleigh 7/1924   Order No. T16-2 Works Serial Number 104
Built as E521, renumbered 521 1/1932, 30521 6/1948

No SR Engine Record Card available

7/7/1924		New Locomotive E521, SOUTHERN olive green
5/12/24-13/12/24	D	Left trailing bearing
9/3/25-19/3/25	D	Wheels and boxes
20/4/25-25/4/25	D	Left driving bearing
15/8/25-25/8/25	D	Right trailing bearing
16/12/25-24/12/25	C	Light repairs
21/5/26-1/6/26	D	Speed indicator
25/4/27-12/7/27	A	KA chimney, dark green, boiler numbered 521, tender 802
23/7/28-13/8/28	D	Left driving and trailing bearings
20/8/29-28/9/29	A	General repairs, Boiler 523, Maunsell superheater
27/4/31-30/4/31	D	Spring hanger, smoke deflectors
11/9/31-12/9/31	(GW)	
10/12/31-23/1/32	A	Maunsell boiler 491, part repaint, renumbered 521
3/2/32-8/2/32	(GW)	
5/2/34-17/3/34	(GW)	part repaint
10/4/34-16/4/34	(GW)	
?-29/2/36	(GW)	Urie boiler? full repaint
?-30/7/38	(GW)	Maunsell boiler 830, full repaint, cylinders panelled
3/1941-9.4.41	(DLB)	Boiler 475, unlined black, gilt lettering
12/1942-?	(RO)	
12/1943		Sunshine lettering
6/5/1944		Boiler 496
1/1946-?	(RO)	
?-28/9/46		Boiler 478
6/1948-?	(GW)	Renumbered SOUTHERN 30521
5/1949-26/6/49	(GW)	Boiler 499, snifting valves off, lined black unlettered
12/1951-6/1/52	(GW)	Maunsell boiler 767, repainted, first emblem
11/6/54-3/7/54	Gen	Boiler 736
5/4/56-21/4/56	H Int	
28/5/56-2/6/56	NC	
15/10/57-9/11/57	Gen	Boiler 473, repainted, second emblem (F)
5/11/59-21/11/59	H Int	
12/1961		Withdrawn, mileage 1,161,139
20/1/62	(GW)	Cut up at Eastleigh

Allocation

1/1925	Bournemouth
9/1925	Eastleigh
10/1940	Bournemouth
1/1945	Eastleigh
11/1950	Nine Elms

E521 between September 1929 and April 1931, when it received smoke deflectors. It now has a Maunsell superheater and lamp irons have been placed in the LSWR style sockets.

30521 by the Eastleigh coaling stage, probably in the late 1950s. The minimal cleaning of the tender seems to reveal the second BR emblem, applied in late 1957. The headcode is for all stations to Eastleigh loco. R.K. Blencowe Collection.

30522

Built Eastleigh 7/1924   Order No. T16-3   Works Serial Number 105
Built as ᴇ522, renumbered 522 4/1932, 30522 ?/1949

No SR Engine Record Card available

30/7/1924		New Locomotive ᴇ522, SOUTHERN olive green
2/11/25-27/11/25	B	Right driving bearing
16/6/26-6/7/26	C	Axleboxes and hornblocks
8/12/26-18/3/27	A	General repairs, dark green, boiler numbered 522, tender 803
10/7/28-2/8/28	C	Light repairs
8/2/29-11/4/29	A	General repairs, Boiler 504, KA chimney, Maunsell superheater
18/6/29-18/6/29	D	Weighing
2/7/29-2/7/29	D	Weighing
23/12/29-6/1/30	C	Framing flawed
20/10/30-26/11/30	A	General repair, Boiler 474, smoke deflectors
2/3/32-4/4/32	B	part repaint renumbered 522
17/5/33-24/6/33	(GW)	Boiler 744
12/10/33-28/10/33	(GW)	
20/8/34-25/8/34	(GW)	
9/5/35-14/6/35	(GW)	full repaint
14/4/36-27/5/36	(GW)	Maunsell boiler? part repaint
9/6/37-8/7/37	(GW)	part repaint
14/3/38-25/4/38	(GW)	Boiler 524 , full repaint, panelled cylinders
22/9/39-7/10/39	(GW)	touch up only
?-18/6/41		Boiler 515, unlined black, gilt lettering
5/1942-?	(RO)	
10/1942-?	(RO)	
4/1944-?	(RO)	
?-29/12/44		Boiler 522, sunshine lettering
5/1945-?	(RO)	
5/1946-?	(RO)	
?-26/4/47		Boiler 502
1/1949-?	(GW)	Snifting valves off, SOUTHERN 30522
9/1950-21/10/50	(GW)	
11/1950-11/11/50	(GW)	
?-21/10/50	(GW)	
11/1951-?	(GW)	
16/12/52-16/1/53	Gen	Maunsell boiler 830, lined black, first emblem
17/2/53-21/2/53	Return	
9/8/54-28/8/54	Gen	Maunsell boiler, repainted
17/4/57-11/5/57	H Int	
6/8/57-31/8/57	H Cas	
5/3/59-28/3/59	Gen	Maunsell boiler, repainted, second emblem (L)
30/12/60-7/1/61	L Cas	
9/1961		Withdrawn, mileage 1,093,943
4/11/61		Cut up at Eastleigh

Allocation

1/1925	Bournemouth
9/1925	Eastleigh
3/1944	Nine Elms
1/1945	Eastleigh
1/1951	Nine Elms
5/1959	Salisbury

E522 at Nine Elms on 26 March 1927. It is as built, with a stovepipe chimney, but now has a cabside numberplate. Livery is Maunsell dark green, applied at its first Class A repair a few weeks earlier. It later received a Maunsell superheater and King Arthur chimney, in 1929.

E522 near Weybridge on a Portsmouth-Waterloo train, consisting of two ex-LSWR 4-car lavatory sets and two loose vehicles, in the late 1920s. E522 now has lamp irons placed in its LSWR style sockets. H. Gordon Tidey.

30523

Built Eastleigh 9/1924   Order No. T16-4   Works Serial Number 106
Built as E523, renumbered 523 10/1931, 30523 6/1948

No SR Engine Record Card available

6/9/1924		New Locomotive E523, SOUTHERN olive green
1/5/25-9/5/25	D	Left driving axlebox
16/6/25-20/6/25	D	Left leading bearing
22/2/26-12/3/26	C	Light repairs
10/1/27-9/4/27	A	KA chimney, dark green, boiler numbered 523, tender 804
16/4/28-28/4/28	C	Right trailing bearing
3/10/28-19/10/28	D	Right driving bearing
29/5/29-19/7/29	A	General repair. Maunsell superheater, boiler 522
22/9/31-31/10/31	A	Boiler 501, smoke deflectors, loco renumbered 523
11/6/33-13/6/33	(GW)	
11/7/33-14/7/33	(GW)	
14/6/34-4/8/34	(GW)	Boiler 514, part repaint
22/9/36-20/10/36	(GW)	Boiler 476, tender not repainted
18/10/37-23/11/37	(GW)	
17/5/38-21/6/38	(GW)	Boiler 496
27/3/40-27/4/40	(GW)	Boiler 755, unlined dark green, Bulleid lettering
5/1940-?	(GW)	
?-10/2/43		Boiler 739, unlined black, sunshine lettering
?-21/4/45		Boiler 743
10/1946-?	(RO)	
8/1947-6/9/47	(RO)	
?-26/3/48	(GW)	
6/1948-19/6/48	(GW)	Snifting valves off, SOUTHERN 30523
6/1949-30/7/49	(GW)	Boiler 521, lined black unlettered
8/1949-27/8/49	(GW)	
?-6/5/51	(GW)	
12/1951-?	(GW)	
2/7/52-15/8/52	Gen	Boiler 478, repainted, first emblem
24/3/54-17/4/54	H Int	
9/9/55-16/9/55L	Cas	
5/3/56-7/4/56	Gen	Boiler 513, repainted
5/6/57-26/6/57	L Cas	At Nine Elms
7/9/57-21/9/57	L Cas	
7/1958-?	(GW)	
9/4/59-2/5//59	H Int	
12/1961	(DB)	Withdrawn, 1,063,049 miles
1/1962	(GW)	to works
3/2/62	(GW)	Cut up at Eastleigh

Allocation

1/1925	Bournemouth	9/1925 Eastleigh	3/1944 Nine Elms
1/1945	Eastleigh	1/1951 Nine Elms	5/1959 Salisbury

E523 at Eastleigh shed, between April 1927 and May 1929. It has received a King Arthur chimney, but still has an Eastleigh superheater. It is in Maunsell dark green livery and lamp irons have been placed in the LSWR sockets.

30523 approaching Vauxhall on the 9.54 Waterloo-Southampton Terminus on 4 July 1959. It had received its second application of lined black with the first emblem in 1956, which it will retain until withdrawal at the end of 1961. The train comprises one of the 1946-built Bulleid 3-car sets 981-984, formed of 63ft vehicles with outside doors to each compartment. A Maunsell SK and an LMS BG have been added fore and aft. Peter Groom.

30524

Built Eastleigh 9/1924   Order No. T16-5   Works Serial Number 107
Built as E524, renumbered 524 3/1932, 30524 2/1949

30/9/1924		New Locomotive E524, Maunsell superheater
2/3/25-4/3/25	D	Left driving bearing
23/3/25-28/3/25	D	Leading axlebox
30/12/25-16/1/26	B	Light repairs
25/10/26-16/11/26	C	Light repairs
23/12/26-22/1/27	(GW)	
23/11/27-10/3/28	A	KA chimney, dark green, boiler numbered 524, tender 805
27/8/28-3/9/28	D	Axleboxes
1/3/30-17/4/30	A	General repairs, Boiler 754, smoke deflectors, full repaint
25/2/32-23/3/32	B	Renumbered 524
5/10/32-12/11/32	A	Boiler 509, tender not repainted
9/1/33-19/1/33	(GW)	
7/6/34-14/7/34	(GW)	Boiler 501, part repaint
26/4/35-25/5/35	(GW)	Boiler 505
14/7/36-26/8/36	A	103,116, full repaint
7/9/37-14/9/37	C	41,291
15/11/38-14/12/38	A	74,759, boiler 509, dark green, Bulleid lettering
31/7/39-4/8/39	D	5,018
12/5/42-8/7/42	A	87,175, boiler 753, unlined black
2/9/43-3/11/43	B	38,629
13/3/45-1/4/45	C	75,695, repair at Bournemouth
1/5/45-25/5/45	C	76,755, mileage extended by 5,000
4/9/45-26/1/46	B	85,529
18/2/46-2/3/46	C	85,529, mileage extended by 20,000
19/6/46-29/6/46	C	96,634
16/1/47-15/2/47	A	114,580, boiler 745, copper stays fitted LNER method, test 2074
5/1/49-29/1/49	C	51.002, renumbered SOUTHERN 30524
23/11/49-2/12/49	L Cas	71,296
12/10/50-3/11/50	L Int	96,629, snifting valves removed
19/8/52-30/8/52	L Cas	155,349 BRITISH RAILWAYS (S) 30524 (G)
7/11/52-4/12/52	Gen	159,205, Maunsell boiler 451, lined black, first emblem
3/1953-?	(GW)	
14/6/54-26/6/54	L Cas	49,816
22/11/54-11/12/54	L Int	65,052
29/3/55-15/4/55	L Cas	74,423, at Nine Elms
22/5/56-16/7/56	Gen	105,124, Maunsell boiler 769, at Brighton Works
11/1957-23/11/57	(GW)	
28/7/58-23/8/58	L Int	58,824
25/2/1961		Withdrawn, mileage 1,071,335
1/7/61		Cut up at Eastleigh

Allocation
1/1925	Bournemouth
9/1925	Eastleigh
10/1940	Feltham
6/1942	Bournemouth
1/1945	Eastleigh
1/1951	Nine Elms
5/1959	Salisbury

E524 on an up train at Southampton West on 14 June 1930, two months after it had received smoke deflectors, with the smokebox side lamp irons moved up. It had carried a King Arthur chimney since 1928. R.K. Blencowe Collection.

30524 approaching Surbiton on a train for Basingstoke or Southampton Terminus during the 1950s. It had received a Maunsell boiler and lined black livery with the first emblem in late 1952. The train, which clearly carries a set number, consists of a strange mixture of vehicles, led by an ex-LSWR corridor brake third, with a single newer corridor vehicle amongst an assortment of LSWR non-corridors, with an ex-SE&CR vehicle in third position. In the background, a London Transport RT bus follows the London United tram route to Tolworth. R.K. Blencowe Collection.

The first H15 in its final state; 30486 at Eastleigh on a stopping train to Bournemouth via Sway in the late 1950s. In June 1957 30486 became the only parallel boilered Urie H15 to carry the second BR emblem, facing forward on both sides, although taper boilered rebuild 30491 also did. It has continuous cabside lining.

S15 The Record

496 at Strawberry Hill, as built in May 1921. It is in the LSWR dark holly green goods livery, with black edging and fine light green lining, which frequently does not show up in photographs. Although carrying the lowest number in a continuous series of twenty, 496 was the last to be built. South Western Circle, D.L. Bradley Collection.

30496 at Clapham Junction, not long after May 1959, when it had its last General Repair and received a Maunsell boiler and the second BR emblem, facing left on both sides. It is coupled to BR Mark 1 carriage, which is still in crimson and cream. Most were green by 1960. RK Blencowe collection, P Winding.

30496

Built Eastleigh 5/1921   Order No. E16-5   Works Serial Number 78
New as 496, renumbered ᴇ496 5/1924, 496 2/1933, 30496 11/1948

27/5/1921		New Locomotive, LSWR goods green
11/10/22-21/10/22		Right trailing journal scored
3/3/24-10/5/24A		General repairs, SOUTHERN lined black, renumbered ᴇ496
29/7/25-1/8/25D		Left driving bearing
9/5/27-19/9/27A		Maunsell superheater, repaint, boiler numbered 496, tender 3200
19/2/29-19/2/29	D	Weighing
22/5/30-16/7/30	A	General repair, Boiler 743, smoke deflectors, dark green
17/1/33-18/2/33	(GW)	Boiler 754, full repaint, loco renumbered 496
16/3/35-16/3/35	(GW)	
28/6/35-20/7/35	A	80,145, Boiler 986, part repaint
23/4/37-14/6/36	B	Repair at Feltham
25/5/38-29/6/38	A	94,523, boiler 501, full repaint, cylinders panelled
10/6/40-9/7/40	B	66,026, part repaint, mileage increased by 10,000
20/6/41-30/7/41	A	92,672, Maunsell boiler 775
30/10/42-2/1/43	B	20,000, Boiler 500, U1 chimney, unlined black
14/9/44-24/10/44	C	70,013, Feltham
30/10/45-22/12/45	A	97,418, Boiler 504
6/6/47-26/7/47B		40,377, new cylinders
15/10/48-13/11/48	A	67,901, Boiler 986, snift valves off, BRITISH RAILWAYS 30496 (G)
4/10/50-20/10/50	H Cas	60,896, Maunsell boiler 771, Test 2081, regulator valves fitted
8/8/51-16/8/51NC		84,089
11/9/52-4/10/52	Gen	116,258, Boiler 521, first emblem
5/11/54-20/11/54	Gen	66,257, boiler 503
10/1955-15/10/55	(GW)	
28/5/56-7/7/56	L Cas	45,229
7/1958-?	(GW)	
10/1958-25/10/58	(GW)	
25/1/57-9/2/57	H Int	61,809
21/4/59-9/5/59	Gen	117,691, Maunsell boiler 783, repainted, second emblem (L)
4/8/61-16/9/61	H Int	72,263, AWS fitted
6/3/63-13/3/63	L Cas	113,146
22/6/63		Withdrawn, Mileage 1,277,029
24/8/63		Cut up at Eastleigh

Allocation
1921	Salisbury
1922	Exmouth Junction
1928	Feltham
11/1941	Southall (GWR)
2/1942	Exeter (GWR)
7/1943	Feltham
4/1948	Nine Elms
12/1949	Feltham

30496 at Eastleigh, 26 August 1956. It has smoke deflector plates, a chimney of the type introduced on the U1 class 2-6-0s and a Maunsell smokebox door. R.K. Blencowe Collection.

30496 at Brighton shed on 11 September 1960. It does not yet have AWS gear, although the Schools 4-4-0 on the left has. The LSWR S15s were, strictly, out of gauge for ex-LB&SCR lines but the extra half inch of platform width was unlikely to cause any trouble and height was no problem on the LB&SCR. It had probably reached Brighton along the coast from Fratton. Peter Groom.

30497

Built Eastleigh 2/1920   Order No. S15-1   Works Serial Number 59
Built as 497, renumbered ᴇ497 9/1924, 497 8/1932, 30497 11/1948

28/2/20		New Locomotive, LSWR goods green
20/12/20-25/12/20		Left driving box
26/10/21-21/10/21		Vacuum ejector and cylinder examination
17/10/22-28/10/22		Heated boxes
7/7/24-13/9/24	A	General repairs, SOUTHERN lined black, ᴇ497
19/8/26-18/12/26	A	General repairs, boiler numbered 497, tender 3201
3/1/28-15/2/28	B	Tubeplate flawed, new Maunsell boiler 931
10/9/29-2/11/29	A	General repairs, smoke deflectors, full repaint, dark green
4/7/32-11/8/32	A	Maunsell boiler 801, renumbered 497
23/9/33-4/10/33	(GW)	
27/4/35-29/5/35	(GW)	Urie boiler 753, part repaint
6/9/35-17/9/35		11,115, repair at Feltham
17/4/36-6/5/36	C	31,795, not repainted
31/8/36-8/9/36	D	40,770, buffer beam repainted
30/11/37-5/1/38	A	80,509, boiler 736, full repaint, cylinders panelled
9/4/38-27/4/38	C	5,098, buffer beam repaired
23/3/39-26/4/39	B	31,520, boiler 475, touch up only
5/10/39-25/10/39	C	39,729, touch up only
19/12/40-5/2/41	A	82,737, boiler 478, unlined dark green, Bulleid lettering
1/1943	(DB)	Int Repair at Swindon Works, not shown on Southern ERC
12/6/43-1/9/43	B	41,065, boiler 514, unlined black
31/5/45-11/6/45	C	99,244, at Feltham
19/9/45-27/10/45	A	106,731, U1 chimney
22/5/47-14/6/47	B	48,115, new RH cylinder
10/2.48-7/3/48	D	57,753, at Eastleigh shed
22/10/48-20/11/48	A	71,877, boiler 513, snift valves off, BRITISH RAILWAYS 30497 (G)
17/12/48-24/12/48	D	
7/5/51-8/6/51	Gen	75,245, boiler 515, first emblem
15/5/53-11/6/53	Gen	60,820, boiler 477, repainted
27/9/55-22/10/55	H Int	not repainted
17/6/57-6/7/57	Gen	118,460, Maunsell boiler 792, second emblem (F)
23/9/59-10/10/59	L Int	62,020, not repainted
3/8/61-2/9/61	Gen	Maunsell boiler 1056, AWS fitted
7/7/1963		Withdrawn, Mileage 1,241,163
7/3/64		Sold, cut up by George Cohen, Kettering

Allocation
1921	Feltham
1928	Feltham
11/1941	Old Oak Common (GWR)
1/1943	Tyseley (GWR)
5/1943	Feltham
4/1948	Nine Elms
12/1949	Feltham

497, the first S15 to be built (in February 1920) at Feltham in the 1920s. It is now at least three years old, as Feltham shed did not open until 1923. The only alteration since it was built is the inward curve of the steam pipe to the injector, alongside the firebox. This looks as though it has been done properly, by a coppersmith. Accidental damage would have added kinks and flattened bits, but no others like this are known. South Western Circle D.L. Bradley Collection.

30497 at Feltham on 21 July 1963. It had emerged from its last General Repair, in 1961, with a Maunsell boiler and BR AWS. No 6F power classification is visible but it does have a yellow triangle below the cabside number, indicating that it is fitted with BR water treatment equipment. Despite the massive load of coal in the tender, it had been withdrawn from service two weeks earlier. Stephen Gradidge.

30498

Built Eastleigh 4/1920   Order No. S15-2   Works Serial Number 60
Built as 498, renumbered ᴇ498 9/1924, 498 8/1932, 30498 2/1950

3/4/20		New Locomotive, LSWR goods green
4/8/21-13/8/21		Left trailing box
26/1/22-4/2/22		Right leading bearing melted out
3/6/24-17/9/24	A	General repairs, SOUTHERN lined black, ᴇ498
8/6/26-4/9/26	A	Heavy repairs, boiler numbered 498, tender 3202
14/11/27-31/1/28	B	Boiler 986 (Urie)
14/2/28-21/3/28	D	Right cylinder and piston
7/9/28-29/9/28	D	Left leading bearing
14/1/30-22/2/30	A	Maunsell superheater, smoke deflectors, repainted dark green
15/7/32-26/8/32	A	Boiler 497, loco renumbered 498
5/3/35-6/4/35	(GW)	Partial repaint
19/7/37-20/8/37	A	87,754, boiler 755, partial repaint
2/3/40-3/4/40	A	94,673, boiler 512, U1 chimney, unlined dark green, Bulleid lettering
26/5/43-30/6/43	A	71,475, boiler 740, unlined black
16/9/44-28/10/44	B	41,603, new RH cylinder
20/5/46-12/7/46	B	93,353, mileage extended by 5,000
22/7/47-23/8/47	A	123,164, boiler 497, snifting valves off
11/9/47-18/9/47	D	
17/1/50-17/2/50	A	74,599, boiler 753, first emblem, 30498
28/5/51-5/6/51	NC	37,116, hot box
27/12/51-5/1/52	L Cas	53,583
29/7/52-23/8/52	Gen	68,502, Maunsell boiler 782
13/9/54-9/10/54	H Int	66,166, 5200 gallon tender 783 ex 30488
11/1954-21/11/54	(GW)	
2/11/56-24/11/56	Gen	126,427, Maunsell boiler 787, repainted
14/11/58-29/11/58	H Int	58,847
30/5/61-30/6/61	Gen	108,481, Maunsell boiler 829, AWS fitted, second emblem (L)
22/6/63		Withdrawn, Mileage 1,191,462
24/8/63		Cut up at Eastleigh

Allocation
1921	Nine Elms
1940	Feltham
11/1941	Old Oak Common (GWR)
2/1942	Exeter (GWR)
5/1943	Feltham
4/1948	Nine Elms
12/1949	Feltham

498, new at Nine Elms in its LSWR goods green livery. It is just possible to pick out the light green line on the front curve of the platform valance.

30498 at Feltham on 2 September 1962. It had received a Maunsell boiler in 1952 and the 5,200 gallon tender from 30488 in October 1954. A General Repair in June 1961 has brought a third Maunsell boiler and a repaint with the second BR emblem, facing left on both sides. It was also fitted with AWS, clearly visible from this side. The painter has managed to get the water treatment triangle somewhat offset. Peter Groom.

30499

**Built Eastleigh 5/1920   Order No. S15-3   Works Serial Number 61
Renumbered ᴇ499 1/1925, 499 1/1934, 30499 1/1949**

1/5/20		New Locomotive, LSWR goods green
26/10/22-11/11/22		Left trailing bearing
28/11/22-2/12/22		Left leading bearing
27/8/23-1/9/23		Right trailing bearing
30/9/24-24/1/25	A	General repairs, SOUTHERN dark green ᴇ499
30/6/25-15/7/25	D	Axleboxes
3/1/28-1/6/28	A	General repairs, boiler numbered 499, tender 3203
25/9/28-10/10/28	D	Right trailing bearing
23/4/31-6/6/31	A	Boiler 476, Maunsell superheater, smoke deflectors, dark green
5/12/33-24/1/34	(GW)	Partial repaint, renumbered 499
12/8/36-12/9/36	A	89,762, boiler 739, complete repaint
3/11/38-30/11/38	A	83,171, boiler 507, complete repaint
24/6/41-6/8/41	A	82,209, Maunsell boiler 785, U1 chimney, unlined black, gilt lettering
10/4/43-21/7/43	B	29,484, Maunsell boiler 782
20/12/45-23/3/46	A	103,083, Boiler 750, unlined black, sunshine lettering
4/12/48-8/1/49	A	74,921, Maunsell boiler 839, snifting valves off, 30499 unlettered
24/1/49-29/1/49	D	Weighing only
29/3/51-2/5/51	Gen	66,133, boiler 509, first emblem
18/8/53-12/9/53	Gen	68,244, boiler 500, repainted
29/9/55-22/10/55	H Int	63,001
13/11/57-30/11/57	Gen	125,139,Maunsell boiler 1057, second emblem (F)
14/8/59-29/8/59	L Int	47,940, not repainted
5/1/61-4/2/61	Gen	Boiler 755, second emblem (L)
4/1961-6/5/61	(GW)	
18/6/62-23/6/62	NC	AWS fitted, not repainted
3/12/62-13/12/62	L Cas	not repainted,
20/12/63-20/12/63		4000 gallon 6-wheel tender 882 ex 30835 at Feltham
1/1964		Withdrawn, Mileage 1,241,024
6/1964		Sold to Woodham Bros, Barry
1980		Sold to Urie S15 Preservation Group
11/1983		Moved to Mid Hants Railway

Allocation
1921	Nine Elms
1940	Feltham
11/1941	Old Oak Common (GWR)
3/1943	Feltham

499 at Nine Elms when new in LSWR goods green, with its green lining invisible. The cylindrical feed water heat exchanger can be seen between the tender bogies.

30499 coaling at Eastleigh; the period is between November 1957, when Maunsell boiler 1057 was fitted, and January 1961, when it took a Urie example. Boiler 1057 was built with multiple washout plugs but is clearly one of those which reverted later to two plugs each side. The tender carries the second BR emblem, facing forward on both sides. N. Hamshere.

30500

Built Eastleigh 5/1920   Order No. S15-4   Works Serial Number 62
Built as 500, renumbered E500 10/1924, 500 3/1933, 30500 10/1948

22/5/20		New Locomotive, LSWR goods green
23/8/21-27/8/21		Boxes
5/4/23-21/4/23		Right leading box hot
30/4/23-5/5/23		Right trailing bearing
18/12/23-12/1/24	B	Defective superheater tube
30/7/24-11/10/24	A	General repairs, SOUTHERN lined black, E500
9/2/25-28/3/25	C	Tubeplate cracked
6/10/27-7/1/28	A	General repairs, boiler 1000 (Urie), tender numbered 3204
16/1/28-17/1/28	D	Driving axlebox
9/8/28-28/8/28	D	Right leading wheel shifted
30/8/29-30/8/29	D	Weighing
27/8/30-11/10/30	A	Maunsell superheater, smoke deflectors, dark green
9/5/32-10/5/32	(GW)	
17/2/33-31/3/33	(GW)	Boiler 743, loco renumbered 500
2/8/34-21/9/34	(GW)	Boiler 509
22/1/35-14/2/35	(GW)	tender damaged
16/8/35-16/8/35	D	
8/10/35-26/10/35	C	75,068
19/3/36-25/4/36	A	90,693, complete repaint
24/8/36-31/8/36	D	11,745
2/6/37-1/7/37	C	33,730
4/10/38-26/10/38	A	72,898, boiler 499
5/11/40-18/12/40	A	67,148, boiler 474, U1 Chimney, unlined light green, Bulleid lettering
13/2/43-10/3/43	A	79,162, boiler 754, unlined black
26/6/46-27/7/46	A	100,450, boiler 513
3/9/48-2/10/48	B	49,932, boiler 751, snifting valves off, SOUTHERN 30500
11/10/48-16/10/48	D	49,932
7/9/50-6/10/50	Gen	105,371, Maunsell boiler 779, first emblem
1/1/53-24/1/53	Gen	69,355, Maunsell boiler 801,
11/1/55-29/1/55	H Int	59,366
19/12/56-18/1/57	Gen	115,560, Maunsell boiler 1047, repainted
3/7/58-2/8/58	H Cas	43,161, not repainted
12/5/59-13/6/59	Gen	58,290, Maunsell boiler 785, second emblem (L)
3/1960-14/5/60	(GW)	Driving axle removed
5/1960-11/6/60	(GW)	
11/8/61-2/9/61	L Int	56,882, AWS fitted, not repainted
5/12/62-21/12/62	L Cas	86,184
3/1963-6/4/63	(GW)	
6/7/1963		Withdrawn, Mileage 1,280,116
19/10/63		Cut up at Eastleigh

Allocation
1921 Nine Elms
1922 Strawberry Hill
1923 Feltham

500 in the mid-1930s. In 1930, it got smoke deflectors, a Maunsell superheater and green livery; it lost the E prefix in 1933. It retains its Urie smokebox door, with a separate handrail on the smokebox front. The stovepipe chimney has lost its capuchon. R.K. Blencowe Collection.

30500 at Eastleigh on 29 October 1949. It became 30500, with SOUTHERN on the tender, in October 1948 but the faded remains of its Southern number are still visible on the buffer beam. The lamp iron above the coupling is still an LSWR socket, with an inserted lamp iron; the near frontal viewpoint shows the handrail stanchions on the side of the smokebox. A.E. West, courtesy M.S. King.

30501

Built Eastleigh 6/1920   Order No. S15-5   Works Serial Number 63
Built as 501, renumbered E501 2/1925, 501 8/1931, 30501 12/1948

22/5/20		New Locomotive, LSWR goods green
19/8/20-28/8/20		Driving bearings
2/9/20-11/9/20		Right trailing bearing
6/4/22-15/4/22		Left leading bearing hot
29/7/24-1/8/24	D	Axleboxes & coupling rods
8/11/24-14/2/25	A	General repairs, SOUTHERN lined black, E501
9/8/27-3/9/27	C	Right trailing bearing, boiler numbered 501, tender 3205
20/7/28-1/12/28	A	General repairs, boiler 514, repainted dark green
4/11/29-14/11/29	D	Right leading bearing, smoke deflectors
21/7/31-29/8/31	A	Boiler 498, Maunsell superheater, part repaint, loco numbered 501
8/3/34-14/4/34	(GW)	partial repaint
15/5/34-18/5/34	(GW)	
28/9/36-24/10/36	A	90,440, boiler 514, partial repaint
17/6/38-27/7/38	B	60,877, partial repaint, mileage extended by 5,000
28/8/39-20/9/39	A	97,995, boiler 500, unlined dark green, Maunsell lettering
15/12/39-20/12/39	C	1,147, collision damage
17/3/41-3/5/41	C	37,039, repair at Nine Elms
28/4/42-3/6/42	D	Repair at Salisbury
30/10/42-25/11/42	A	83,206, boiler 503, unlined black
23/4/43-26/5/43	C	10,163
6/7/45-1/9/45	A	75,478, boiler 511, U1 chimney
5/1/48-24/1/48	B	71,250, Maunsell boiler 839, not repainted
27/10/48-27/11/48	A	91,638, boiler 741, snift valves off, BRITISH RAILWAYS 30501 (G)
20/3/51-27/4/51	Gen	64,434, boiler 524, first emblem
9/1952-?	(GW)	
25/2/53-21/3/53	Gen	56,084, boiler 523
24/3/55-16/4/55	Gen	66,568, boiler 746, repainted
10/1/57-2/2/57	H Int	54,313
10/1957-6/10/57	(GW)	
14/4/59-9/5/59	Gen	115,349, Maunsell boiler 450, repainted second emblem (L)
1/3/61-25/3/61	H Int	57,389
21/4/61-24/4/61	NC	58,053
?-11/11/61	(GW)	
22/6/63		Withdrawn, Mileage 1,288,684
31/8/63		Cut up at Eastleigh

Allocation
1921	Nine Elms
11/1941	Feltham

148

E501 at Nine Elms; this is after February 1925, when it acquired the Southern lined black livery. It is otherwise as built and still has LSWR lamp sockets.

30501 at Eastleigh on 25 March 1950. At a Class A repair in late 1948, it lost its snifting valves and got its BR number and BRITISH RAILWAYS tender lettering in Gill sans characters, with the A power classification below the cabside number. W. Gilburt.

30502

Built Eastleigh 7/1920   Order No. A16-1 Works Serial Number 64
Built as 502, renumbered ᴇ502 6/1925, 502 7/1932, 30502 7/1950

17/7/20		New Locomotive, LSWR goods green
5/8/20-7/8/20		Right driving bearing heated
22/7/21-30/7/21		Heated bearing
22/12/21-7/1/22		Left leading bearing heated
9/3/25-13/6/25	A	General repairs, SOUTHERN lined black, ᴇ502
18/8/26-19/8/26	D	Light repairs
14/9/26-22/1/27	A	General repairs, full repaint, boiler numbered 502, tender 3206
2/12/29-18/1/30	A	Boiler 497, Maunsell superheater, smoke deflectors, dark green
8/6/32-16/7/32	A	Boiler 512, partial repaint, loco renumbered 502
23/7/34-6/9/34	(GW)	Boiler 747, part repaint
17/11/36-18/12/36	A	78,643, boiler 475, full repaint
3/3/37-20/3/37	C	3,022
26/7/38-31/8/38	B	59,055, boiler 986, cylinders panelled, mileage extended by 5,000
29/4/40-29/5/40	A	117,358, boiler 496, unlined dark green, Bulleid lettering
10/11/42-19/12/42	B	70,455, mileage extended by 10,000
28/10/43-1/12/43	A	98,446, boiler 1000 (Urie), unlined black
9/1/47-1/2/47	A	99,521, boiler 505, U1 chimney
23/5/50-5/7/50	A	99,433, Maunsell boiler 803, snifting v off, first emblem 30502
12/11/52-6/12/52	Gen	72,429, Maunsell boiler 1401, repainted
21/12/54-8/1/55	H Int	66,563, tender 3207 ex 30503
27/11/56-29/12/56	Gen	116,179, boiler 476, repainted
18/12/58-10/1/59	L Int	60,050
23/2/60-19/3/60	Gen	88,838, Maunsell boiler 828, second emblem (L)
15/12/1962		Withdrawn, Mileage 1,276,916
23/3/63		Cut up at Eastleigh

Allocation
1921	Nine Elms
1922	Strawberry Hill
1928	Nine Elms
11/1941	Feltham

502 at Nine Elms in 1932; Maunsell superheater and smokebox door, no capuchon. It has been renumbered 502, without the E prefix, but has not been fully repainted. South Western Circle John Eyers Collection.

502, still with Urie stovepipe chimney and snifting valves, has overrun the end of Waller's Ash up loop and gone to earth opposite Weston signalbox during 1946. Although three miles south of Micheldever station, it is within a mile of Micheldever village, to the east. The chimney will be replaced in early 1947 but the snifting valves and Bulleid 'sunshine' lettering will be there until 1950. R.K. Blencowe Collection.

30502 at Christchurch on a train from Southampton Terminus to Bournemouth West on 12th May 1961. R.K.Blencowe collection.

30503

Built Eastleigh 8/1920   Order No. A16-2   Works Serial Number 65
Built as 503, renumbered ɛ503 11/1924, 503 3/1934, 30503 1/1950

21/8/20		New Locomotive, LSWR goods green
10/4/23-5/5/23		Right leading bearing and wheels
13/8/24-21/8/24	D	Hot trailing axlebox
23/9/24-29/11/24	A	General repairs, SOUTHERN lined black, ɛ503
30/8/26-9/10/26	D	Light repairs, boiler numbered 503, tender 3207
1/2/28-22/6/28	A	General repairs, boiler 498
20/3/31-2/5/31	A	Boiler 741, Maunsell superheater, smoke deflectors, dark green
18/1/32-26/1/32	(GW)	
4/1/33-6/1/33	(GW)	
30/1/34-9/3/34	(GW)	partial repaint, renumbered 503
29/7/36-12/9/36	A	86,972, Maunsell boiler 783, full repaint
9/8/38-14/9/38	B	71,942, mileage extended by 10,000
7/11/38-10/11/38	D	71,957
15/5/39-7/6/39	A	89,867, boiler 477, part repaint, green smoke deflectors
31/8/39-31/8/39	D	
1/4/42-27/5/42	A	88,664, boiler 738, U1 chimney, unlined black
5/2/45-17/3/45	A	114,209, boiler 509, King Arthur chimney
21/11/47-29/11/47	D	70,874
10/1/48-21/2/48	B	71,919, Maunsell boiler 451, snifting valves off, not repainted
12/12/49-20/1/50	A	119,230, Maunsell boiler 799, 30503, first emblem
10/1/52-19/1/52	H Cas	61,948, boiler 744, not repainted
12/9/52-4/10/52	L Int	76,867
6/12/54-8/1/55	H Int	141,750, U1 chimney returned, 5200 gall tender 780 ex 30482
13/5/55-14/5/55	L Cas	150,721
9/1955-8/10/55	(GW)	
4/2/57-9/3/57	Gen	186,111, Maunsell boiler 797, repainted
18/6/5-11/7/59	H Int	63,774
5/4/61-29/4/61	Gen	106,785, Maunsell boiler 1406, AWS, second emblem (L)
6/1962-7/7/62	(GW)	
24/9/62-29/9/62	L Cas	40,874
29/6/63		Withdrawn, Mileage 1,287,774
5/10/63		Cut up at Eastleigh

Allocation
1921	Nine Elms
1922	Strawberry Hill
1923	Feltham
1928	Nine Elms
1940	Feltham

503, in work stained LSWR goods green, standing beside the nearly new lifting shop at Feltham, 1 March 1924. H.C. Casserley, courtesy R.M. Casserley.

30503 at Boscombe on an up stopping train. It was fitted with a short King Arthur chimney in 1945; Maunsell boiler and BR number with the large first emblem came in January 1950. 30503 ran with five different Maunsell boilers after 1936, but got a Urie boiler in January 1952, dating the photograph to 1950-51. The triangular additional balance weight on the leading coupled wheel shows that the form of these weights varied from one locomotive to another. R.K. Blencowe Collection.

30504

Built Eastleigh 9/1920   Order No. A16-3   Works Serial Number 66
Built as 504, renumbered E504 11/1925, 504 3/1932, 30504 10/1948

11/9/20		New Locomotive, LSWR goods green
13/12/20-18/12/20		Right leading bearing heated
29/11/21-3/12/21		Right driving bearing melted
24/3/22-25/3/22		In collision, buffer beam bent
12/1/23-20/1/23		Left leading bearing heated
3/5/23-12/5/23		Leading bearings
15/9/24-24/9/24	C	Trailing axleboxes
19/8/25-26/11/25	A	General repairs, SOUTHERN lined black, E504
4/8/27-17/8/27	C	Axleboxes, boiler numbered 504, tender 3208
12/10/28-2/2/29	A	Boiler 515, Maunsell superheater, dark green
26/9/29-2/11/29	B	Boiler 507
28/2/30-17/4/30	B	Smoke deflectors, repainted
4/2/32-5/3/32	A	Boiler 477, repainted, loco renumbered 504
14/3/34-2/5/34	(GW)	Boiler 510, part repaint
21/2/36-14/3/36	C	Repair at Feltham, mileage extended by 5,000
17/3/36-24/3/36	D	68,087, Drummond tender 222 ex 292.
12/11/36-12/12/36	A	92,068, boiler 751, repainted (not tender)
22/10/37-22/10/37	D	
31/8/39-27/9/39	A	86,818, boiler 752, unlined dark green, Maunsell lettering
12/8/42-30/9/42	A	90,546, boiler 498
17/8/45-26/10/45	A	92,054, boiler 503, unlined black
54//46-18/4/46	C	16,116
9/2/48-28/2/48	B	52,491, Maunsell boiler 767, snifting valves off, U1 chimney
4/10/48-23/10/48	B	67,974, SOUTHERN 30504, mileage extended by 15,000
10/1/50-28/2/50	L Cas	104,010, at Basingstoke
21/6/51-13/7/51	Gen	141,114, boiler 503, first emblem
4/9/51-13/9/51	N/C	3,383
13/10/52-31/10/52	L Cas	36,354, at Guildford
18/12/52-24/12/52	L Cas	38,955
25/1/54-20/2/54	Gen	72,134, boiler 740, repainted
6/2/56-25/2/56	H Int	59,616
11/4/58-3/5/58	Gen	116,883, boiler 521, 5200 gallon tender 787 ex 30487, second emblem (F)
30/7/58-2/8/58	N/C	3,392
19/8/59-28/8/59	L Cas	37,291
12/8/60-27/8/60	H Int	62,387
30/4/62-8/5/62 N/C		110,904, AWS fitted
17/11/62		Withdrawn, Mileage 1,218,025
12/1962	(GW)	To Eastleigh Works
2/2/63		Cut up at Eastleigh

Allocation

1921	Nine Elms	8/1930	Nine Elms
5/1930	Salisbury	10/1930	Feltham

504 backing out of Southampton Docks, opposite the Terminus station, in the late 1930s. In 1936 it had lost its Urie tender to ex-LB&SCR 4-6-4T 2331, when this was rebuilt as a 4-6-0, following electrification of the Brighton line, and had received the Drummond bogie tender from withdrawn C8 class 4-4-0 No.292. It has a Maunsell smokebox door, but retained its stovepipe chimney until early 1948. R.K. Blencowe Collection.

30504 at Southampton Central on 20 April 1957. It is in the down bay, with the headcode for a light engine from Eastleigh shed to Southampton, which does not give any indication of where it will be going next with that ex-LSWR carriage, rebuilt on an SR underframe. Although it is over three years since its last General Repair, 30504 looks smart enough. R.K. Blencowe Collection.

30505

Built Eastleigh 10/1920   Order No. A16-4   Works Serial Number 67
Built as 505, renumbered E505 5/1926, 505 12/1931, 30505 8/1948

1/10/20		New Locomotive, LSWR goods green
17/10/21-22/10/21		Right driving bearing hot
29/6/23-7/7/23		Left leading bearing
28/7/24-1/8/24	D	Trailing bearing,
20/10/24		Cabside numberplate, tender lettered LSWR 505
14/12/25-22/5/26	A	SOUTHERN lined black, E505, boiler numbered 505, tender 3209
18/8/28-4/1/29	A	General repairs, boiler 512, repainted dark green
3/9/29-3/9/29	D	Weighing (may have been in store Jan – Sept 1929)
10/3/31-10/3/31	D	Weighing
31/10/31-11/12/31	A	Boiler 755, Maunsell superheater, smoke deflectors, loco renumbered 505
15/8/33-5/9/33	(GW)	
3/5/34-14/6/34	(GW)	partial repaint
23/12/35-30/12/35	C	50,912 Drummond tender 226 ex 296, tender repainted
8/10/36-7/11/36	A	72,673, boiler 522, repainted (not tender)
21/2/39-22/3/39	C	73,403, mileage extended by 10,000
20/12/39-24/1/40	A	96,672, boiler 502, unlined dark green, Bulleid lettering
3/5/40-15/5/40	D	6,161
16/9/42-17/10/42	A	85,795, Maunsell boiler 790, U1 chimney, unlined black
12/3/46-6/4/46	A	94,818, boiler 500
20/1/48-25/5/48		53,957 repair at Feltham
5/8/48-28/8/48	C	57,005, BRITISH RAILWAYS (G) 30505 (S)
7/12/49-27/1/50	A	96,482, Maunsell boiler 789, snifting v off, first emblem
26/6/51-1/7/51	N/C	45,341
8/4/52 – 9/5/52	Gen	66,113, boiler 474
8/12/53-16/12/53	N/C	49,075
1/9/54-25/9/54	H Int	66,415
25/9/56-20/10/56	Gen	115,218, Maunsell boiler 837, 5000 gallon tender 855 ex 30741
12/6/58-21/6/58	N/C	44,337
11/12/58-17/1/59	L Int	60,952
26/10/59-7/11/59	H Cas	76,954, Maunsell boiler 1052
22/6/61-29/7/61	H Int	114,551, AWS fitted
3/1962-7/4/62	(GW)	
19/9/62-6/10/62	N/C	139,125
17/11/62		Withdrawn, Mileage 1,177,241
12/1962	(GW)	To works
8/12/62		Cut up at Eastleigh

Allocation
1921	Nine Elms
1928	Feltham

E505 arriving at Feltham yard on a freight in the 1920s. Under the dirt, the tender appears to be in normal SOUTHERN livery, either black, or green from 1929. It received a Maunsell superheater and smoke deflectors in 1931.

30505 at Eastleigh on 18 June 1949. A Drummond tender had appeared at the end of 1935 and a U1 chimney in 1942. In August 1948 came BR number and BRITISH RAILWAYS tender lettering, in Gill sans lettering but with Southern style numerals. It now has a smokebox numberplate. D.L. Bradley.

30506

Built Eastleigh 10/1920   Order No. A16-5   Works Serial Number 68
Built as 506, renumbered ᴇ506 12/1924, 506 7/1932, 30506 8/1949

23/10/20		New Locomotive, LSWR goods green
5/10/22-28/10/22		General repairs
1/5/23-5/5/23		Left trailing bearing
25/9/24-13/12/24	A	General repairs, SOUTHERN lined black, ᴇ506
31/3/27-13/7/27	A	General repairs, full repaint, boiler numbered 506, tender 3210
13/3/29-13/3/29	D	Weighing
11/12/29-1/2/30	A	Boiler 753, Maunsell superheater, repainted dark green
3/6/32-9/7/32 A		Boiler 746, smoke deflectors, loco renumbered 506
19/6/34-29/8/34	(GW)	Boiler 511, part repaint
13/4/35-18/4/35	(GW)	Drummond tender 221 ex 291, tender repainted
4/10/35-4/10/35	D	
27/1/37-27/2/37	A	90,397, boiler 1000 (Urie), repainted (not tender)
29/8/39-27/9/39	A	81,455, boiler 747, unlined dark green, Bulleid lettering
12/1/40-17/1/40	D	5,634
25/3/42-20/5/42	A	79,058, boiler 523, unlined black
19/6/45-3/8/45	A	76,184, boiler 524, U1 chimney
10/1/46-25/1/46	C	12,152
2/3/1948-30/3/48	C	65,282
7/7/49-19/8/49	A	93,464, boiler 754, snifting valves off, renumbered 30506, unlettered
16/1/50-27/1/50	L Cas	11,997
10/2/50-24/2/50	D	11,997
24/3/52-19/4/52	Gen	71,092, boiler 752, first emblem
19/6/53-27/6/53	H Cas	33,769
29/7/54-14/8/54	L Int	61,757
4/9/56-22/9/56	Gen	115,265, boiler 745, 5000 gallon tender 859 ex 30745
18/11/58-29/11/58	L Int	62,290
9/2/61-25/3/61	Gen	115,350, Maunsell boiler 451, second emblem (L)
13/11/62-24/11/62	L Cas	41,125, AWS fitted
1/1964		Withdrawn, Mileage 1,227,897
6/1964		Sold to Woodham Bros, Barry
10/1964		Arrived at Barry scrapyard
4/1976		To Urie Locomotive Society, Mid Hants Railway
7/1987		To service, Maunsell boiler 799 SOUTHERN 506, dark green

Allocation
1921	Nine Elms
7/1927	Exmouth Junction
1928	Feltham

E506 at Feltham during the 1920s, in Southern lined black with cabside numberplate and with lamp irons placed in its LSWR sockets. In early 1930 it was fitted with a Maunsell superheater and took green livery.

30506 at Eastleigh between 1952 and 1956. It had received a Drummond tender in 1935, a U1 chimney in 1945 and lost its snifting valves in August 1949, when it was renumbered. It received the first emblem on its tender during a General Repair in April 1952; in September 1956 it went into works for another General Repair at which it received the Urie tender from 30745. D.L. Bradley.

30507

Built Eastleigh 11/1920   Order No. C16-1   Works Serial Number 69
Built as 507, renumbered E507 3/1925, 507 1/1932, 30507 3/1950

13/11/20		New Locomotive, LSWR goods green
31/5/21-11/6/21		Left leading driving bearing
2/7/21-9/7/21		Left driving bearing heated
24/7/22-5/8/22		Right leading bearing hot
1/5/23-5/5/23		Left trailing bearing
19/3/24-26/3/24	B	Left leading bearing
5/11/24-10/3/25	A	General repairs, SOUTHERN lined black, E507
14/8/25-22/8/25	D	Left driving bearing
27/7/26-30/10/26	A	General repairs, boiler numbered 507, tender 3211
9/8/28-1/9/28	D	Right driving bearing
?-8/12/28	(GW)	
8/6/29-25/7/29	A	General repairs, Maunsell boiler 742 and superheater
31/12/31-30/1/32	A	Boiler 522, smoke deflectors, dark green, renumbered 507
22/6/34-22/6/34	(GW)	Derailment damage
3/8/34-3/8/34	(GW)	
2/11/34-3/12/34	(GW)	Boiler 524, tender not repainted
16/8/35-21/8/35	D	18,445, Drummond tender 223 ex 293, tender repainted
28/9/36-7/10/36	D	60,261, tender damaged
12/8/37-11/9/37	A	77,753, boiler 754, repainted (not tender)
18/9/39-13/10/39	C	71,578, at Feltham
10/7/40-7/8/40	A	95,191, Maunsell boiler 805, U1 chimney, unlined dark green, Bulleid lettering
27/3/43-12/5/43	A	91,716, boiler 513 , unlined black
10/7/45-25/8/45	C	75,190, at Feltham
3/4/46-18/5/46	B	89,361, boiler 476, mileage extended by 15,000
8/5/47-7/6/47	A	111,901, boiler 749, narrow piston rings fitted
2/2/50-10/3/50	A	70,243, boiler 500, snifting valves off, 30507, large first emblem
28/9/51-10/10/51	H Cas	43,858, at Feltham
17/2/53-7/3/53	Gen	77,825, boiler 751, small first emblem
26/7/54-31/7/54	L Cas	37,090
17/8/54-21/8/54	L Cas	37,090
5/10/55-29/10/55	H Int	5200 gallon tender 781 ex 30483
18/12/57-11/1/58	Gen	127,649, Maunsell boiler 1405, second emblem (L)
19/1/60-6/2/60	L Int	61,649
6/1961-8/7/61	(GW)	
28/11/61-16/12/61	Gen	111,743, Maunsell boiler 1402, AWS fitted
15/12/63		Withdrawn, Mileage 1,259,244
7/3/64		Sold to George Cohen, Kettering for scrap

Allocation
1921	Strawberry Hill
1923	Feltham

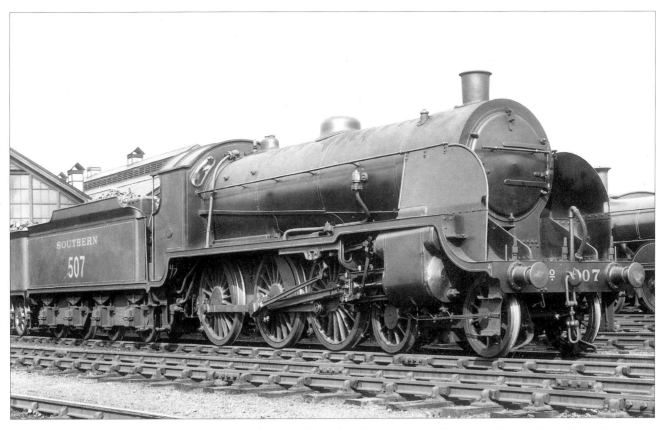

507 at Eastleigh in the 1930s. In January 1932 it received smoke deflectors, green livery and lost the E prefix to its number. It also has a Maunsell superheater and smokebox door. With the fitting of smoke deflectors, the wide footsteps on the front drop of the platform were replaced by narrow ones, outside the deflectors. The small grab rails on the front part of the main frame were replaced by vertical stanchions, next to the outer lamp brackets.

30507 at Feltham about 1960. Having run with a Drummond tender from 1935, it received the 5,200 gallon tender from H15 30483 in 1955 and a Maunsell boiler at a General Repair in January 1958, at which it was repainted with left-facing second emblems on the tender. It has electrification warning signs on the smoke deflectors and the top of the firebox and bushed connecting rod big ends. Stephen Gradidge.

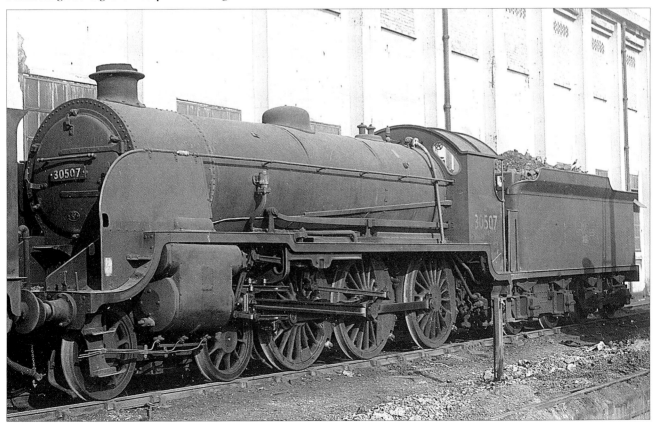

30508

Built Eastleigh 11/1920   Order No. C16-2   Works Serial Number 70
Built as 508, renumbered ᴇ508 11/1925, 508 4/1932, 30508 7/1949

13/11/20		New Locomotive, LSWR goods green
9/2/21-19/2/21		Right leading bearing
31/5/21-11/6/21		Left driving bearing
12/1/22-14/1/22		Left trailing box hot
29/7/22-5/8/22		Left leading bearing hot
26/2/23-3/3/23		Left trailing bearing hot
4/6/25-6/11/25	A	General repairs, SOUTHERN lined black, ᴇ508
13/6/29-29/7/29	A	General repairs, Maunsell boiler 801, tender numbered 3211
23/7/30-23/7/30	D	Weighing
10/9/30-10/9/30	D	Weighing
9/3/32-16/4/32	A	Boiler 478, smoke deflectors, dark green, renumbered 508
19/1/35-16/2/35	(GW)	part repaint
25/3/35-30/3/35	(GW)	Boiler 738, Drummond tender 224 ex 833
24/4/56-24/4/36	D	
18/9/37-16/10/37	A	85,827, boiler 478, full repaint
24/11/39-12/1/40	B	71,440 at Feltham, mileage extended by 10,000
30/9/40-30/10/40	A	93,224, boiler 754, unlined light green, Bulleid lettering
11/9/42-14/10/42	A	69,481, boiler 504, unlined black
12/4/45-16/5/45	C	85,476, at Guildford
15/11/45-19/1/46	A	102,609, Maunsell boiler 929, U1 chimney
4/3/46-16/3/46	C	2,092
17/7/47-16/8/47	C	44,695
27/5/49-8/7/49	A	91,471, boiler 478, Snifting valves off, 30508, unlettered
12/3/52-5/4/52	Gen	80,633, boiler 499, first emblem
24/9/53-2/10/53	L Cas	44,854
7/9/54-25/9/54	H Int	70,631
17/10/56-10/11/56	Gen	121,530, Maunsell boiler 764, 5000 gallon tender 3230 ex 32329
5/12/58-3/1/59	H Int	60,337
10/9/59-24/9/59	N/C	At Guildford
13/1/60-6/2/60	Gen	84,359, Maunsell boiler 786, second emblem (L)
16/4/62-5/5/62	L Int	71,414, AWS fitted
16/11/63		Withdrawn, Mileage 1,247,861
1/1964	(GW)	To works
18/1/64		Cut up at Eastleigh

Allocation
1921	Strawberry Hill
1923	Feltham
6/1929	Exmouth Junction
9/1929	Feltham
11/1963	Exmouth Junction *

* Nominal transfer, to enable the Western Region to claim the scrap value of the locomotive. This was to balance the potential scrap value of Western Region allocated locomotives of Southern or BR design, which were transferred to the Southern Region for further use.

508 at Strawberry Hill, with some of the newness wearing off.

30508 at Feltham on 29 October 1961. In November 1956 30508 acquired a Maunsell boiler and a Urie 5,000 gallon tender, in place of the Drummond tender which it had run with since 1935. This was tender 3230 from withdrawn N15X 4-6-0 32329, the one which Maunsell S15 833 had lost in 1934. It retains the curved rear footsteps and handrail, which were fitted when it was coupled to 2329, but has lost its auxiliary vacuum reservoirs and now has straight front footsteps, to match the S15. 30508 also has bushed big ends to its connecting rods. Stephen Gradidge.

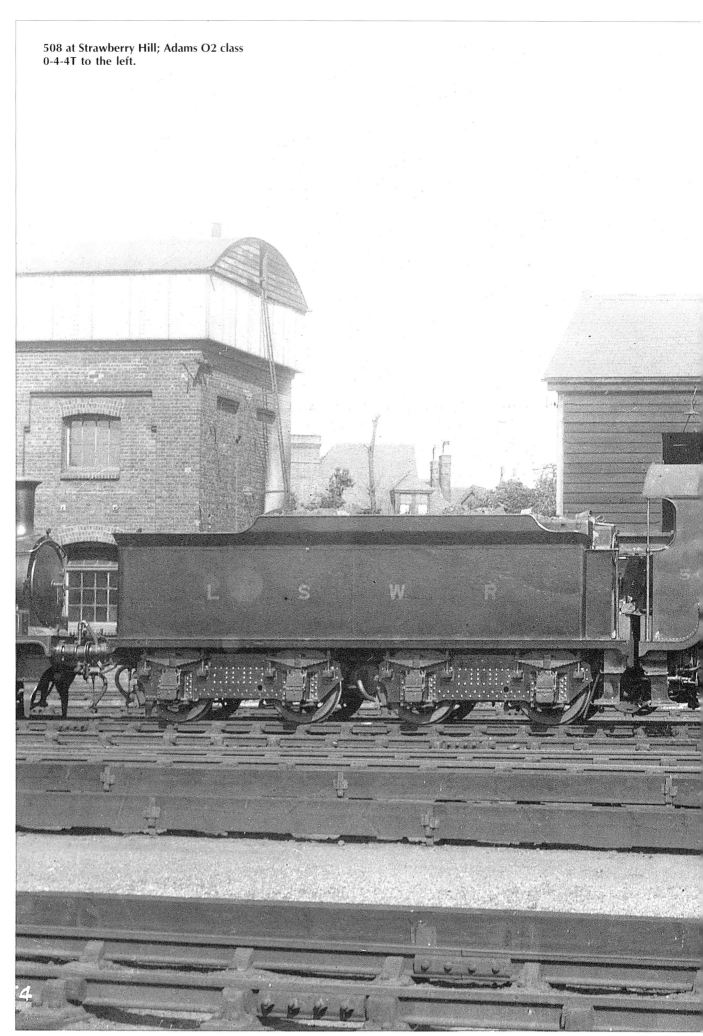

508 at Strawberry Hill; Adams O2 class
0-4-4T to the left.

30509

**Built Eastleigh 12/1920   Order No. C16-3   Works Serial Number 71
Built as 509, renumbered E509 6/1926 , 509 7/1932, 30509 5/1948**

17/12/20		New Locomotive, LSWR goods green
19/7/22-29/7/22		Left trailing bearing melted
16/8/23-22/9/23		Axleboxes and coupling rods
28/9/23-6/10/23		Left leading bearing hot
15/1/24-18/1/24	C	Right leading bearing hot
30/3/25-25/4/25	D	Superheater
8/7/25-30/7/25	B	Right driving bearing
15/2/26-30/6/26	A	General repairs, SOUTHERN lined black, E509
30/8/27-7/9/27	C	Left trailing bearing, boiler numbered 509, tender 3213
12/2/29-20/4/29	A	Maunsell superheater, repainted dark green
14/6/32-15/7/32	A	Boiler 753, smoke deflectors, renumbered 509
20/7/33-20/7/33	(GW)	
31/12/34-29/1/35	(GW)	Boiler 743, Drummond tender 220 ex 290, full repaint
27/7/36-27/7/36	D	
20/10/37		Mileage extended by 5,000 at Feltham
13/6/38-13/7/38	A	93,968, boiler 515, cylinders panelled, tender not repainted
28/2/41-8/4/41	A	91,086, boiler 476, unlined black, gilt lettering
9/6/41-16/6/41	D	120
29/2/44-29/3/44	A	93,615, Boiler 478, sunshine lettering
19/6/45-21/7/45	C	45,646 at Ashford Works
5/12/45-11/12/45	C	63,530, at Feltham
31/5/46-6/7/46	B	68,485, boiler 738, U1 chimney
29/8/47-13/9/47	D	100,685
3/4/48-8/5/48	A	107,865, boiler 501, snift valves off, BRITISH RAILWAYS 30509 (S)
3/10/50-27/10/50	A	68,583, boiler 751, first emblem
7/8/51-14/8/51	N/C	22,790
19/9/52-11/10/52	Gen	52,366, boiler 754, repainted
12/1952-7/12/52	(GW)	
18/6/54-10/7/54	H Cas	49,156
10/2/55-26/2/55	L Int	5000 gallon tender 3210 ex 32328
8/1955-6/8/55	(GW)	
23/5/56-9/6/56	Gen	99,475, boiler 755
9/6/58-11/7/58	H Int	60,552
7/10/60-12/11/60	Gen	127,297, Maunsell boiler 1404, second emblem (L)
27/7/62-4/8/62	N/C	50,255, AWS fitted
7/7/63		Withdrawn, Mileage 1,193,769
7/3/64		Sold to George Cohen, Kettering, for Scrap

Allocation
1921	Strawberry Hill
1923	Feltham
1928	Eastleigh
10/1935	Feltham

30509 at Feltham in June 1948, recently repainted with its BR number and tender lettering in green shaded Southern style characters. It had lost its snifting valves at the same time and had only got a U1 chimney two years earlier. It has been running with a double sided Drummond 4,000 gallon tender since 1935. R.K. Blencowe Collection.

30509 at Feltham on 15 September 1956, now running with 5,000 gallon Urie tender 3210 from N15X 32328, which was the original tender of S15 506. It retains the curved footsteps at all four corners and the auxiliary vacuum cylinders, which were added in 1935. R.K. Blencowe Collection.

30510

Built Eastleigh 1/1921   Order No. C16-4   Works Serial Number 72
Built as 510, renumbered E510 1/1925, 510 11/1933, 30510 4/1949

8/1/21		New Locomotive, LSWR goods green
19/6/22-24/6/22		Right leading bearing heated
11/7/22-15/7/22		Driving wheels
4/4/23-14/4/23		Left leading bearing and tubes
5/9/23-8/9/23		Left trailing bearing hot
8/4/24-10/4/24	C	Right trailing bearing
1/11/24-24/1/25	A	General repairs, SOUTHERN lined black E510
20/4/25-2/5/25	D	Patches leaking
27/8/25-12/9/25	C	Tubes
3/3/27-3/3/27	(GW)	
25/4/27-25/4/27	(GW)	Repair in yard
29/12/27-21/4/28	A	Old boiler numbered 510, boiler 500, tender numbered 3214
19/12/28-19/12/28	D	Weighing
21/1/29-29/1/29	D	Right driving bearing
23/8/29-23/8/29	D	Weighing
14/10/29-14/10/29	D	Weighing
9/1/30-9/1/30	D	Weighing
4/4/30-25/4/30	D	Right driving axlebox
7/10/30-7/10/30	D	Weighing
3/11/30-3/11/30	D	Weighing
21/1/31-28/2/31	A	Maunsell superheater, KA chimney, smoke deflectors, dark green
12/3/31-18/3/31	D	Leading bearing
5/5/31-5/5/31	D	Weighing
11/10/33-20/11/33	(GW)	Accident damage, boiler 512, renumbered loco 510, tender 3214
10/9/35-10/9/35	D	
28/10/35-2/11/35	D	Drummond tender 225 ex 295, tender repainted.
21/4/36-21/4/36	D	83,955
9/6/36-16/6/36	D	
10/11/36-5/12/36	A	100,716, boiler 746, U1 chimney, tender not repainted
23/5/39-21/6/39	A	73,990, boiler 506, dark green, black and yellow lining
22/1/40-24/1/40	D	17,130
16/6/41		Mileage extended by 5,000 at Feltham
4/11/42-2/12/42	A	106,453, boiler 737, unlined black
8/1/43-20/2/43	C	
18/7/44-26/8/44	C	47,670
15/2/45-30/3/45	C	62,113
10/5/46-6/7/46	A	90,716, Maunsell boiler 1052
7/3/49-14/4/49	A	76,479, boiler 508, snifting valves off, 30510 unlettered
7/7/49-15/7/49	L Cas	30,320
16/2/51-17/3/51	Gen	51,845, boiler 522, first emblem
13/2/52-20/2/52	L Cas	25,800 at Nine Elms
24/4/53-9/5/53	L Int	59,925

8/1953-23/8/53	(GW)	
3/9/54-24/9/54	Gen	78,288, Maunsell boiler 453, repainted
26/10/55-10/11/55	L Cas	32,519
12/1955-10/12/55	(GW)	
11/1/57-2/2/57	H Int	62,548, 5000 gallon tender 850 ex 30736
31/3/59-25/4/59	Gen	131,295, Maunsell boiler 1408, second emblem (L)
4/10/60-14/10/60	L Cas	44,970
28/6/61-5/8/61	L Int	65,480, AWS fitted
29/6/1963		Withdrawn, mileage 1,188,192
8/1963	(GW)	To works
14/9/63		Cut up at Eastleigh

Allocation
| 1921 | Strawberry Hill |
| 1923 | Feltham |

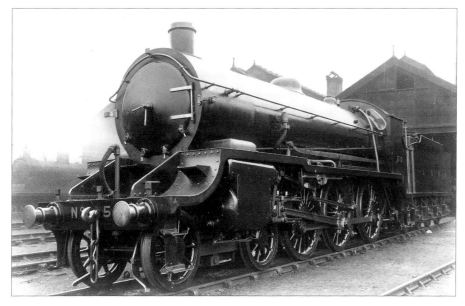

Left. 510 at Strawberry Hill when new.

Below. E510 in 1931-33, when running with a King Arthur type chimney, smoke deflectors and Maunsell superheater, but before losing its E-prefix. It retains its Urie smokebox door, with lamp irons on the door. E.W. Fry.

30511

Built Eastleigh 1/1921   Order No. C16-5   Works Serial Number 73
Built as 511, renumbered ᴇ511 10/1925, 511 9/1933 , 30511 6/1949

29/1/21		New Locomotive, LSWR goods green
4/8/21-13/8/21		Right driving box
9/6/22-17/6/22		Left trailing box hot
14/8/22-19/8/22		Right driving bearing heated
28/8/23-1/9/23		Right trailing bearing
22/11/23-1/12/23		Right leading bearing
4/6/25-3/10/25	A	General repairs, SOUTHERN lined black, ᴇ511
13/2/28-30/6/28	A	Old boiler numbered 511, boiler 510, tender numbered 3215
15/10/30-22/11/30	A	Maunsell superheater, smoke deflectors, dark green
2/8/33-5/9/33	(GW)	Boiler 499, loco renumbered 511,
9/7/35-9/7/35	D	
22/10/35-22/10/35	D	
19/12/35-18/1/36	A	80,996, boiler 507, full repaint
27/2/37-27/2/37	D	
29/8/38-21/9/38	A	89,067, boiler 740, tender not repainted
8/1/41-19/2/41	A	72,832, boiler 497, U1 chimney, unlined dark green, Bulleid letters
16/3/43-14/4/43	A	81,607, boiler 755, unlined black
9/6/45-21/4/45	B	62,812, boiler 505
19/10/46-9/11/46	A	96,707, boiler 496
23/5/49-24/6/49	H Cas	67,726, boiler 474, snifting valves off, SOUTHERN 30511
13/3/50-31/3/50	L Cas	91,623
10/12/51-10/1/52	Gen	139,876, Maunsell boiler 931, first emblem
16/2/54-13/3/54	Gen	64,909, boiler 509, repainted
16/2/56-17/3/56	Gen	59,291, boiler 741
11/9/56-14/9/56	N/C	14,361
1/2/57-8/2/57	L Cas	24,218
12/3/58-10/4/58	Gen	53,955, boiler 751, tender repainted, second emblem (F)
30/6/60-13/8/60	H Int	64,228
27/3/62-21/4/62	Gen	108,588, Maunsell boiler 763, AWS, second emblem (L)
6/1962-1/9/62	(GW)	
7/7/63		Withdrawn, Mileage 1,287,933
12/1963	(GW)	To works
11/1/64		Cut up at Eastleigh

Allocation
1921	Strawberry Hill
1923	Feltham

511 at Strawberry Hill, which is still dealing with steam suburban traffic. There is a Drummond M7 0-4-4T on the left and an Adams T1 0-4-4T to the right.

30511 at Eastleigh on 26 March 1954, immediately after a General Repair. It had received smoke deflectors in 1930 and a U1 chimney in 1941. R.K. Blencowe Collection.

30512

**Built Eastleigh 2/1921   Order No. E16-1   Works Serial Number 74
Built as 512, renumbered ᴇ512 9/1925 , 512 8/1931, 30512 6/1949**

26/2/21		New Locomotive, LSWR goods green
5/9/21-10/9/21		No detail
26/5/22-3/6/22		Right leading box hot
13/3/23-24/3/23		Tyres turning
13/6/23-16/6/23		Left leading bearing
22/10/23-27/10/23		Left trailing bearing hot
19/1/24-28/1/24	C	Piston rods etc.
6/5/25-5/9/25	A	General repair, SOUTHERN lined black ᴇ512
30/4/28-24/10/28	A	Boiler 511, dark green, tender numbered 3216
23/6/31-1/8/31	A	Maunsell superheater, smoke deflectors, renumbered 512
31/5/34-24/7/34	(GW)	Boiler 477, part repaint
20/6/36-29/7/36	C	69,691, not painted, mileage extended by 5,000
2/4/37-6/5/37	A	93,428, boiler 512, full repaint
28/9/38-19/10/38	C	43,715, not painted
3/1/40-31/1/40	A	83,383, boiler 751, unlined dark green, Bulleid lettering
5/12/42-18/1/43	A	90,917, boiler 506, unlined black
12/9/44-11/10/44	C	58,756, at Feltham
20/1/45-10/3/45	B	64,139, boiler 515, mileage extended by 10,000
4/5/46-22/6/46	A	102,711, boiler 474, U1 chimney
21/4/49-27/5/49	A	82,219, Maunsell boiler 835, sv off, 30512, unlettered
?-20/1/51	(GW)	
11/9/51-5/10/51	L Int	70,214, first emblem
4/1/54-29/1/54	Gen	144,213, Boiler 986 (Urie)
12/1/56-11/2/56	H Int	60,051
10/7/56-18/7/56	L Cas	72,883
21/2/58-15/3/58	L Int	116,696
25/1/60-13/2/60	Gen	176,986, Maunsell boiler 1401, second emblem (L)
15/5/62-2/6/62	L Int	68,411, AWS fitted
1/1963-2/3/63	(GW)	
4/4/64		Withdrawn, mileage 1,291,002
6/1964		Sold to Woodham Bros, Barry
1/1965		Cut up at Barry

Allocation
1921	Strawberry Hill
1923	Feltham

512 during the1930s. Repainted green in 1928, Maunsell superheater and smoke deflectors appeared in 1931, the E prefix disappearing. It retains its Urie smokebox door and continuous boiler handrail; tender coping black. South Western Circle John Eyers Collection.

30512 at Eastleigh between 1954 and 1959. Having run with a Maunsell boiler, it has reverted to a Urie boiler and has just been repaired, with the paintwork touched up. It has small first BR emblems on the tender and 6F power classification on the cabside. D.L. Bradley.

30513

Built Eastleigh 3/1921   Order No. E16-2   Works Serial Number 75
Built as 513, renumbered E513 7/1924, 513 9/1932 , 30513 11/1949

12/3/21		New Locomotive, LSWR goods green
3/11/22-11/11/22		Right trailing bearing hot
20/12/22-23/12/22		Left driving and trailing bearings
1/8/23-4/8/23		Both leading bearings
22/4/24-7/7/24	B	General repairs, SOUTHERN lined black, E513
7/2/27-14/7/27	A	General repairs, full repaint, boiler numbered 513, tender 3217
19/11/28-19/22/28	D	Weighing
8/4/30-31/5/30	A	Boiler 502, Maunsell superheater
7/4/30-21/3/31	(GW)	Smoke deflectors, dark green (In store 6/30 – 3/31?)
8/8/32-10/9/32	A	Renumbered 513
21/11/32-24/12/32	(GW)	
13/6/35-13/7/35	A	83,081, boiler 501, tender not repainted
31/1/38-2/3/38	A	84,183, boiler 513, full repaint, cylinders panelled
27/8/40-2/10/40	A	80,771, boiler 508, unlined dark green, Bulleid lettering
7/8/42-16/9/42	A	67,041, boiler 745, unlined black
26/9/44-28/10/44	C	71,320, mileage increased by 9,000
10/8/45-31/8/45	C	98,146, at Feltham
17/12/45-30/1/46	C	109,912, at Feltham, mileage increased by 10,000
24/9/46-19/10/46	A	126,727, boiler 746, U1 chimney
14/2/48-25/3/48	B	39,566, not repainted
14/10/49-18/11/49	A	82,856, Maunsell boiler 802, snifting valves off, renumbered 30513, first emblem
7/8/51-21/8/51	L Cas	55,504
15/2/52-8/3/52	Gen	71,079, boiler 506
5/1952-25/5/52	(GW)	
24/6/54-31/7/54	Gen	70,730, Maunsell multi-plug boiler 838, repainted
12/7/56-18/8/56	L Int	57,998
16/10/57-9/11/57	L Cas	90,442
24/10/58-22/11/58	Gen	117,208, boiler 740, second emblem (L)
7/2/61-4/3/61	L Int	65,860
6/4/63		Withdrawn, mileage 1,231,659
5/1963	(GW)	To works
22/6/63		Cut up at Eastleigh

Allocation
1921	Strawberry Hill
1923	Feltham

513 at Strawberry Hill, 1 October 1921. H.C. Casserley, courtesy R.M. Casserley.

513 at Eastleigh on 6 August 1949. It retained Southern unlined black livery and snifting valves until a Class A repair in October 1949. A.E. West, courtesy M.S. King.

30514

Built Eastleigh 4/1921   Order No. E16-3   Works Serial Number 76
Built as 514, renumbered E514 4/1925, 514 4/1934, 30514 9/1948

2/4/21		New Locomotive, LSWR goods green
19/6/23-23/6/23		Left trailing box hot
18/9/23-29/9/23		Right leading bearing heated
6/11/23-10/11/23		Steam pipe elbow casting split
30/8/24-6/9/24	D	Trailing boxes
5/1/25-24/4/25	A	General repairs, SOUTHERN lined black, E514
23/3/28-1/10/28	A	General repairs, boiler 503, dark green, tender numbered 3218
18/2/30-18/2/30	D	Weighing
20/4/31-30/5/31	A	Maunsell superheater, smoke deflectors, short KA chimney,
4/12/33-4/12/33	(GW)	
5/2/34-17/4/34	(GW)	Dark green, boiler 739, loco renumbered 514
16/4/36-16/4/36	D	
17/7/36-5/9/36	A	83,545, boiler 752, full repaint, stovepipe chimney
5/7/39-26/7/39	A	89,045, boiler 736, part repaint
23/1/42-11/3/42	A	83,909, boiler 505, U1 chimney, unlined black
3/5/45-23/6/45	A	110,848, boiler 739
8/4/47-26/4/47	C	54,931
16/7/47-9/8/47	C	56,941, snifting valves off
10/12/47-20/12/47	D	64,422
16/8/48-11/9/48	A	78,891, boiler 738, BRITISH RAILWAYS 30514 (G)
12/1/51-10/2/51	A	69,537, Urie boiler 986, first emblem
30/4/53-22/5/53	Gen	62,927, boiler 502, repainted
17/6/55-8/7/55	H Int	63,712
14/8/57-31/8/57	Gen	122,447, Maunsell boiler 776, second emblem (F)
3/2/59-20/2/59	L Cas	45,189
28/10/59-14/11/59	H Int	62,241
24/7/61-19/8/61	Gen	111,936, Maunsell boiler 1410, AWS fitted, 2nd emblem (L)
7/7/63		Withdrawn, mileage 1,193,977
7/3/64		Sold to George Cohen, Kettering, for scrap

Allocation
1921	Strawberry Hill
1923	Feltham

514 at Strawberry Hill on 17 March 1923. H.C. Casserley, courtesy R.M. Casserley.

30514 at Basingstoke shed on 1 September 1962. It has the Waterloo-Southampton Terminus headcode, which was also carried by Basingstoke trains. AWS was fitted and left facing second emblems were applied during its final General Repair in August 1961. R.K. Blencowe Collection.

30515

Built Eastleigh 4/1921   Order No. E16-4 Works Serial Number 77
Built as 515, renumbered E515 1/1926, 515 9/1931, 30515 12/1948

23/4/21		New Locomotive, LSWR goods green
5/5/21-2/7/21		Scarab oil fuel apparatus fitted
17/10/21-29/10/21		Reconversion to coal burning
5/6/23-9/6/23		Right driving bearing
11/2/24-29/2/24	B	Boxes and motion
8/9/25-8/1/26	A	General repairs, lined black, E515
7/6/26-12/6/26	D	Oil fuel apparatus refitted
17/12/26-21/12/26	D	Removal of oil fuel apparatus
25/7/27-30/7/27	C	Left trailing bearing, boiler numbered 515, tender 3219
16/7/28-21/7/28	D	Steam chest liners, smoke deflectors fitted
9/8/28-30/11/28	A	General repairs, boiler 739, dark green
9/9/29-2/10/29	B	Change of wheels
27/4/31-30/4/31	D	Weighing
11/8/31-18/9/31	A	Maunsell superheater, renumbered 515
16/12/33-27/1/34	(GW)	Boiler 751, part repaint
19/5/36-27/6/36	A	85,962, boiler 744, part repaint
23/5/38-23/5/38	D	
7/12/38-11/1/39	A	90,226, boiler 739, full repaint, cylinders panelled
26/2/40-8/3/40	C	35,782, at Nine Elms
28/1/41-31/5/41	B	56,429, at Nine Elms, mileage extended by 25,000
9/1942	(DB)	General Repair at Ashford, boiler 736, unlined black (not on ERC)
2/4/45-18/5/45	C	84,564, at Feltham
5/10/4-8/11/45	A	93,987, boiler 508, U1 chimney (DB states Ashford, ERC shows Eastleigh)
29/10/48-4/12/48	A	67,395, boiler 498, snift valves off, BRITISH RAILWAYS 30515 (G)
6/12/48-24/12/48	D	
19/1/51-17/2/51	Gen	69,700, boiler 476, repaint, first emblem
18/5/53-13/6/53	Gen	66,229
23/6/55-9/7/55	L Int	62,454
7/9/56-22/9/56	H Cas	93,532, Maunsell boiler 773
3/9/57-21/9/57	L Int	117,110
8/1958-23/8/58	(GW)	
20/11/59-19/12/59	Gen	165,801, Maunsell boiler 768, second emblem (L)
5/2/62-31/3/62	H Int	60,868, new front frames & cylinders, AWS fitted
20/7/63		Withdrawn, 1,188,683 miles
12/1963	(GW)	to works
11/1/1964		Cut up at Eastleigh

Allocation
1921	Eastleigh
1922	Strawberry Hill
1922	Salisbury
1928	Nine Elms
11/1941	Feltham

515 at Eastleigh works, probably immediately after fitting with oil burning equipment in July 1921. 515 and N15s 737 and 739 were so altered, using the Scarab system, during the coal miners strike in 1921. All three were fitted for oil burning again during the 1926 General Strike. See also page 44. South Western Circle D.L. Bradley Collection.

30515 at Eastleigh on 21 March 1950, with the usual Southern modifications. In December 1948 it lost its superheater snifting valves, but clearly didn't need a new smokebox, as there is a patch where the snifting valves had been. With the combination of dirt and glare, the BRITISH RAIL WAYS tender lettering is not apparent. A.E. West ,courtesy M.S. King.

30823

Built Eastleigh 3/1927   Order No. E90-1   Works Serial Number 138
Built as E823, renumbered 823 4/1932, 30823 9/1948

10/3/27		SOUTHERN E823, boiler 823, flare top tender 3220, lined black
25/2/29-28/3/29	C	Piston valves etc.
23/12/29-8/2/30	A	Smoke deflectors, dark green
25/2/32-9/4/32	A	tender not repainted, loco renumbered 823
17/8/3-16/9/33	(GW)	
10/10/34-18/12/34	(GW)	Boiler 931
27/10/36-28/11/36	A	91,938, boiler 805, tender not repainted
24/10/38-16/11/38	A	92,256,boiler 833, full repaint, panelled cylinders
17/4/39-20/5/39	B	11,714, boiler 1054, boiler repainted
27/11/39-22/12/39	C	30,278
19/2/41-31/3/41	A	80,759, boiler 836, unlined black, gilt lettering
16/2/43-24/3/43	A	75,233, boiler 786, sunshine lettering
29/8/44-6/10/44	C	62,456
29/10/45-8/12/45	A	107,251, boiler 831
19/3/46-13/4/46	C	10,257, new right hand cylinder
30/9/46		Tender 3221 ex 824 at Exmouth Junction
15/9/47-4/10/47	C	68,127
24/8/48-18/9/48	A	104,702, boiler 823, snift valves off, BRITISH RAILWAYS 30823(G)
24/9/48-18/9/48	D	
12/10/48-30/10/48	D	
4/4/49-8/4/49	L Cas	12,350
23/1/51-9/2/51	NC	Hot box
22/1/52-9/2/52	Gen	104,819, boiler 793, first emblem
5/2/54-20/2/54	L Int	82,993
16/9/55-15/10/55	Gen	147,296, boiler 775, repainted
24/10/57-9/11/57	H Int	88,555
16/9/59-17/10/59	Gen	158,902, boiler 806, second emblem (L)
8/12/61-23/12/61	L Int	74,628, AWS fitted
6/3/63-27/3/63	L Cas	115,587
29/11/64		Withdrawn, mileage 1,411,643
		Sold to J. Cashmore, Newport for scrap

Allocation
1927	Exmouth Junction
6/1951	Salisbury
12/1963	Feltham

E823 at Exmouth Junction on 4 August 1928. It is not as clean as it might be, but the locomotives, as well as their crews, are probably getting plenty of work during the holiday season, with the 'passed cleaners' out firing most of the time. Under the dirt, the livery is black with fine green lining. It still carries LSWR style lamp sockets, with no lamp irons in them. H.C. Casserley, courtesy R.M. Casserley.

30823, now at Salisbury but on a return visit to its old home at Exmouth Junction, at some date between 1952 and 1959. The small first BR emblem was applied in early 1952. R.K. Blencowe Collection.

30824

Built Eastleigh 3/1927   Order No. E90-2   Works Serial Number 139
Built as E824, renumbered 824 9/1932, 30824 1/1950

29/3/27		SOUTHERN E824, boiler 824, flare top tender 3221, lined black
30/12/27-14/1/28	D	Steam chest liners
15/4/29-6/6/29	A	General repairs
13/4/31-22/5/31	A	Smoke deflectors, dark green
20/7/32-1/9/32	(GW)	Loco renumbered 824
2/8/33-2/9/33	(GW)	Boiler 453, tender not repainted
23/2/35-6/3/35	(GW)	
3/7/35		Mileage extended by 5,000 at Exmouth Junction
6/1/36-8/2/36	A	97,700, boiler 840, full repaint
7/12/37-12/1/38	A	93,221, boiler 763, full repaint, panelled cylinders
6/3/40-3/4/40	A	94,465, boiler 784, unlined dark green, Bulleid lettering
22/4/40-26/4/40	(GW)	
25/7/42-9/9/42	A	94,469, boiler 742, unlined black
16/4/45-2/6/45	A	98,104
30/9/46		Tender 3220 ex 823 at Exmouth Junction
6/6/47-5/7/47	A	81,914, boiler 457
7/12/49-13/1/50	A	88,668, boiler 454, snifting valves off, 30824, first emblem
15/9/52-10/10/52	Gen	87,023, boiler 772, repainted
15/10/54-6/11/54	H Int	89,571
5/11/56-24/11/56	Gen	164,207, boiler 823, repainted
17/1/57-26/1/57	L Cas	2,326
15/10/57-15/10/57	N C	33,840
20/1/59-7/2/59	L Int	74,039
15/9/60-16/9/60	N C	115,412, AWS fitted
13/4/61-10/6/61	Gen	135,366, boiler 1412, tender 3202 ex 30482, second emblem (L)
3/8/63-5/10/63	L Int	76,019
5/9/65		Withdrawn, mileage 1,389,966
		Sold to J. Cashmore, Newport for scrap

Allocation

1927	Exmouth Junction
6/1951	Salisbury
12/1963	Feltham
1/1965	Eastleigh
1/1965	Feltham
6/1965	Eastleigh

E824 at Exmouth Junction between May 1931, when it received smoke deflectors and green livery, and July 1932, when it lost the E prefix to its number.

30824 at Nine Elms on 17th July 1964; AWS battery box on the left-hand platform. It also has a good load of what the late Bert Hooker called 'Best Nine Elms Anti Glow' coal. The painter has got the yellow triangle on the cab better placed on this side. Peter Groom.

30825

**Built Eastleigh 4/1927　　Order No. E90-3　Works Serial Number 140
Built as E825, renumbered　825 3/1932, 30825 5/1948**

30/4/27		SOUTHERN E824, boiler 824, flare top tender 3222, lined black
7/5/27-7/5/27	(GW)	Repair in yard
15/12/27-5/1/28	D	Steam chest liners
7/10/29-16/11/29	A	General repair
1/2/32-5/3/32	A	smoke deflectors, dark green, loco renumbered 825
17/6/32-6/7/32	C	
8/6/34-28/7/34	(GW)	Boiler 448, part repaint
13/5/36-20/6/36	A	89,709, full repaint
17/12/37		Mileage extended by 10,000 at Exmouth Junction
5/9/38-28/9/38	A	99,940, boiler 766, panelled cylinders, tender not repainted
21/8/39-27/9/39	B	40,744, cylinders
25/9/40-23/10/40	A	84,554, boiler 788, unlined light green, Bulleid lettering
22/4/43-9/6/43	A	98,884, boiler 824, unlined black
16/10/45-1/12/45	A	94,911, boiler 450
2/4/48-1/5/48	A	100,770, boiler 1055, snifting valves off, BRITISH RAILWAYS 30825(S)
9/2/50-17/3/50	H Cas	61,928
24/3/52-12/4/52	L Int	140,043, first emblem
2/3/53-12/3/53	L Cas	176,676, at Brighton Works
5/4/54-8/5/54	Gen	211,314, boiler 1408, repainted
21/9/54-25/9/54	L Cas	16,088
15/5/56-2/6/56	L Int	76,549
7/11/58-6/12/58	Gen	158,600, boiler 799, second emblem (L)
19/11/60-26/11/60	L Int	65,623
8/5/62-12/5/62	N C	117,933
7/9/1963		tender 3223 ex 30826 at Eastleigh shed
5/1/64		Withdrawn, mileage 1,384,665
		Sold to Woodham Bros, Barry for scrap,
1/1981		Boiler 799 sold to Mid Hants Railway for 30506
1/1986		Frames and wheels to Shipyard Services, Essex

Allocation
1927	Exmouth Junction
6/1951	Salisbury

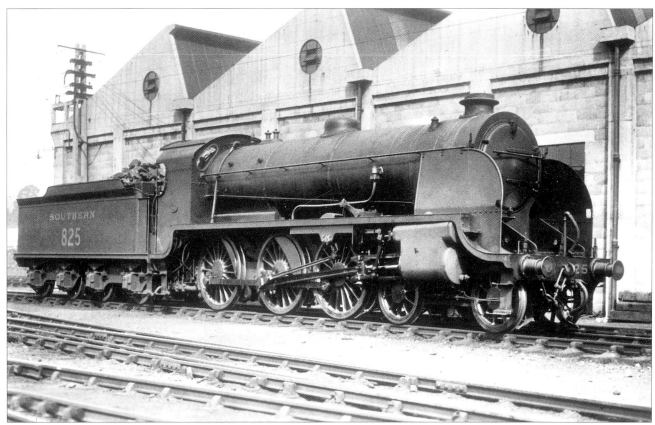

E825 at Exmouth Junction, about 1930; smoke deflectors, with the smokebox side lamp irons in the raised position. It appears to have an E prefix on the tender. Livery is indeterminate under the dirt, but probably black.

30825 at Feltham on 23 April 1962; second BR emblem on the tender. Stephen Gradidge.

30826

Built Eastleigh 5/1927   Order No. E90-4 Works Serial Number 141
Built as E826, renumbered 826 11/1931, 30826 6/1949

14/5/27		SOUTHERN E826, boiler 826, flare top tender 3223, lined black
20/1/28-8/2/28	D	Steam chest liners
8/7/29-28/8/29	A	General repairs
9/5/30-9/5/30	D	Weighing
5/1/31-5/1/31	D	Weighing
12/10/31-14/11/31	A	Boiler 929, smoke deflectors, dark green, renumbered 826
15/3/34-4/5/34	(GW)	part repaint
9/3/36-4/4/36	A	83,955, boiler 769, tender not repainted
21/2/38-23/3/38	A	88,702, boiler 801, full repaint, panelled cylinders
22/3/39-26/4/39	B	39,775, cylinder damage, part repaint, mileage extended by 5,000
22/7/40-21/8/40	A	97,065, boiler 838, unlined dark green, Bulleid lettering
5/11/41-24/12/41	B	42,018, boiler 448
24/6/43-28/7/43	A	102,825, boiler 805, unlined black
10/5/44-15/5/44	D	29,897
3/7/45-21/7/45	C	Mileage extended by 10,000 at Exmouth Junction
23/4/46-15/6/46	A	112,818, boiler 836
31/1/48-12/3/48	C	64,131, at Exmouth Junction
31/3/48-31/3/48	D	64,131*, weighing only
26/4/49-27/5/49	A	97,307, boiler 800, snifting valves off, 30826(G) unlettered
22/10/51-27/10/51	N/C	97,435
5/11/51-15/11/51	N/C	first emblem
25/8/53-19/9/53	Gen	170,935, boiler 1407
2/9/55-8/10/55	L Int	76,869, at Brighton Works
20/6/57-3/8/57	Gen	141,894, boiler 801, second emblem (F)
2/9/59-19/9/59	L Int	85,354
8/8/60-20/8/60	L Cas	120,098, AWS fitted
20/2/61-4/3/61	L Cas	127,528
1/12/1962	(DLB)	Withdrawn, 1,364,577 miles
7/9/63		Tender 3222 ex 30825 at Eastleigh shed
1/1964	(GW)	To works
18/1/64		Cut up at Eastleigh

* That's what it says. Exmouth Junction to Eastleigh with no added mileage!

Allocation
1927	Exmouth Junction
8/1950	Salisbury

30826 at Eastleigh on 5 June 1949; recent BR number, unlettered tender. R.K. Blencowe Collection.

30826 on an up train at Yeovil Junction, 22 July 1958. Second BR emblem, facing forward on both sides, applied in August 1957. The arched cutouts in the frames of the tender bogies show that it retains its original tender 3223. R.C. Riley, transporttreasury.co.uk

30827

Built Eastleigh 6/1927   Order No. E90-5   Works Serial Number 142
Built as ᴇ827, renumbered 827 1/1932, 30827 4/1949

16/6/27		SOUTHERN ᴇ827, boiler 827, flare top tender 3224, lined black
20/12/27-12/1/28	D	Steam chest liners
30/4/28-11/5/28	D	Left trailing bearing
28/11/29-18/1/30	A	smoke deflectors, dark green
7/12/31-16/1/32	A	Boiler 826, full repaint, renumbered 827
16/8/34-19/9/34	(GW)	Boiler 449, part repaint
9/9/36-8/10/36	A	96,442, boiler 823, full repaint
5/10/37-28/10/37	C	48,017
1/9/38-28/9/38	A	84,540, boiler 780, full repaint, panelled cylinders
14/9/40-23/10/40	A	93,012, boiler 804, unlined light green, Bulleid lettering
12/7/41-28/7/41	C	17,860
24/3/43-5/5/43	A	77,039, boiler 836, unlined black
19/1/46-23/2/46	A	112,124, boiler 930
4/3/46-23/3/46	C	
25/6/47-12/7/47	C	47,558
3/4/48-17/5/48	C	78,091 at Exmouth Junction
15/3/49-23/4/49	A	107,786, boiler 838, snifting valves off, 30827(G) unlettered
20/6/50-13/7/50	H Cas	43,987, at Salisbury
9/4/52-10/5/52	L Int	114,307, first emblem
31/5/54-19/6/54	Gen	196,894, boiler 930
28/5/56-16/6/56	Gen	74,266, boiler 835, repainted
17/7/56-21/7/56	N/C	379
30/5/58-28/6/58	H Int	69,918
18/8/60-10/9/60	Gen	146,885, boiler 455, AWS fitted, second emblem (L)
5/1/62-9/1/62	L Cas	45,549
3/1962-21/4/62	(GW)	
5/1/64		Withdrawn, mileage1,358,001
2/1964	(GW)	To works
22/2/64		Cut up at Eastleigh

Allocation
1927   Exmouth Junction
1/1950   Salisbury

E827 emerges from the west end of Honiton tunnel on a down stopping train, 4 August 1928. Little over a year after building, conventional lamp irons have already been placed in the LSWR sockets. H.C. Casserley, courtesy R.M. Casserley.

827 heading a stopping train on the Exeter-Salisbury main line, near Milborne Port perhaps, in 1947 or 1948. In Bulleid unlined black livery, it has lost its vacuum pump but still has snifting valves on the smokebox. The train is an ex-LSWR 4-car non corridor lavatory set, reduced to three cars and with additional vans. 827 did not get British Railways livery until April 1949. R.K. Blencowe Collection.

30827 in Eastleigh Works on 23 April 1949. According to the Engine Record Card, it returned to traffic on that day but George Woodward notes a more realistic 30 April. It carries multi-plug boiler 838 and the uneven spacing of the right-hand plugs is apparent. The painters have begun to apply BR unlined black livery and the driving wheels are on rollers, to allow the valve timing to be set up, although some components of the valve gear are still missing. J.H. Aston.

30828

Built Eastleigh 7/1927   Order No. E90-6   Works Serial Number 143
Built as E828, renumbered 828 7/1931, 30828 12/1949

6/7/27		SOUTHERN E828, boiler 828, flare top AVR tender 3225, lined black
10/1/29-10/1/29	D	AVR tender to E858, Urie tender ex E770, renumbered 3225
13/4/29-13/4/29	D	Tender repairs
27/11/29-17/1/30	A	smoke deflectors, dark green
18/3/31-18/3/31	D	Weighing
7/7/31-18/7/31	C	renumbered 828
20/5/32-25/6/32	A	Boiler 795, not repainted
30/6/34-25/8/34	(GW)	Boiler 778, part repaint
20/8/36-19/9/36	A	83,020, tender not repainted
25/9/36-25/9/36	D	
13/7/37-17/7/37	D	28,469
28/7/37-29/7/37	D	33,262
9/12/37-24/12/37	C	43,387
2/2/39-1/3/39	A	79,225, boiler 931, full repaint, cylinders panelled
2/1/40-10/1/40	D	26,908
13/1/42-18/3/42	A	97,886, boiler 1056, unlined black
21/8/44-7/10/44	A	100,707
29/11/46-4/1/47	B	82,189, mileage extended by 10,000
21/7/47-30/8/47	A	98,152, boiler 826, snifting valves off
2/11/49-2/12/49	A	78,919, boiler 449, 30828, first emblem
22/5/52-20/6/52	L Int	97,881
21/9/53-3/10/53	H Cas	148,031
30/4/54-22/5/54	L Cas	166,264, new right hand cylinder
22/11/54-18/12/54	Gen	184,838, boiler 763, repainted
21/12/1956-19/1/57	L Int	71,077
28/5/58-28/6/58	Gen	124,801, boiler 781, second emblem (F)
26/11/59-12/12/59	L Cas	52,262
16/9/60 -8/10/60	H Int	72,977
8/5/63-25/5/63	L Cas	155,610
5/1/64		Withdrawn, 1,287,124 miles
6/1964		Sold to Woodham Bros, Barry for scrap
9/1978		Tender 3225 sold to Maunsell Locomotive Society for 30847
3/1981		Sold to Eastleigh Railway Preservation Society with tender 3227 ex 30830

Allocation
1927   Salisbury

828 stands at Weybridge on a down stopping train during the 1930s. It received smoke deflectors and green livery in 1930 and lost its E prefix in 1931.

30828 at Eastleigh on 1 October 1950. It still has the rearward extension to the left hand crosshead, to carry the vacuum pump drive. It received its British Railways number, and large first emblems on the tender, in December 1949. R.K. Blencowe Collection.

828 heading a train of sheeted open wagons on the main line near Salisbury in the 1930s. The tender bogies have straight bottoms to their frames, showing that it is a Urie tender, transferred from a King Arthur in 1929. The original tender had been similar, but had arched cutouts to the bogie frames and auxiliary vacuum reservoirs behind the coal space. R.K. Blencowe Collection.

30829

Built Eastleigh 7/1927   Order No. E90-7   Works Serial Number 144
Built as E829, renumbered 829 9/1931, 30829 12/1948

Date	Type	Details
28/7/27		SOUTHERN E829, boiler 829, flare top AVR tender 3226, lined black
1/8/28-1/9/28	D	Right trailing and left driving bearings
8/10/28-13/10/28	D	Right driving bearing
7/2/29-26/3/29	D	AVR tender to E859, Urie tender ex E766, renumbered 3226
17/3/30-2/5/30	A	smoke deflectors
31/8/31-21/9/31	(GW)	renumbered 829 in lined black
21/11/32-31/12/32	(GW)	
3/1/33-13/1/33	(GW)	
21/12/34-21/12/34	(GW)	
28/3/35-4/5/35	(GW)	Boiler 831, full repaint, dark green
24/5/37-28/6/37	A	85,128, boiler 838, full repaint
15/2/38-26/2/38	C	22,548
30/1/39-8/2/39	C	59,601
20/7/39-2/8/39	C	72,432
6/5/40-29/5/40	A	93,784, boiler 763, unlined dark green, Bulleid lettering
5/1/43-10/2/43	A	98,152, boiler 827, unlined black
3/5/45-14/7/45	A	86,000, boiler 828
22/5/47-21/6/47	C	77,676, mileage increased by 10,000
12/11/48-18/12/48	A	119,478, boiler 785, snifting valves off, 30829 (G) unlettered
1/5/51-2/6/51	Gen	94,332, boiler 790, first emblem
13/6/51-20/6/51	Return	
27/2/53-20/3/53	H Int	66,385
21/2/55-19/3/55	Gen	145,412, boiler 784, repainted
13/3/57-20/3/57	H Int	65,916
7/5/59-6/6/59	Gen	138,222, boiler 791, second emblem (L)
31/3/60-9/4/60	N/C	23,622, AWS fitted
7/6/61-1/7/61	L Int	61,317
30/11/1963		Withdrawn, 1,209,387 miles
12/1963	(GW)	to works
4/1/64		Cut up at Eastleigh

*   Tender number 887 applied when it was coupled later to King Arthur 770

Allocation
1927   Salisbury throughout

30829 at Eastleigh on 26 March 1955, immediately following its second repaint with the first emblem on the tender. It now has the 6F power classification above the cabside number. The tender emblem is set higher than at a previous repaint. R.K. Blencowe Collection.

30829 at Yeovil Town, 22 August 1959. A further General repair and the tender now carries left facing second BR emblems. There is a U class 2-6-0 behind 30829 and ex-GWR 0-6-0PT 9732, probably transferred from Yeovil Pen Mill shed, which closed at about this time. A.E. West, courtesy M.S. King.

30830

Built Eastleigh 8/1927   **Order No. E90-8**   **Works Serial Number 145**
Built as ᴇ830, renumbered 830 9/1932, 30830 3/1950

27/8/27		SOUTHERN ᴇ830, boiler 830, flare top AVR tender 3227, lined black
1/3/29-1/3/29	D	Weighing
15/3/29-16/3/29	D	AVR tender to ᴇ860, Urie tender ex ᴇ765, renumbered 3227
5/9/29-5/10/29	C	
26/2/30-11/4/30	A	General repairs, smoke deflectors
22/7/32-2/9/32	A	Boiler 777, renumbered 830, lined black
4/2/35-7/3/35	(GW)	Boiler 773, full repaint, dark green
22/6/36-25/7/36	C	52,906, part repaint
3/4/37-7/5/37	A	81,675, boiler 928, tender not repainted
22/11/38-18/1/39	B	53,878, mileage increased by 5,000
5/4/40-1/5/40	A	88,261, boiler 783, unlined dark green, Bulleid lettering
4/1942	(DB)	General Repair at Ashford, boiler 454 (Not on ERC)
19/6/43-2/8/43	C	36,377, mileage increased by 10,000 at Salisbury
6/11/43-29/12/43	B	43,603, mileage increased by 15,000, unlined black
27/3/45-9/6/45	A	84,340, boiler 449
22/3/46-5/4/46	C	35,450
12/11/47-13/12/47	A	92,889, boiler 1056, snifting valves off
?-1/10/49	(GW)	
27/2/50-24/3/50	A	80,873, boiler 841, repaint, 30830 first emblem
6/12/50-19/1/51	L Cas	29,948 at Salisbury
1/10/52-25/10/52	Gen	90,387, boiler 824
29/10/54-20/11/54	Gen	88,050, boiler 825
21/1/57-23/2/57	H Int	79,994
19/6/59-11/7/59	Gen	162,168, boiler 928, second emblem (L)
20/5/60-28/5/60	N/C	24,315, AWS fitted
11/10//61-4/11/61	L Int	76,534
26/7/64		Withdrawn, 1,259,236 miles
12/1964		Sold to Woodham Bros, Barry for scrap
11/1980		Tender 3227 to Eastleigh Railway Preservation Soc for 30828
9/1987		To Maunsell Locomotive Society without tender

Allocation
1927	Salisbury
12/1963	Feltham

E830 at Exmouth Junction on 24 August 1930. It had received smoke deflectors four months earlier and the smokebox side lamp irons have been moved up, right into the driver's line of sight. Fortunately, it will be doing most of its work on the Salisbury-Exeter main line, with discs top and bottom in the middle. H.C. Casserley, courtesy R.M. Casserley.

30830 at Feltham on 7 April 1964, with bushed connecting rod big ends. After being sold for scrap to Woodham Bros of Barry in December 1964, 30830 is currently on the North Yorkshire Moors Railway, awaiting rebuilding. Peter Groom.

30831

Built Eastleigh 9/1927   Order No. E90-9   Works Serial Number 146
Built as E831, renumbered 831 10/1932, 30831 3/1949

24/9/27		SOUTHERN E831, boiler 831, flare top AVR tender 3228, lined black
31/10/29-19/12/29	A	smoke deflectors, tender to E852, Urie tender ex E769 renumbered 3228, dark green
3/1/30-3/1/30	D	Weighing
13/1/31-29/1/31	D	Piston valves
26/9/32-029/10/32	A	Boiler 772, loco renumbered 831
8/11/33-25/11/33	(GW)	
11/9/34-9/10/34	(GW)	
21/9/35-19/10/35	A	88,327, boiler 454, full repaint
25/11/36-10/12/36	C	40,924
12/10/37-23/10/37	C	65,878
2/3/38-2/3/38	D	
17/5/38-20/6/38	A	85,442, boiler 769, cylinders panelled, tender not repainted
12/10/40-6/11/40	A	86,113, boiler 795, unlined light green, Bulleid lettering
4/1942	(DB)	Repair at Ashford
5/8/42-4/9/42	C	50,603, unlined black
7/8/43-15/9/43	A	84,738, boiler 785
3/5/44-20/5/44	C	23,855
17/1/46-23/11/46	A	106,550,boiler 456
27/1/49-11/3/49	L Int	67,130, SOUTHERN 30831
10/8/50-1/9/50	H Cas	115,549, boiler 1410, snifting valves off, first emblem
21/2/52-8/3/52	L Int	68,684
21/12/53-16/1/54	Gen	248,751, boiler 1405, repainted
7/11/55-26/11/55	H Int	67,466
16/8/57-7/9/57	Gen	131,626, boiler 828, second emblem (F)
22/10/59-21/11/59	Gen	78,380, boiler 453, second emblem (L)
20/4/60-23/4/60	N/C	10,232, AWS fitted
9/8/61-2/9/61	L Int	53,114
16/11/63		Withdrawn, 1,304,943 miles
11/1963	(GW)	to works
7/12/63		cut up at Eastleigh

Allocation
1927   Salisbury

E831, probably in Eastleigh works yard, in 1930-32. Smoke deflectors, green livery and the tender from King Arthur 769 in December 1929. G.H. Butland.

30831 heading a short freight on the main line, approaching Wilton on 5 October 1963. It has only another month to run. R.K. Blencowe Collection.

30832

Built Eastleigh 10/1927   Order No. E90-10 Works Serial Number 147
Built as E832, renumbered 832 10/1932, 30832 9/1948

15/10/27		SOUTHERN E832, boiler 832, flare top AVR tender 3229, lined black
9/3/28-16/3/28	D	Right trailing bearing
18/8/28-30/8/28	D	Piston valve liners
24/7/29-3/8/29	D	Leading and driving axleboxes
4/1/30-20/2/30	A	Smoke deflectors, dark green
3/3/30-3/3/30	D	AVR tender to E853, Urie tender ex E767, renumbered 3229
10/10/32-29/10/32	C	Renumbered 832
10/2/33-20/3/33	(GW)	Boiler 801, boiler repainted
15/5/34-19/5/34	(GW)	Tender damaged
30/4/35-1/6/35	(GW)	Full repaint
31/7/36-29/8/36	B	45,811, disc wheels on tender
19/5/37-11/6/37	C	72,034
2/11/37-27/11/37	A	83,133, boiler 450, cylinders panelled
10/1/39-10/1/39	D	
18/10/39-8/11/39	A	63,146, boiler 1056, unlined dark green, Maunsell lettering
24/11/41-31/12/41	A	79,899, boiler 773, unlined black
12/9/43-5/11/43	C	60,383, at Salisbury
18/6/44-16/9/44	C	94,511, mileage extended by 5,000, at Salisbury
4/7/45-23/8/45	A	110,192, boiler 827
9/7/47-16/8/47	B	60,447, new right hand cylinder
24/8/48-18/9/48	A	92,499, boiler 737, snift valves off, BRITISH RAILWAYS 30832 (G)
17/2/50-25/3/50	H Int	50,273, boiler 770
8/2/51-3/3/51	H Int	85,194, first emblem
19/3/53-18/4/53	Gen	170,364, boiler 742, repainted
13/5/55-8/7/55	H Int	83,555, at Brighton Works
24/5/57-22/6/57	Gen	146,238, boiler 1411, second emblem (F)
3/6/59-20/6/59	H Int	77,324
23/8/61-23/9/61	H Int	142,873, AWS fitted
11/1/64		Withdrawn, 1,205,892 miles
1/1964	(GW)	to works
25/1/64		cut up at Eastleigh

Allocation
1927   Salisbury throughout

30832 at Exmouth Junction, probably between 1955 and 1957. The smokebox numberplate is set higher than usual, following Brighton Works practice. On Maunsell doors, the plates were generally on the centreline of the door but LB&SCR doors all had centre darts, requiring the plate to be mounted higher. R.K. Blencowe Collection.

30832 at Honiton on the 3.34pm Templecombe-Exeter Central, 20 September 1960. It still has that high set smokebox numberplate, after an Eastleigh overhaul and boiler exchange. The train comprises a Bulleid 3-car set with doors to each compartment and a 2-car set, which had been brought as far as Templecombe by the 1 pm Waterloo-Exeter, together with a Seaton coach, detached from the stopping train at Seaton Junction. The Southern thus provided direct transit from Waterloo to the intermediate stations on the main line, and the branches. South Western Circle John Eyers Collection.

30833

Built Eastleigh 11/1927   Order No. E158-1 Works Serial Number 148
Built as E833, renumbered 833 10/1932, 30833 1/1949

12/11/27		SOUTHERN E833, boiler 833, flat side tender 3230, lined black
15/11/27-16/11/27	(GW)	
18/5/28-18/5/28	D	Flat side tender to E851, Urie tender ex E764, renumbered 3230
11/2/29-16/2/29	D	Piston valves etc.
16/6/30-7/7/30	D	Piston valves etc, smoke deflectors
20/10/30-29/11/30	A	General repairs
27/4/31-29/4/31	D	Wrapper plate
17/9/32-12/10/32	C	renumbered 833
20/3/33-4/4/33	(GW)	
2/5/34-30/6/34	(GW)	Boiler 800, full repaint, dark green
?-6/11/34	(GW)	Drummond tender 224 ex 294
25/3/35-30/3/35	(GW)	Urie tender 3212 ex 508
4/11/35-3/12/35	D	56,667
24/6/36-25/7/36	A	77,285, boiler 800 retained, tender not repainted
3/9/36-15/10/36	D	4,551, 6-wheel tender 880 ex 763
29/10/37-4/12/37	B	27,271, part repaint
15/5/38-25/8/38	C	36,261, at Brighton Works
21/8/39-4/10/39	C	57,256, at Brighton Works
3/12/40-15/1/41	A	77,764, boiler 839, unlined light green, Bulleid lettering
24/2/43-16/3/43	C	43,674, at New Cross Gate
1/1/45-10/2/45	A	90,626, boiler 793, unlined black
19/4/45-28/4/45	C	3,937
24/5/46-29/6/46	C	42,416
8/4/47-12/5/47	C	61,373, at Feltham
8/1/48-7/2/48	B	75,498, snifting valves off, mileage extended by 19,000
12/10/48-12/10/48	D	89,884, weighing only
2/12/48-1/1/49	B	96,293, boiler 1410, SOUTHERN 30833
3/3/49-4/3/49	D	97,433, at Nine Elms
11/7/50-25/8/50	A	139,153, boiler 769, first emblem
13/8/52-6/9/52	Gen	52,229, boiler 827, repainted
18/10/54-6/11/54	H Int	65,084
28/2/56-9/3/56	L Cas	98,056, at Brighton Works
11/9/56-29/9/56	Gen	109,177, boiler 840, repainted
27/5/57-8/6/57	N/C	12,937
7/1/58-18/1/58	L Cas	26,153, at Ashford Works
1/1/59-7/2/59	H Int	44,496
15/12/59-9/1/60	N/C	64,585
1/4/60-30/4/60	H Cas	69,505, boiler 805, AWS fitted
6/9/61-30/9/61	H Int	108,322
10/5/62-12/5/62	N/C	125,051, 6- wheel tender 708 ex 30908, second emblem
23/5/65		Withdrawn, 945,634 miles
		Sold to J Buttigeg for scrap

Allocation

1927	Feltham	12/1942	Feltham
10/1936	Brighton	1/1965	Eastleigh
1941	New Cross Gate	1/1965	Feltham

E833, probably at Feltham in 1928-32. 833 held the record for the largest number of tender changes of any S15, possibly the record for any Southern locomotive. It had been built with a flat sided bogie tender, but lost it in May 1928 and now has the Urie tender from King Arthur E764. The straight edged footstep backing plates do not match the curved ones on the engine. This tender was given up to an ex-LB&SCR 4-6-4T, rebuilt as a 4-6-0 in 1934. 833 then ran very briefly with a Drummond tender, before exchanging this for the Urie tender from S15 508. It has its original multi plug boiler.

30833 at Salisbury in June 1949. In 1936 it was transferred to Brighton and given its fifth tender, the 4,000 gallon six wheeled one seen here. Repainted in Southern unlined black in 1945, it received its BR number, on the Southern livery, in January 1949. R.K. Blencowe Collection.

30834

**Built Eastleigh 11/1927   Order No. E158-2 Works Serial Number 149
Built as E834, renumbered 834 11/1932, 30834 2/1949**

26/11/27		SOUTHERN E834, boiler 834, flat side tender 3231, lined black
28/8/28-29/8/28	D	Flat side tender to E854, Urie tender ex E763, renumbered 3231
25/7/29-17/8/29	D	Left driving bearing
7/4/30-30/5/30	A	General repairs, smoke deflectors
27/6/30-28/6/30	D	Tender change
21/7/30-22/7/30	D	Tender change
31/3/31-1/4/31	D	Firebox
18/10/32-17/11/32	A	Boiler 831, renumbered 834
14/2/35-16/3/35	(GW)	Boiler 835, repaint, dark green
27/10/36-5/11/36	D	70,815, 6-wheel tender 881 ex 764, steam de-sanding
15/12/36-21/1/37	A	74,406, tender not repainted
25/9/39-25/10/39	B	50,657, part repaint, mileage extended by 5,000
1/5/41-11/6/41	A	82,212, boiler 1054, unlined black, gilt lettering
16/4/45-9/6/45	A	97,755, boiler 1049, sunshine lettering
3/10/47-25/10/47	B	70,049, snifting valves off, mileage extended by 5,000
12/1/49-12/2/49	A	96,829, boiler 793, repainted 30834, unlettered
15/8/50-24/8/50	L Cas	46,545
10/8/51-7/9/51	Gen	71,514, boiler 804, first emblem
18/5/53-29/5/53	L Cas	45,738, at Brighton Works
9/10/53-6/11/53	Gen	54,421, boiler 770, repainted
21/11/55-17/12/55	H Int	65,253
12/11/57-23/11/57	H Int	116,868
18/9/58-27/9/58	L Cas	136.936
12/8/59-22/8/59 *	Gen	156,371, boiler 1403, second emblem (L)
22/3/61-12/4/61	L Cas	At Guildford
1/8/61-23/8/61	L Cas	55,359, AWS fitted
10/10/62-10/11/61	L Int	82,426
3/3/64-14/3/64	L Cas	112,907
1/11/1964	(DLB)	Withdrawn, 952,561 miles
		Sold to Birds Commercial Motors, Morriston, for scrap

*This seems very quick for a General Repair. GW records 30834 off works 5/9/59

Allocation
1927	Feltham
11/1936	Brighton
1941	New Cross Gate
12/1942	Feltham

30834 at Eastleigh in June 1949, repainted with its BR number and an unlettered tender. The sniffing valves have gone but the crosshead extension and widened lower slide bar, to carry the vacuum pump, are still present. Power classification A below the cabside number. R.K. Blencowe Collection.

30834 at Feltham on 11 March 1961. When transferred to Brighton in 1936 it had received the six wheeled tender from King Arthur 764. At its last General repair in August 1959, it got left-facing second emblems on the tender. Behind it is a Schools 4-4-0, not a common sight at Feltham but they did get used on goods trains occasionally. Peter Groom.

30835

Built Eastleigh 12/1927   Order No. E158-3 Works Serial Number 150
Built as E835, renumbered 835 5/1932, 30835 9/1948

10/12/27		SOUTHERN E835, boiler 835, flat side tender 3232, lined black
28/8/28-29/8/28	D	Flat side tender to E855, Urie tender ex E768, renumbered 3232
16/1/29-2/2/29	D	Piston valves
26/2/30-5/4/30	A	General repair, smoke deflectors
4/3/31-4/3/31	D	Weighing
17/4/31-17/4/31	D	Firebox
18/4/32-26/5/32	A	dark green, renumbered 835
12/7/34-1/9/34	(GW)	Boiler 830, part repaint
19/7/35-19/7/35	D	
11/6/36-25/7/36	B	68,518, part repaint, mileage extended by 10,000
10/12/36-24/12/36	D	80,348, 6wh tender 882 ex 765
31/5/38-29/6/38	A	104,599, boiler 930, cylinders panelled, tender not repainted
3/8/42-7/10/42	A	82,653, boiler 833, unlined black
5/8/43-17/8/43	C	20,254
8/5/44-1/7/44	B	41,484
22/9/45-1/10/45	D	85,492, at Ashford Works
27/3/46-4/5/46	A	99,638, boiler 1048
16/8/48-18/9/48	B	65,067, SOUTHERN 30835, mileage extended by 10,000
26/1/49-5/2/49	C	74,636
26/9/49-14/10/49	L Cas	93,478, snifting valves off
9/8/50-7/9/50	Gen	117,920, boiler 451, first emblem, storm sheets fitted
20/9/51-13/10/51	H Int	28,115
23/9/52-10/10/52	H Cas	56,516, boiler 769
17/12/53-2/1/54	H Cas	83,117
9/7/54-6/9/54	L Cas	96,387, at Brighton Works
8/11/55-3/12/55	Gen	117,018, boiler 1056, repainted
7/2/57-16/2/57	L Cas	29,529
17/5/57-21/5/57	N/C	32,903
19/7/57-2/9/57	L Cas	38,660, at Brighton Works
1/2/58-22/2/58	Gen	47,270, boiler 824, second emblem (F)
9/9/60-1/10/60	L Int	59,725, AWS fitted
5/9/62-29/9/62	L Cas	94,338
20/12/63		Urie tender 3203 ex 30499 at Feltham
22/11/1964		Withdrawn, 923,425 miles
		Sold to Birds Commercial Motors, Morriston, for scrap

Allocation

1927	Feltham	12/1942	Feltham
12/1936	Brighton	7/1951	Redhill
1941	New Cross Gate	6/1963	Feltham

E835 at Feltham about 1931, still carrying the multi washout plug boiler with which it was built. Unusually, it has an E prefix in sans serif characters on the left side of the buffer beam. It had a Urie tender from August 1928 and smoke deflectors in April 1930. Under the dirt, it is still black. It will get green livery and lose its E prefix in May 1932. The photographer is clearly with a group, some of whom are in the cab and tender. G.L. Turner   .

30835 at Reading Southern shed on 20 September 1958, with GWR signals prominent behind. It had received a six wheel tender when transferred to Brighton in 1936 and was now based at Redhill. The second BR emblems had appeared on its tender in February, in the early form, which faced forward on both sides. Peter Groom.

30836

Built Eastleigh 12/1927   Order No. E158-4 Works Serial Number 151
Built as E836, renumbered 836 3/1932, 30836 9/1949

24/12/27		SOUTHERN E836, boiler 836, flat side tender 3233, lined black
30/10/28-30/10/28	D	Flat side tender to E856, Urie tender ex E771, renumbered 3233
10/11/28-17/1/29	D	Pistons etc.
30/5/30-24/7/30	A	General repair, smoke deflectors, dark green
8/5/31-9/5/31	D	Wrapper plate
18/2/32-22/3/33	B	Renumbered 836
18/2/33-29/3/32	(GW)	Boiler 737
16/9/33-4/10/33	(GW)	
27/10/34-27/11/34	(GW)	Boiler 456, full repaint
16/7/3-17/8/35	C	23,608, accident damage
26/3/36-6/5/36	B	43,708, boiler 450
7/6/37-3/7/37	A	80,661, boiler 834, 6-wh tender 883 ex 766, full repaint
17/3/39-3/4/39	D	30,840, at Brighton Works
3/8/40-16/10/40	B	55,604, Boiler 790, unlined malachite green, Bulleid lettering
25/2/41		Mileage extended by 5,000 at Brighton Works
30/6/42-7/9/42	A	85,137, boiler 451, unlined black
15/10/42-23/10/42	D	Aircraft attack damage repair, at Brighton Works
20/2/45-28/4/45	A	67,429, boiler 452
23/7/45-28/7/45	C	6,731
22/1/46-2/2/46	C	26,276
7/5/46-16/5/46	C	35,343
19/9/47-11/10/47	A	68,975,boiler 779, snifting valves off
14/11/47-18/2/48	C	1,720, at Feltham
31/8/49-23/9/49	L Cas	46,036, SOUTHERN 30836
26/4/50-26/5/50	A	62,526, boiler 1056, first emblem
4/11/52-29/11/52	L Int	69,363
27/4/53-2/5/53	L Cas	81,967
18/8/5-14/9/53	L Cas	88,254, at Brighton Works
7/4/54-20/5/54	H Cas	101,520, at Brighton Works
23/6/55-30/7/55	Gen	123,299, boiler 780, repainted
31/1/56-10/2/56	L Cas	12,233
26/6/56-11/7/56	L Cas	22,539
4/12/56-15/12/56	L Cas	33,145
27/2/57-20/3/57	L Cas	37,826, at Brighton Works
21/6/57-29/6/57	N/C	40,979
27/9/57-19/10/57	Gen	48,930, boiler 742, second emblem (F)
17/6/60-2/7/60	H Int	56,282, AWS fitted
8/1960-20/8/60	(GW)	
26/9/62-27/10/62	H Cas	87,920, boiler 826
14/6/64		Withdrawn, 871,613 miles
		Sold to J. Cashmore for scrap

Allocation

1927	Feltham
7/1937	Brighton
1941	New Cross Gate
12/1942	Feltham
7/1951	Redhill
6/1963	Feltham

Maunsell S15 E836 from the rear, showing the back of its original flat sided tender, as coupled to E833-E837, but replaced by Urie tenders during 1928. These had footsteps at all four corners, with a handrail on the rear corner. The three auxiliary vacuum reservoirs are placed between the rear bulkhead of the coal space and the two water fillers. Livery is black with green lining. The stance of the driver shows the disparity between the height of the cabside cutout and the front of the tender.

E836 at Waterloo in 1930-32. In October 1928 it had got a Urie tender and smoke deflectors and green livery in July 1930. It has the E prefix and number on the buffer beam in serif characters, dating the photograph to before February 1932, when it lost the E. It has arrived at Waterloo on a train and is waiting for the signal to run light to Nine Elms.

30837

Built Eastleigh 1/1928   Order No. E158-5 Works Serial Number 152
Built as E837, renumbered 837 9/1932 , s837 2/1948, 30837 4/1948

2/1/28		SOUTHERN E837, boiler 837, flat side tender 3234, lined black
27/11/28-27/11/28	D	Flat side tender to E857, Urie tender ex E772, renumbered 3234
10/12/28-17/1/29	D	Pistons etc.
4/9/29-4/9/29	D	Weighing
5/11/29-5/11/29	D	Weighing
14/5/30-28/6/30	A	General repair, smoke deflectors, dark green
24/2/31-11/3/31	C	Steam chest liners
29/8/32-30/9/32	A	Boiler 836, Loco renumbered 837
4/10/32-7/10/32	(GW)	
18/2/33-24/2/33	(GW)	
18/8/33-4/9/33	(GW)	
1/6/34-1/6/34	(GW)	tender derailment
6/4/35-11/5/35	(GW)	tender not repainted
24/3/37-8/5/37	B	60,081, boiler 806, 6-wh tender 884 ex 767, steam de-sanding
11/1/38-2/2/38	A	70,467, boiler 840, cylinders panelled, tender not repainted
28/7/39-19/8/39	C	29,133, cylinders repainted
24/10/41-26/11/41	A	73,937, boiler 841, unlined black?
29/1/42-11/2/42	C	1,035, at Brighton Works
29/1/44-8/2/44	C	54,218, unlined black
26/1/45-10/3/45	A	82,401, boiler 823
26/6/46-20/7/46	C	50,514
25/9/1946-19/10/46	D	54,139
13/8/47-16/8/47	C	73,584
28/1/48-28/2/48	A	84,381, boiler 1402, snifting valves off, BRITISH RAILWAYS s837
20/4/48-24/4/48	D	1,983, renumbered 30837
19/1/49-29/1/49	C	23,577
15/5/51-8/6/51	H Int	94,882, first emblem
27/9/51-28/9/51	N/C	102,766
23/1/52-2/2/52	H Cas	107,935, boiler 791
10/3/52-13/3/52	Return	108,795
4/3/53-11/4/53	L Cas	136,790, at Brighton Works
18/2/54-21/3/54	Gen	156,839, boiler 737, repainted
10/11/55-3/12/55	H Cas	35,846, boiler 833
28/2/57-23/3/57	L Int	63,970
25/2/58-14/3/58	L Cas	89,000, at Redhill
11/8/59-5/9/59	Gen	119,660, boiler 825, second emblem (L)
21/10/60-22/10/60	N/C	24,370
16/3/61-8/4/61	L Cas	33,196
9/8/61-23/8/61	N/C	37,397, AWS fitted
21/6/62-23/6/62	L Cas	59,967, tender 712 ex 30912, second emblem (L)
27/11/62-29/12/62	L Int	73,485
3/6/64-26/6/64	L Cas	
19/9/65		Withdrawn, 911,016 miles
		Sold to J. Cashmore for scrap

Allocation

1928	Feltham	12/1942	Feltham	1/1965	Eastleigh
5/1937	Brighton	7/1951	Redhill	1/1965	Feltham
1941	New Cross Gate	6/1961	Feltham		

837 at Eastleigh, 14 March 1937. 837 was coupled to a Urie bogie tender in November 1928; smoke deflectors and green livery came in June 1930. It is now due for a class B repair, during which it will be coupled to a six wheel tender, for transfer to the Central section. R.K. Blencowe Collection.

30837 at Eastleigh station on 1 August 1962; headcode for light engines to Eastleigh shed. A month earlier, it had been coupled to the tender from Schools 4-4-0 30912. It was green and so had to be repainted black; the locomotive then had to be cleaned to match.

30838

Built Eastleigh 5/1936   Order No. E630-1 Works Serial Number 247
Built as 838, renumbered s838 2/1948, 30838 8/1949

23/5/36		New, boiler 1047, flat side tender 3235, SOUTHERN dark green
30/9/36-5/10/36	D	6,075
16/2/39-17/2/39	D	60,517, brakework alterations
4/8/39-9/10/39	C	71,708, mileage extended by 10,000 at Brighton Works
17/5/40-12/6/40	A	93,083, boiler 1048, unlined dark green, Bulleid lettering
23/3/42-11/4/42	C	56,569
3/2/43-3/3/43	A	80,570, boiler 797, unlined black
6/7/45-31/8/45	A	77,434, boiler 448
30/10/46-30/10/46	C	41,511, at Nine Elms
29/1/48-28/2/48	A	74,953, boiler 1401, snifting valves off BRITISH RAILWAYS s838
20/3/48-20/3/48	D	
28/7/49-26/8/49	L Cas	44,139, renumbered 30838, unlettered
1/5/50-26/5/50	L Int	61,971
6/11/50-6/11/50	N/C	77,197, at Nine Elms
29/8/52-27/9/52	Gen	126,505, boiler 783, first emblem
5/5/54-29/5/54	Gen	58,140, boiler 1049, repainted
22/3/55-2/4/55	L Cas	31,009, at Brighton Works
19/4/56-9/6/56	H Int	65,445, at Brighton Works
6/6/57-27/6/57	H Cas	96,172
24/4/58-17/5/58	Gen	120,561, boiler 794, second emblem (F)
9/12/59-19/12/59	H Int	49,246
1/1960-2/1/60	(GW)	
7/4/60-14/4/60	N/C	54,525, AWS fitted
24/4/61-5/5/61	L Cas	84,165
30/1/62-24/2/62	Gen	100,168, boiler 839, second emblem (L)
27/8/62-1/9/62	N/C	11,595
20/2/63 -1/3/63	L Cas	21,749
23/12/63-3/1/64	L Cas	40,081
19/9/65		Withdrawn, 827,196 miles
		Sold to Birds Commercial Motors,Risca, for scrap

Allocation
1/1936	Hither Green
10/1939	Feltham
1/1965	Eastleigh
1/1965	Feltham

S838 at Eastleigh, 8 May 1949. 837 and 838 were the only S15s to get S prefixes in early 1948. Lettering is Southern style, with hand painted characters where the letters could not be derived from SOUTHERN transfers. The snifting valves were removed at the same time. On the left is a Schools 4-4-0, in malachite green with Gill sans lettering. W. Gilburt.

30838 at Feltham on 12 July 1959, now with the second BR emblem, facing forward on both sides. Peter Groom.

30839

Built Eastleigh 5/1936   Order No. E630-2 Works Serial Number 248
Built as 839, renumbered 30839 10/1948

29/5/36		New, boiler 1048, flat side tender 3236, SOUTHERN dark green
4/11/36-9/11/36	D	7,258, steam de-sanding fitted
6/3/39-7/3/39	D	64,645, brakework alterations
10/4/40-8/5/40	A	90,395, boiler 1050, unlined dark green, Bulleid lettering
10/8/42-1/10/42	C	76,472, mileage extended by 10,000 at Stewarts Lane
15/3/43-21/4/43	A	90,420, boiler 456, unlined black
11/12/45-11/12/45	C	74,157, at Nine Elms
31/5/46-22/6/46	B	78,549, boiler 799, mileage extended by 5.000
3/3/47-5/4/47	A	97,879
11/6/47-13/6/47	D	2,447, at Nine Elms
28/9/47-29/9/47	D	10,852, at Nine Elms
16/2/48-10/4/48	C	23,476
15/9/48-16/10/48	C	33,750, SOUTHERN 30839
21/11/49-23/12/49	A	68,036. boiler 825, snifting valves off, first emblem
17/11/50-17/11/50	N/C	29,427, at Nine Elms
4/2/52-27/2/52	Gen	62,654, boiler 930
19/1/54-13/2/54	Gen	64,086, boiler 1410, repainted
8/2/56-3/3/56	H Int	72,144
3/2/57-20/2/57	L Cas	100,736, at Guildford
21/5/57-1/6/57	L Cas	106,724
28/4/58-24/5/58	Gen	134,160, boiler 1001, tender repainted, second emblem (L)
3/6/60-2/7/60	Gen	62,358, AWS fitted
30/5/62-23/6/62	Gen	55,536, boiler 457
19/9/65		Withdrawn, 795,995 miles
		Sold to Birds Commercial Motors, Risca, for scrap

Allocation
1/1936	Hither Green
10/1939	Feltham
1/1965	Eastleigh

839 at Hither Green on 10 April 1937. The balance weight on the driving wheel is squared off at the clockwise end. Although the Eastern section S15s, 838-842, were restricted to goods trains, they were painted in the passenger green livery. H.C. Casserley, courtesy R.M. Casserley.

Hither Green April 1937. The casing over the exhaust steam pipe is invisible from this angle. These casings varied and the smoke deflector plates must have been fitted individually to each casing. R.K. Blencowe Collection.

30839 at Salisbury on 22 August 1963; AWS receiver below the coupling. R.K. Blencowe Collection.

30840

Built Eastleigh 6/1936   Order No. E630-3 Works Serial Number 249
Built as 840, renumbered 30840 8/1949

30/6/36		New, boiler 1049, flat side tender 3237, SOUTHERN dark green
29/4/37-30/4/37	D	21,095, steam de-sanding fitted
27/2/39-28/2/39	D	65,680, brakework alterations
28/2/40-3/4/40	A	94,069, boiler 1051, unlined dark green, Bulleid lettering
9/7/42-2/9/42	A	71,873, boiler 784
14/10/43-15/10/43	D	34,482, unlined black
21/4/45-16/6/45	A	75,079, boiler 1047
17/4/47-19/4/47	C	56,133, at Nine Elms
27/1/48-20/3/48	B	73,233, boiler 448, snifting valves off, mileage extended by 5,000
11/7/49-26/8/49	A	108,960, boiler 929, 30840 unlettered
11/10/50-27/10/50	L Cas	34,412
13/6/52-11/7/52	Gen	80,247, boiler 831, first emblem
10/3/54-9/4/54	Gen	58,131, boiler 1053, repainted
5/4/55-16/4/55	L Cas	34,441, at Brighton Works
19/4/56-5/5/56	H Int	65,964
3/3/58-20/3/58	Gen	120,562, boiler 795, second emblem (F)
4/9/59-12/0/59	L Cas	44,300
14/3/60-2/4/60	L Int	58,562, AWS fitted
6/7/62-25/8/62	Gen	120,426, boiler 1407, second emblem (L)
13/9/64		Withdrawn, 781,397 miles
		Sold to Shipbreakers (Queenborough) for scrap

Allocation
1936   Hither Green
10/1939   Feltham

840 at Dover in the late 1930s; green livery looking somewhat work worn. R.K. Blencowe Collection.

30840 at Reading South, 6 March 1963; second **BR** emblem, facing left, on both sides of the tender. The 2-6-0 on the right carries overhead electrification warning signs, but very few S15s received these. **R.K. Blencowe Collection.**

30841

Built Eastleigh 7/1936   Order No. E630-4 Works Serial Number 250
Built as 841, renumbered 30841 10/1948

Date	Type	Details
15/7/36		New, boiler 1050, flat side tender 3238, SOUTHERN dark green
1/6/37-3/6/37	D	21,427, steam de-sanding fitted
26/10/37-3/11/37	C	28,831
15/3/39-16/3/39	D	57,004, brakework alterations
12/3/40-17/4/40	A	87,320, boiler 1049, unlined dark green, Bulleid lettering
11/4/41-15/4/41	D	30,227
19/6/42-5/8/42	A	73,922, boiler 931, unlined black
28/3/44-13/5/44	B	52,178, boiler 777
5/7/44-15/7/44	C	52,178
6/3/45-14/4/45	A	76,091, boiler 778
6/4/46-13/4/46	C	40,086
31/10/46-1/11/46	C	53,976, at Nine Elms
31/10/47-22/11/47	B	77,467, boiler 452, snifting valves off
14/1/48-24/1/48	C	80,397
8/9/48-2/10/48	A	98,471, BRITISH RAILWAYS 30841 (G)
4/9/50-22/9/50	L Int	79,049
31/1/52-23/2/52	Gen	121,148, boiler 491
20/1/54-6/2/54	H Int	77,218, first emblem
23/6/54-2/7/1954	L Cas	92,141, at Brighton Works
27/9/55-1/10/55	L Cas	133,405
4/1/56-4/2/56	Gen	142,701, boiler 1051, repainted
6/6/58-28/6/58	L Int	83,369
11/1/61-11/2/61	Gen	164,615, boiler 1409, second emblem (L)
24/8/61-2/9/61	N/C	9,524, AWS fitted
5/1/64		Withdrawn, 837,002 miles
6/1964		Sold to Woodham Bros, Barry for scrap.
9/1972		To East Anglian Transport Museum, Chappel
1974		To Service on Stour Valley Railway, named *Greene King*
8/1975		Ran in Rail 150 cavalcade at Shildon
10/1977		To Nene Valley Railway
11/1978		To North Yorkshire Moors Railway

Allocation
1936	Hither Green
10/1939	Feltham
6/1948	Exmouth Junction
9/1963	Feltham

841 in the late 1930s. An M7 0-4-4T on the left suggests that the photograph was taken at Feltham, to which 841 was transferred in October 1939, rather than Hither Green.

30841 leaving Axminster on the 3.34pm Templecombe to Exeter Central train, 2 August 1958. The bridge carries the Lyme Regis branch over the main line. The down line has been relayed with flat bottom rail whilst the up line still has chaired bullhead rail. A.E. West, courtesy M.S. King.

30842

Built Eastleigh 8/1936   Order No. E630-5 Works Serial Number 251
Built as 842, renumbered 30842 9/1949

11/8/36		New, boiler 1051, flat sided tender 3239, SOUTHERN dark green
25/8/36-3/9/36	D	Hot axleboxes
27/8/37-15/9/37	C	27,705, steam de-sanding fitted
24/3/39-5/4/39	C	62,166, brakework alterations
15/11/39-20/12/39	A	77,965, boiler 450, unlined dark green, Bulleid lettering
2/5/42-13/6/42	A	78,456, boiler 840, unlined black
23/11/43-5/1/44	B	51,008, mileage extended by 20,000
1/11/45-1/12/45	A	120,501
1/8/47-23/8/47	C	46,447
14/2/48-6/3/48	B	60,304, boiler 1001, snifting valves off
15/7/48-15/9/48	C	70,085, at Exmouth Junction
26/7/49-9/9/49	A	98,194, boiler 827, 30842 unlettered
10/1949-1/10/49	(GW)	Large first emblem applied 24/9/49
16/2/51-16/3/51	H Int	54,071
10/6/52-11/7/52	Gen	105,104, boiler 799, tender not repainted
30/8/54-18/9/54	L Int	99,557
9/8/55-13/8/55	L Cas	134,916
24/10/55-17/11/55	H Int	144,750 small first emblem.
12/2/58-8/3/58	Gen	219,938, boiler 780, second emblem (F)
28/3/60-9/4/60	L Int	66,361, AWS fitted
9/11/62-15/12/62	Gen	188,657, second emblem (L)
7/3/63-29/3/63	L Cas	749
4/1963-26/5/63	(GW)	
5/9/65		Withdrawn, 898,348 miles
		Sold to J.Cashmore for scrap

Allocation
1936	Hither Green
10/1939	Feltham
6/1948	Exmouth Junction
9/1963	Feltham
1/1965	Eastleigh
1/1965	Feltham
6/1965	Eastleigh

842 passing Tonbridge on an up goods. The route is shown as Ramsgate to Bricklayers Arms via Canterbury West and Tonbridge. Bulleid Pacific Preservation Society.

30842 leaving Salisbury on an up goods train, 6 May 1954. It was repainted as 30842 with an unlettered tender in September 1949 but large first emblems were applied two weeks later. It still has the A power classification below the cabside number. W. Gilburt.

30843

Built Eastleigh 9/1936   Order No. E630-6 Works Serial Number 252
Built as 843, renumbered 30843 6/1948

26/9/36		New, boiler 1052, flat side tender 3240, SOUTHERN dark green
23/2/39-24/2/39	D	69,014, brakework alterations
2/6/39-28/6/39	A	98,982, dark green, black/yellow lining, half green deflectors, Maunsell lettering
19/8/39-23/9/39	C	2,298
10/4/40-13/4/40	D	6,925
21/9/42-27/10/42	A	98,048, boiler 930, unlined black
18/9/45-24/10/45	A	79,420, boiler 767
13/12/47-17/1/48	B	64,614, snifting valves off
29/5/48-26/6/48	B	74,578, SOUTHERN 30843, mileage extended by 10,000
28/6/49-19/8/49	A	110,937, boiler 836, repainted, unlettered
5/4/51-4/5/51	L Int	64,366
16/12/52-10/1/53	H Int	128,167, new right hand cylinder
16/5/53-28/5/53	H Cas	140,372
8/11/54-4/12/54	Gen	194,815, boiler 789, first emblem
28/11/55-10/12/55	L Cas	38,721
21/2/57-9/3/57	L Int	74,991
10/7/59-15/8/59	Gen	152,561, boiler 1047, second emblem (L)
30/3/60-7/4/60	L Cas	13,242, AWS fitted
15/2/62-17/3/62	L Int	61,919
20/9/64		Withdrawn, 856,824 miles
		Sold to Shipbreakers (Queenborough) for scrap

Allocation
10/1936   Feltham
1/1948   Exmouth Junction
9/1963   Feltham

843 at Eastleigh in the late 1930s, with Drummond D15 class 4-4-0 470 on the left and a 700 class 0-6-0 on the right.

30843 stands on the up line at Axminster, 15 June 1957 as passengers board a corridor carriage in the Lyme Regis bay. As the branch train was generally comprised of non-corridor stock, this is probably a through carriage, to be attached to an up train on the main line. The tail lamp on the buffer beam of 30843 suggests that it has arrived tender first from Exmouth Junction. It now has the small first emblem on its tender and 6F power classification on the cabside. A.E. West, courtesy M.S. King.

30843 has moved into the goods yard at Axminster and the tail lamp on the buffer beam has gone. Although it is two and a half years since its last repaint, the Exmouth Junction cleaners are now doing their job rather better than in 1950. A.E. West, courtesy M.S. King.

30844

Built Eastleigh 10/1936   Order No. E630-7 Works Serial Number 253
Built as 844, renumbered 30844 7/1950

6/10/36		New, boiler 1053, flat side tender 3241, SOUTHERN dark green
2/3/39-3/3/39	D	93,747, brakework alterations
21/7/39-23/8/39	A	108,909, boiler 837, dark green, black/yellow lining, half green deflectors.
16/5/41-20/5/41	D	60,487
6/6/42-15/7/42	A	95,321, boiler 450, unlined black
22/5/44-19/7/44	C	60,875, at Feltham
31/5/45-14/7/45	A	80,092, boiler 784
15/12/45-15/12/45	C	16,590, at Nine Elms
2/12/47-27/12/47	A	87,807, boiler 781, snifting valves off, repainted
2/6/50-7/7/50	A	83,146, boiler 832, first emblem, 30844
27/6/52-2/8/52	H Int	73,894
7/7/1953-10/7/53	L Cas	110,621
21/1/54-6/2/54	L Cas	129,353
22/6/54-9/7/54	L Int	140,040
11/1/55-21/1/55	L Cas	160,330
29/12/55-28/1/56	Gen	188,897, boiler 737, repainted
21/4/58-16/5/58	H Int	72,182
24/9/59-24/10/59	Gen	118,248, boiler 833, second emblem (L)
21/6/62-28/7/62	L Int	72,903, AWS fitted
14/6/64		Withdrawn, 873,763 miles
		Sold for scrap to Woodham Bros, Barry

Allocation
10/1956	Feltham
11/1946	Exmouth Junction
9/1963	Feltham

844 at Feltham on 25 September 1937, still less than a year after construction. H.C Casserley, courtesy R.M. Casserley.

30844 leaving Yeovil Junction on the 3.20pm Exeter Central-Templecombe train on 6 May 1960. Following a General repair in October 1959, it carries multiple washout plug boiler 833, fitted at its last General Repair in October 1959. The train is a 1947-built Bulleid 3-set. South Western Circle, John Eyers Collection.

30844 at Feltham on 5 July 1964, a month after withdrawal. AWS fitted at a Light Intermediate repair in July 1962. 30844 was one of six S15s sold to Woodham Bros for scrap, and sadly the only one actually to be scrapped there. Peter Groom.

30845

Built Eastleigh 10/1936   Order No. E630-8 Works Serial Number 254
Built as 845, renumbered 30845 3/1948

27/10/36		New, boiler 1054, flat side tender 3242, SOUTHERN dark green
1/11/38-1/11/38	D	
14/3/39-5/4/39	A	89,972, boiler 778, brakework alterations
22/4/41-23/4/41	D	68,789
26/7/41-3/9/41	A	76,533, boiler 800, unlined black
1/6/44-12/8/44	A	96,079, boiler 771
13/10/44-11/11/44	B	1,522
6/9/45-19/11/45	B	31,820
15/11/46-5/12/46	C	60,812, at Feltham
20/2/48-25/3/48	A	102,935, boiler 784, snift valves off, BRITISH RAILWAYS 30845 (S)
28/12/50-26/1/51	A	98,266, boiler 833, first emblem
4/4/52-12/4/52	L Cas	45,646
14/1/53-14/2/53	Gen	70,218, boiler 794
11/8/54-28/8/54	H Int	71,168
21/3/56-14/4/56	L Int	129,008
14/2/58-14/3/58	Gen	185,901, boiler 452, second emblem (F)
14/8/59-5/9/59	H Int	45,000
23/3/62-14/4/62	H Int	109,653
4/5/62 5/5/62	L Cas	111,324, AWS fitted
27/7/63		Withdrawn, 858,845 miles
8/1963	(GW)	to works
7/9/63		cut up at Eastleigh

Allocation
10/1956   Feltham
11/1946   Exmouth Junction

845 at Eastleigh on 11 June 1939, after its first Class A repair. Panelled lining on the cylinders. George Woodward records that the tender was not repainted.

30845 is prepared for a test run at Eastleigh Works on 28 August 1954. For once, the Engine Record Card appears to be entirely honest, indicating completion of a Heavy Intermediate repair on that very day. Stephen Gradidge.

30845 at Exmouth Junction in 1960-62. AWS was to be fitted in May 1962. R.K. Blencowe Collection.

30846

Built Eastleigh 11/1936   Order No. E630-9 Works Serial Number 255
Built as 846, renumbered 30846 4/1948

18/11/36		New, boiler 1056, flat side tender 3243, SOUTHERN dark green
8/2/39-13/2/39	D	80,698, brakework alterations
3/8/39-13/9/39	A	96,722, boiler 1053, dark green, black/yellow lining, Bulleid lettering
15/4/42-19/8/42	A	Miles not recorded, boiler 1053, at Ashford Works, unlined black
11/6/45-7/10/45	A	71,201, boiler 774
30/4/46-30/4/46	C	17,983, at Nine Elms
16/3/48-17/4/48	A	89,221, boiler 771, snift valves off, BRITISH RAILWAYS 30846(S)
31/7/50-25/8/50	Gen	77,154, boiler 763, first emblem
8/12/52-3/1/53	L Int	89,873
5/10/53-8/10/53	N/C	122,304
25/8/54-18/9/54	Gen	160,004, boiler 783, repainted
7/1/55-8/1/55	L Cas	11,855
21/6/56-7/7/56	L Int	63,957
27/8/58-27/9/58	Gen	132,826, boiler 1049, second emblem (F)
14/11/60-26/11/60	L Int	61,381
16/8/62-24/8/62	L Cas	107,684, AWS fitted
26/1/63		Withdrawn, 845,017 miles
2/1963	(GW)	to works
23/2/63		cut up at Eastleigh

Allocation
1937	Feltham
11/1946	Exmouth Junction
6/1951	Salisbury

846 at Feltham on 25 September 1937. H.C Casserley, courtesy R.M. Casserley.

30846 on a down stopping train at Axminster on 25 August 1956. The front coupling is correctly attached to the hook below the buffer beam. An LNER passenger brake van is the leading vehicle of the train. A.E. West, courtesy M.S. King.

30847

Built Eastleigh 12/1936   Order No. E630-10 Works Serial Number 256
Built as 847, renumbered 30847 8/1948

30/12/36		New, boiler 1057, flat side tender 3244, SOUTHERN dark green
11/1/38-11/1/38	D	Tender leaking
29/3/38-29/3/38	D	
27/7/38-17/8/38	C	69,863, light repairs to tender
21/2/39-22/2/39	D	92,445, brakework alterations
16/6/39-10/7/39	A	107,137, dark green, yellow/black lining, half green deflectors, Maunsell lettering
15/2/40-20/2/40	D	21,674
2/11/40-5/11/40	D	48,958
23/3/41-28/4/41	C	Mileage extended by 5,000 at Exmouth Junction
28/8/41-30/8/41	D	71,389
9/4/42-3/6/42	A	97,566, boiler 789, unlined black
6/4/44-19/5/44	A	72,414, boiler 770
23/8/46-12/10/46	A	98,561, boiler 737
24/7/48-28/8/48	A	74,470, boiler 455, snift valves off, BRITISH RAILWAYS 30847 (G)
24/11/50-22/12/50	L Int	75,377
19/2/53-28/3/53	Gen	152,941, boiler 795, first emblem
20/9/54-9/10/54	L Int	64,257
17/4/56-12/5/56	Gen	122,618, boiler 802, repainted
20/3/58-19/4/58	L Int	69,560
5/1958-17/5/58	(GW)	Second Emblem (F)
9/5/60-11/6/60	Gen	127,850, boiler 456, AWS, 2nd emblem (L), 3500 gal tender 914 ex 30805
3/9/62-21/9/62	N/C	
5/1/64		Withdrawn, 931,829 miles
6/1964		Sold for scrap to Woodham Bros, Barry
8/10/78		To Maunsell Locomotive Society, Bluebell Railway, with Urie tender 3225 ex 30828.
1993		Restored to service, tender 3225 rebuilt with flat sides.

Allocation
1937	Exmouth Junction
6/1951	Salisbury
7/1959	Redhill
9/1963	Feltham

30847 at Exmouth Junction shed on 22 August 1950. BRITISH RAILWAYS lettered tender, but invisible under the dirt. No shed plate is carried yet. A.E. West, courtesy M.S. King.

30847 at Reading shed on 31 May 1963. At its General Repair in June 1960, it was coupled to a 3,500 gallon six wheel tender from King Arthur 30805. This was narrower than the locomotive and with the platform set higher. 30847 hides its miserable appendage in the shed; the similar tender on the right is coupled to a Maunsell mogul, with width and platform height to match the tender. Peter Groom.

30488 at Reading WR shed on 1 March 1953. It had been involved in a collision on the Western Region main line and was taken there before going to Eastleigh for repair. The buffer to buffer coupling of locomotive and tender suggests that the tender drawbar is unusable, making any further movement difficult. Note the tail lamp on the cab fallplate and the storm sheet hanging from the cab roof. Initial Photographics.

30496 passing Eastleigh on a Southampton-Nine Elms goods, 21 July 1962.